Greenhill Books

At
Hitler's Side

'Nicolaus von Below was almost constantly at Hitler's side
for eight years. In his memoirs . . . he provides a thoughtful record
of those years from the point of view of a professional army
officer. . . Von Below's book is probably a unique document in
that it represents a serious attempt, by a comparatively uncompli-
cated but unfailingly sincere man, to come to terms with matters
he would ordinarily have considered totally beyond him.'
—Gitta Sereny

'Since as Luftwaffe Adjutant Nicolaus von Below saw
Hitler on an almost daily basis from 1937 down to the last days in
the bunker, I found his memoirs indispensable in writing the
second volume of my biography of the Dictator and now greatly
welcome their appearance in English translation.'
—Ian Kershaw

'An intimate glimpse into the decision-making process of the
Nazi military leadership . . . A brief history of the war from the
perspective of someone who witnessed it at the highest levels and
then interspersed this history with his remembered observations
and occasional references to surviving correspondence.'
—Library Journal (USA)

'We are presented with an absorbing account which provides
more insight about the intimate detail about life with the Führer
than many other . . . It is our good fortune that the late Nicolaus
von Below miraculously survived Hitler's ruthlessness and the
Bomb Plot attempt to kill Hitler (and the author) on 20 July
1944. Otherwise we would not, even belatedly, have been made
privy to these important memoirs.'
—Kenneth Macksey
Tank: The Journal of the Royal Tank Regiment

Greenhill Books

'This excellent volume . . . His accounts of his dealing
with Hitler's allies and generals during both good and bad times,
and Hitler's reactions to their views and news, provide a detailed
insight into the working of the Nazi and Axis machine
both in peace and war.'
—*The British Army Review*

'Von Below writes clearly, honestly and objectively, and gives
yet another insight into the mind of the one man who alone
changed the course of 20th century history. Well worth reading.'
—*Pennant: The Journal of the Forces Pension Society*

'At Hitler's Side *is the ideal title for Nicolaus von Below's
unique book because Below was Hitler's Luftwaffe adjutant from
1937 to 1945. Von Below, an intelligent but unimaginative man,
was an effective witness of Hitler's war. He flew to many of the
battlefields to get first hand reports just as Montgomery used
young liaison officers to find out what was going on. Von Below
throws new light on the strange, sinister twilight world in
which Hitler overran Europe.*'
— *The Guards Magazine*

At Hitler's Side

The Memoirs of Hitler's Luftwaffe Adjutant
1937–1945

Nicolaus von Below

Translated by Geoffrey Brooks

GREENHILL BOOKS, LONDON
STACKPOLE BOOKS, PENNSYLVANIA

Greenhill Books

This edition of
At Hitler's Side
first published 2004
by Greenhill Books, Lionel Leventhal Limited,
Park House, 1 Russell Gardens, London NW11 9NN
www.greenhillbooks.com
and
Stackpole Books, 5067 Ritter Road, Mechanicsburg,
PA 17055, USA

Original German edition: *Als Hitlers Adjutant 1937–45*
© 1980 by v. Hase & Koehler Verlag, Mainz, Germany
English translation copyright © Lionel Leventhal Limited, 2001

British Library Cataloguing in Publication Data
Below, Nicolaus von
At Hitler's side : the memoirs of Hitler's Luftwaffe adjutant,
1937–1945 – (Greenhill military paperback)
1.Below, Nicolaus von – Friends and associates   2.Hitler, Adolf, 1889–
1945   3.Germany. Luftwaffe – Officers – Biography   4.World War, 1939–
1945 – Biography   5. Germany – History – 1933–1945
I. Title
943′.086′092

ISBN 1-85367-600-4

Library of Congress Cataloging-in-Publication Data available

Publishing History
At Hitler's Side was first published in German as *Als Hitlers Adjutant*
1937–45 in 1980 by v.Hase & Koehler Verlag, Mainz

Edited, designed and typeset by Roger Chesneau
Printed and bound in Great Britain by
Creative Print and Design (Wales), Ebbw Vale

Contents

Illustrations

Pages 129–144

Illustrations 6, 7, 8, 12, 23 and 24 courtesy of Dirk von Below.

Abbreviations

AA	anti-aircraft
ADC	aide-de-camp
BEF	British Expeditionary Force
C-in-C	Commander-in-Chief
FHQ	Führerhauptquartier (Führer Headquarters)
HQ	headquarters
JG	Jagdgruppe (Fighter Group)
LVZ	Luftverteidigungszone (Air Defence Zone)
NSDAP	Nationalsozialistische Deutsche Arbeiter Partei (National Socialist German Workers' Party)
NSKK	Nationalsozialistisches Kraftfahrkorps (National Socialist Motorised Corps)
OKH	Oberkommando des Heeres (Army High Command)
OKW	Oberkommando der Wehrmacht (Armed Forces High Command)
POW	prisoner-of-war
PRO	Public Record Office
RAF	Royal Air Force
RLM	Reichsluftfahrtministerium (German Air Ministry)
SA	Sturmabteilung (Storm Troop; 'Brownshirts'. A uniformed force, formed in 1921 to steward Nazi Party meetings, which grew to a peak membership of 400,000 until the purge of its leaders in 1934, when many of its members transferred to the SS.)
SD	Sicherheitsdienst (SS Security/Intelligence Service)
SKL	Seekriegsleitung (Naval War Office)
SS	Schutzstaffel (Protection Squad. Originally Hitler's personal bodyguard 'Stosstrupp Adolf Hitler', renamed 'SS-Leibstandarte Adolf Hitler', the first SS division. Gradually

expanded to become, as the Waffen-SS, an elite fighting force, and, as the Allgemein-SS, a military-political organisation responsible for intelligence and the execution of State policy.)

USAAF United States Army Air Forces

Introduction

For almost eight years, from 16 June 1937 to 29 April 1945, I served as Luftwaffe Adjutant attached to the *Adjutantur der Wehrmacht beim Führer und Reichskanzler* and experienced the rise and fall of National Socialist Germany in the closest proximity to Hitler. Describing my reminiscences has been an extraordinarily difficult task. My diaries were destroyed at the end of the war: some of them I placed in the fire myself; Hitler's naval adjutant Puttkamer was responsible for burning those at Obersalzberg; and as Allied troops advanced towards my in-laws' estate, my wife destroyed the remaining documents I kept there.[1]

During my captivity I made notes which form the foundation to this memoir. My wife and brother have assisted me. I have attempted to remain uninfluenced by other witnesses and the flood of inaccurate literature concerning those times. In particular I am thinking about the fantasies surrounding the last few weeks in the bunker. I am not a member of that choir which now condemns vociferously what once they so admired and who always knew at the time, or sometimes even before it, exactly how things were bound to turn out for the worst.

I was a career airman and looked to the future. More than once I attempted to return to squadron duty but Hitler would not let me go. When I pressed him for my release at the outbreak of war, he told me that the war would soon end. My repeated requests during the Western campaign were refused with the observation that he, Hitler, would be the one to decide how long I remained his adjutant. He did not like new faces. So flying had to be my consolation, and I took every opportunity to try out every German aircraft from the Fieseler Storch to the Me 262.

To the last Hitler wanted me at his side. While convalescing from my injuries in the autumn of 1944 I became inwardly estranged from him. I realised that the mutual relationship of trust that had developed between us had blinded me to the black side of his regime. I saw that he alone prevented the end to a struggle which had become pointless.

I hope that my reminiscences will contribute in some way to a further understanding of that chain of events which changed the world so decisively following the outbreak of war in 1914, and to which I was for a few years a witness.

My Career Prior to Appointment

I had never wanted to be anything other than a soldier. Towards the end of my secondary education I applied to join Infantry Regiment No 12 (Halberstadt) as an officer cadet. I was rejected on account of slight myopia. My uncle Otto von Below, former General der Infanterie and C-in-C 14./Seventeenth Army, pulled a few strings and at last I was accepted in April 1928.

My early career took an unusual turn. Following certain psycho-technical tests prior to induction into Wehrkreiskommando VI (Münster), and even before recruit training, I was sent with twenty other cadets to the German Commercial Flying School at Schleissheim. My joy and pride can be imagined. I suppose I must have displayed a talent for flying, for I was one of the ten cadets of the group sent for training as fighter pilots to Lipezk near Voronezh in the Soviet Union between May and September 1929. We rose at five every morning, and although we wore civilian clothes there was no mistaking the military character of the establishment. We seldom had contact with Russian civilians or airmen.

I served with Infantry Regiment 12 from 1 October 1929 until the spring of 1933. The only interruptions were tactical infantry training at Dresden, where I became acquainted with future generals such as List, Hube and Rommel, and two flying courses of four weeks' duration at Rechlin run by the future SS-General Wilhelm Bittrich.

I was promoted to Leutnant on 1 October 1932 and was tranferred from the Army into the disguised Luftwaffe on 1 July 1933. I spent a few unprofitable weeks training in Italy. The Italian instructors had no intention of being of any use whatever to us. I had learned more at Lipezk.

My first posting in Germany was to a small squadron at Staaken airfield near Berlin, where we flew as targets for the Army. I learnt little new, but the nearness of the Reich capital was a compensation. In the autumn of 1934 I was appointed Staffelkapitän to the fighter squadron JG 132 (Döberitz). My commanding officer was Major Ritter von Greim.

After six months I became adjutant to the fighter group under the future General von Döring. Our most prominent trainees were Kesselring and Wever, both of whom I got to know on the friendliest terms.

On 20 February 1936 I went with 7 Staffel III./JG 134 to Lippstadt to take part in the occupation of the demilitarised Rhineland. On 7 March we took off, circled Cologne and landed at Düsseldorf-Lohausen, our new home airfield.

On 15 June 1937 I was at the estate of my future in-laws at Nienhagen near Halberstadt when I received a telephone call ordering me to report next morning to the Head of the Personnel Bureau at the Reich Air Ministry (RLM), Oberst Ritter von Greim. I was given such precise instructions for my uniform dress and accoutrements that I knew I should be in the presence of Hitler. Hauptmann Mantius, Hitler's Luftwaffe adjutant, had been killed in a flying accident a few weeks previously and I detected a possible connection. Next morning I left very early for Berlin and reported to Oberst von Greim punctually at nine. He told me I had to report to Göring at ten, when all would be revealed.

Göring asked me a few questions before he came to the point. I was to be offered the position of Luftwaffe adjutant to Hitler. Would I be prepared to accept it? If I could not be Hitler's follower 'heart and soul' then I should say so at once: I should have to serve the Führer 'from innermost conviction'. (The reason for this I discovered later: Greim and the Chief of the Luftwaffe General Staff had recommended me to Göring, who knew of my scepticism concerning National Socialism. I agreed: in 1934 I had taken the oath of unconditional loyalty and obedience to Adolf Hitler and I could not see how this appointment could require me to go beyond that.)

The post would be held for two years. I was subordinated entirely to Hitler. My duties, insofar as they affected the Luftwaffe High Command, could be discussed with Göring's personal adjutant, Oberst Bodenschatz, but he would not interfere in my sphere of duty. I should report to the Wehrmacht Adjutantur in the Reich Chancellery at one that afternoon: he, Göring, would be with the Führer and introduce me personally.

The first person I met in the Adjutantur was the naval adjutant, Korvettenkapitän Karl Jesko von Puttkamer. My first impression was of a tall, blond, good-looking and taciturn cigar-smoker. He escorted me through a very long corridor to the Führer's residence. Our duty rooms were in the former Vossisch Palace which stood on the corner of Voss

Strasse and the Wilhelmsplatz and was a massive edifice dating from the time of the founder. The adjacent Brüning Chancellery was built in 1930. Hitler had added a balcony to its simple limestone façade. A basement corridor connected the Vossisch Palace through the Brüning building to the Old Reich Chancellery which was known as the 'Führer Residence' because Hitler lived there. This attractive eighteenth-century edifice, in the form of a square open on one side to the Wilhelmstrasse, had been purchased in 1871 as the official residence for Bismarck and used ever since by all Reich Chancellors. An entrance hall led into the great Hall of the Palace at its centre. After I had been introduced to the Party, SA and SS men who crowded there, shouts from the street of *Sieg Heil!*, the calling out of the guard, shouted orders, rifles being presented in salute, the sound of a car drawing up to the entrance and the heel-clicking of the SS guard heralded the arrival of Göring. Everybody gave him the Hitler salute and he responded jovially to all sides. He would rarely offer his hand except to a Reich Minister or high Party functionary. I was told to wait, and shortly a manservant arrived and bade me follow him. I passed through two clumsy-looking double-winged doors set at a right angle and on entering the so-called small saloon saw Hitler and a standing Göring together on the far side. I saluted and was about to recite the usual form of military introduction when Göring interrupted and presented me to Hitler. Without formality or military stiffness, Hitler offered me his hand in greeting.

After Göring had departed lunch was taken. One passed through the smoking room (the name being a legacy from Bismarck's time) into the dining room, which was a large, almost square, well-proportioned room decorated in tasteful light colours. At its centre was a large round table with twelve chairs. Four smaller round tables each with six chairs were positioned round about. Hitler sat at the large table with his back to the window. On the opposite wall above a long sideboard hung Kaulbach's painting *The Entry of the Sun Goddess*. I sat at one of the peripheral tables and noticed how Hitler would often glance at me as if to etch my features into his memory. This was a habit I observed of him frequently. Table conversation was free.

The first days in my new role were not happy. I knew nobody. The Army and Luftwaffe adjutants were distant and unfriendly. I was sceptical about the NSDAP but came constantly into contact with Party people. Bodenschatz, Göring's personal ADC, was a great comfort. He knew how to steer clear of court intrigues and would withdraw into 'no man's land', a remote office with no telephone, when trouble brewed.

My first day as Hitler's Luftwaffe ADC was 23 June 1937. My duty was to remain in readiness at the Führer Residence to act as liaison between Hitler and the Luftwaffe High Command during the hours when Hitler was acting officially. At all other times he was attended by his personal aides. Nevertheless, when I heard that same evening that the Milan Scala was performing *La Bohème* at Charlottenberg I hinted to Hitler's chief ADC, SA-Obergruppenführer Wilhelm Brückner, that I would not refuse an invitation and he agreed at once, since he had been looking for somebody to accompany Hitler. Puttkamer and Hossbach always found some way to avoid listening to music and Hitler expressed surprise that a military officer in his entourage had such an interest. He asked if I knew *La Bohème* and seemed astonished that I had heard it in Hanover, Dresden and Berlin. I had not suspected until then Hitler's close affinity to music. On that evening he was full of Bayreuth, Wagner and Dietrich Eckart, the folk writer to whom he had dedicated *Mein Kampf*.

During the Bayreuth Festival itself, Hitler always stayed with Winifred Wagner, the daughter-in-law of the composer. In her house he was at home, the private man. I felt how he transferred his energies to his surroundings—his cheerfulness, his affection, his humour. With no other family did I observe this deep feeling of kinship, nor hear him speak in the familiar grammatical form which otherwise he used so sparingly. The Wagner home and music were his refuge.

On 27 July Hitler invited us to be his guests at Bayreuth. From the 'Prince's Gallery', his large private box, we watched *Siegfried* and *Götterdämmerung*. After supper Brückner took my wife by the arm and presented her to Frau Wagner and Hitler, who kissed her hand. From then on we belonged to his private circle.

The Daily Routine of the Luftwaffe Adjutant

Our daily timetable had to accord with Hitler's routine. He was very easy to get on with, being amiable and correct towards his staff. In Berlin I would spend about an hour a day taking applications before joining the other adjutants at midday in our Reich Chancellery office. Hitler would not normally appear earlier from his private quarters. Because of his insomnia Hitler worked into the early hours, when he found the quietness he needed for reflection. We would start with a mutual question-

and-answer session to clarify outstanding matters. He would then keep his pre-lunch appointments, which were scheduled to finish by 2 p.m. If he overran the meal would be delayed. Table conversation could be very interesting or extremely tedious, depending on how many times one had been over the subject before.

Further appointments followed after lunch. If this involved Hitler meeting with a Luftwaffe officer I would have to be on hand, but otherwise my duties were finished until Hitler reappeared that evening. During the afternoon he would retire to his private rooms to read or rest, although in good weather he enjoyed a walk in the Reich Chancellery park.

With the exception of the most urgent business, during the day he never used a desk except to sit on it. It was his rather odd custom to burst into a sudden dictation, and his adjutants would have to scribble down instructions and intentions and later practically recast them. These would be sudden inspirations and incomplete ideas. Errors in taking down the notes could have serious consequences, and so many of his intentions were misrepresented that an official reading a draft would draw attention to a doubtful assertion with the observation 'Does the Führer know that?' This story filtered throughout the Reich, so that eventually any statement which caused a raised eyebrow would be greeted by this catchphrase in response. A serious weakness of the whole system of dictatorial government in Germany was that nobody was able to say with any certainty what Hitler had really meant when he dictated something at speed and his original idea had passed through several pairs of hands.

The evening meal was normally taken at 8 p.m. with a smaller circle. Speer or Heinrich Hoffmann, Baur his pilot, one or two military adjutants and one of the medical officers would be there, and his personal ADCs would look round to make up the numbers with guests who enjoyed Hitler's conversation. During dinner a list of the newest films, including foreign releases, would be presented by Goebbels and Hitler's choice would be shown afterwards in the orchestral room. Hitler's house servants, his SS guards and guests' chauffeurs were all invited. After the film he would sit before the fireplace with his guests and staff. Drinks, from tea to champagne, would be served—and cakes and sandwiches if the evening looked like being a long one. The evening conversation rarely tailed off much before two the next morning. Hitler's female secretaries ate at table and joined in the social evening at the Berghof and later at Führer HQs, but not at the Reich Chancellery.

Hitler's Staff

There were four personal adjutants with high SA or SS ranks. Wilhelm Brückner was Chief ADC. He was ever helpful and a friendly adviser. As our wives got along well we had an excellent private relationship. Both Brückner and Julius Schaub had been in prison with Hitler at Landsberg. Fritz Wiedemann had been Hitler's superior office in the Great War; I had no contact with him. The fourth personal ADC was Albert Bormann, younger brother of Martin Bormann. On account of a personal feud they never spoke.

There were additionally four female secretaries; three to five personal manservants, one of whom during the day had always to be within call; the housekeeper Kannenberg; Hans Baur, Hitler's pilot; Erich Kempka, his chauffeur; Gesche and Schädle, commanders of the Begleit-kommando; the heads of the plain-clothes police detachments, Ratten-huber and Högl; and four physicians, Brandt, von Hasselbach, Haase and Morell.

An important role was played by the unusually popular SS-Ober-gruppenführer Sepp Dietrich, who as commander of the SS-Leibstandarte Adolf Hitler and Chief of the Begleitkommando was responsible for Hitler's personal safety. Two others must be mentioned not belonging to Hitler's personal staff but always close to him—Press officer Reichsleiter Dr Dietrich, and Reichsleiter Martin Bormann. Until 1941 Bormann was Party Chief and liaison man between Hitler and Hess; later, as Hit-ler's secretary, he became involved in matters of policy.

This circle, including the military adjutants, was Hitler's personal reti-nue. Each went with him from place to place. Regular duty could be as much as sixteen hours daily, but despite this there was no increase in staff size from first to last. Despite their differing social origins the staff worked well together and without friction. The danger lay therein that each was subordinated to Hitler directly and felt answerable to him alone.

The Führer's Residences

The Führer-Standard at the flagstaff on the Chancellery roof and a lively coming and going of visitors were the hallmarks of Hitler's presence. The lower rooms of the Führer Residence had been furbished by Speer and Troost and a successful blend of chambers and home had been achieved. The hall faced the courtyard behind large central doors permanently shut, and facing the garden was the small saloon which connected the large orchestral room and the smoking room. The orchestral room had a door into the hall. This room was where Hitler received visitors and officials, and occasionally relatives and friends. These were mostly tea invitations and rarely lasted an hour. Hitler's table guests assembled in the smoking room before the meal. From the smoking room one passed into the dining room, beyond which was the winter garden and the banqueting hall.

The winter garden was a room about 30 metres long and ten wide with a long window overlooking the garden, and was preferred by Hitler during the day. A wide carpet ran from the dining room door to the garden entrance at the far end of the winter garden, and Hitler was fond of strolling the length of this carpet immersed in conversation. At first this was with Göring, Goebbels and Hess, and often for up to three hours at a time; as military problems began to increase it became more common for the military adjutants to accompany him.

The Führer's private suite, consisting of library, sitting room, bedroom and washroom, were located on the first floor. A small room was reserved for Eva Braun. Beyond these were the servants' quarters. The upper landing led to a side wing accommodating the typing and overnight rooms for the secretaries. Three floors down were the rooms for the adjutants, Press officer and Sepp Dietrich. These latter were the innermost circle who had to be on hand at short notice day and night. On the other side of the upper landing was a small dining room used by Hitler for access to the congress hall in the central part of the building when in use for military conferences during the war. It was at the Old Reich Chancellery that I was destined to spend the greater part of my service life in the Third Reich. Other time was spent at the various *Führer* HQs: at the Berghof, Hitler's retreat on the Obersalzberg mountain near the town of Berchtesgaden; and at the New Reich Chancellery, which was opened officially in January 1939.

The Führer's special train often served as his HQ during manoeuvres and operations. Hitler was very keen on living in his train. Weather permitting, he would often alight with his staff and take a walk. The train was not luxurious but practical. Outwardly it consisted of two locomotives pulling eight coaches of uniform shape and dark green colour. The first was a machinery and luggage coach. Next came Hitler's car with a long table and eight chairs forward. A corridor led to several compartments—two for Hitler, one each for his two senior adjutants, one for his two manservants and three for domestic purposes. The third coach was for SS and police, the fourth was the dining car, the fifth and sixth were for guests, adjutants, physicians and secretaries, the seventh was for the Press and the eighth was the rear machinery coach. All persons had to be in possession of a valid Reichsbahn first class ticket for the journey. We of the retinue had an annual season ticket, but it was the job of the personal ADCs to obtain tickets and distribute them to the guests before the train set off.

Hitler and the Luftwaffe
On 19 September 1937 I was in company with Hitler on manoeuvres. I watched a number of generals making their reports to him and remember how Manstein and Halder both avoided giving details since they thought that Hitler had no grasp of strategy or tactics. This amused me. On the last day of the manoeuvres the Luftwaffe displayed the use of heavy and light flak guns against ground targets at the Wustrow Flak Firing Range on the Baltic coast. The use of 8.8cm flak against tanks brought strong comments from some Army officers, who saw this as the Luftwaffe meddling in Army business!

Visiting an 8.8cm Luftwaffe flak battery, Hitler inspected the guns and fire control then drew me into conversation. It was general talk—the grouping of flak units into batteries according to calibre size and such like—but this was not a layman speaking, and he showed appreciation of operational use. He could also recite important technical data but wanted to know the rate of fire for the weapons. I had no idea and was about to summon the battery commander when he told me not to bother and we walked on. I told him that as a fighter pilot I knew next to nothing about flak. Hitler then spoke of flak as being of greater importance for air defence than fighters. I argued with him the importance of the fighter arm but he replied that the main task of the Luftwaffe was ground attack and therefore bombers.

In October 1937 Jeschonnek told me that the Luftwaffe was forced to plan its building programme to suit the raw material allotment. Flak and the construction of air raid bunkers came a poor second with Göring after aircraft production, contrary to Hitler's order that the same degree of urgency applied to each. Göring was always trying to convince Hitler that the fighter arm was the best defence against enemy air attack. Hitler would not accept this. When the fighter defence was found wanting from

19

1943 onwards, Hitler bitterly criticised Göring in the light of his 1938 instruction. He had foreseen what the experts considered impossible.

On 22 November 1937 Hitler visited the Messerschmitt factory at Augsburg to mark the spectacular success of the Bf 109 in breaking the world record with a speed of 610.95kph. Milch and Udet headed a delegation of officers and engineers from the Reich Air Ministry Technical Office. There was ill-feeling between Milch and Messerschmitt, which had originated from the time Milch had been General Director at Lufthansa. This discord had soured the relationship between Messerschmitt and the RLM, with the result that Germany's best aircraft designer was not put to the best use.

While Hitler was touring the works, Messerschmitt approached him in one of the work halls and, signalling for two great hangar doors to be opened, revealed the mock-up of a four-engined aircraft. At this the RLM gentlemen became very uneasy and the horror on Milch's face was evident. Hitler listened very attentively to Messerschmitt's description of the aircraft's capabilities. It was a projected four-engined long-range bomber, a forerunner to the Me 264, later built but not series-produced. Messerschmitt said it had a range of 6,000km with a one-tonne bomb load at 600kph. The RLM people expressed doubt at these figures. Hitler was non-committal: he was less well read about aircraft than about ships, panzers or guns. He said, however, that it must be possible to build a bomber which could outfly a fighter: if a fighter could manage 600kph, then a bomber needed 650kph. This would mean that armour and weapons on such a 'fast bomber' would be sacrificed for speed. Milch said that a contract with these specifications had been placed some time ago. Messerschmitt interjected that the speed was not possible at all at present because the necessary engine had not been developed. Hitler said it was right that the four-engined bomber should have priority. Milch replied that the Luftwaffe was subject to limits on raw materials, and he considered that a two-engined fast bomber was preferable. The discussion then broke up.

Over the next few weeks I tried to get to the bottom of all this intrigue. I found that, at General Staff, Jeschonnek was the coming man. I had got on well with him from the start and I used him subsequently as my contact at Luftwaffe High Command. Jeschonnek talked to me about bomber planning. Hitler's insistence on a fast bomber was not new. Wever, first Chief of the Luftwaffe General Staff, had demanded it. However the Luftwaffe had awarded to Junkers Dessau and others the building contract for a twin-engined bomber with the specification that as far as possible armament and equipment was secondary to speed. This aircraft, the Ju 88, had achieved 500kph on trials. To my objection that fighters could do 100kph more, Jeschonnek said that the existing record had been achieved with a 'souped-up' engine. The Me 109 series model would come off the production line with a standard engine, weapons and radio installation and fly no faster than 500kph. The next Ju 88 variant would have more powerful motors. These would be ready in about a year. Jeschonnek believed that the Ju 88 was the ideal bomber for the Luftwaffe. If a long-range bomber were needed—why, another variant of the Ju 88 would fit the bill here. Göring had now abandoned the four-engined series ordered by Wever. The first of these designs, the Ju 89 and the Do 19, had flown but were either to be scrapped or put to other uses. The Ju 89 became the Ju 90 commercial airliner.

Göring had decided in favour of the Ju 88 on account of the raw materials situation: for one four-engined bomber two twin-engined aircraft could be built, and this looked good in the production figures. I asked who had instigated and authorised this decision. Jeschonnek could not answer. He said he must have been at Greifswald at the time. He was convinced that the Augsburg Me 264 would never get off the ground. The fatal decision had already been taken not to provide the Luftwaffe with a long-range four-engined bomber.

Göring's decision in 1938 to erect an Air Defence Zone (LVZ) along the western frontier arose because the Army did not want the Westwall or Siegfried Line and Göring saw the opportunity to put himself in Hitler's good books. The LVZ was a second line of defence behind the Westwall along the entire western frontier. Many 8.8cm flak guns were planned in emplacements for a dual flak/anti-tank role. The Army expressed annoyance at this interference in its business. In mid-May 1939 Hitler inspected the Westwall, accompanied by a large entourage and huge Press following. Generalleutnant Kitzinger earned special praise from Hitler for the skilful installation of the flak batteries. All who saw it were very impressed by the great achievement of construction in so short a time. Even though only two-thirds complete, the fortifications were easily a match for any French artillery and tanks of the time.

In autumn 1938 Göring could not imagine that there could ever be an air force superior to the Luftwaffe. Even war itself seemed beyond the bounds of probability. He had taken seriously Hitler's instruction to increase five-fold the Luftwaffe's strength. I asked Jeschonnek how long this would take. He said two years; fuel and pilot training were the main problems. But Jeschonnek rubber-stamped the aircraft building programme: the Ju 88 would become the standard bomber. According to Udet, the He 177 was a very promising successor. Göring wanted to award Junkers the contract to mass produce the Ju 88 but Jeschonnek knew, as did the technical experts, that many teething problems remained to be overcome. Koppenberg, General Director of Junkers, had promised that nothing would stand in the way. Göring, Udet and Jeschonnek had the fullest confidence in him; only Milch had doubts. The He 177 was still a doubtful proposition, particularly the innovation of two pairs of engines in tandem. The prototype would fly in the summer of 1939, and series production was supposed to commence before the end of 1940.

I had the impression that Jeschonnek was putting the case in such a way that there seemed no doubt about the viability of the whole Luftwaffe programme. It was obvious to me, however, that only the fighter programme with the proven Me 109 was definite. The Ju 88 and the He 177 projects seemed questionable, and I did not conceal from Jeschonnek that I would put the situation to Hitler exactly as I saw it. Even the General Staff preliminary planning and the 'England' war games had highlighted our basic weaknesses. In principle, we had no bomber able to make a long flight over the open sea or for any penetration cross-country with a reasonable bomb load. I put it to Jeschonnek that Göring should be influenced to put the state of the Luftwaffe plainly to Hitler. If nothing else, this made clear to him Hitler's growing interest in Luftwaffe questions.

It had become Hitler's custom to ask me for details about squadrons, flak batteries, bomb and munition stocks and weapons. I had a notebook packed with this sort of information. Hitler knew this and one day he asked me, 'Have you got your clever little book with you?'—he wanted some detail or other. One did not have to have all the facts and figures, but it was important that what one did have was accurate. I found out that eventually he placed more reliance on the details in my notebook than on what Göring supplied him from memory.

On 19 November 1938 I had a chance to speak privately with Hitler. I was concerned that he was basing his plans on false information. As I suspected, he was under the impression that the Ju 88 was proven and ready for operations. He accepted my contradiction in silence. As for the He 177, he showed his instinct for simple technical solutions and expressed doubts about the arrangement of engines in tandem for a four-engined aircraft. Göring had told his people at RLM that Hitler was not competent to speak on the subject. I came to the view gradually that Göring was deliberately circulating a false assertion about Hitler's technical understanding and knowledge. At the time Hitler trusted Göring implicitly and was happy to leave Luftwaffe details in his hands, but as time went on Hitler took more interest in the Luftwaffe than Göring suspected.

Just before Christmas 1938 my wife and I attended the Paris International Aircraft Exhibition, where amongst others the British Spitfire was on display and attracted a great deal of interest. It was in an unfinished state, so we gained only an outward impression. It resembled the Me 109. As I knew the flying qualities of the latter I could see that the Spitfire would probably be equal. No engine was fitted but we heard rumours.

Hitler listened attentively to my report. I stated frankly that we had to reckon with the British fighter being superior because the British built better engines. In the end it probably came down to the design. Hitler decided that he had no time to lose. At RLM I explained my impressions to Jeschonnek and their effect on Hitler. Göring was not interested in my report. I assumed he knew everything worth knowing from Udet. Later I discovered that he knew nothing. For the first time I became aware of Göring's peculiarity of underestimating foreign developments. According to him no nation in the world could overtake Germany's armaments potential. One could not contradict him for fear of being labelled defeatist. Hitler, sceptical and curious by nature, was different. He was especially interested in foreign weapons and armaments capacity. He scoured overseas technical journals avidly and had all foreign texts of interest translated. His eye had been trained by architecture and painting. Many ill-informed technical experts suffered embarrassment at his hands.

Following the political developments in February 1939, Jeschonnek had begun to think in terms of war with Britain. Göring had told him frequently that Hitler did not want war with Britain, as I could confirm, but Jeschonnek always replied, 'The devil is a squirrel.' What he had considered impossible in 1938 he now made the foundation stone of his deliberations. The absence of a long-range bomber worried him very much. The Ju 88 was running up against many difficulties. He complained that Göring did not recognise the significance of technology. Since Wever's death in 1936, it had been neglected in the Luftwaffe.

On the morning of 3 July 1939, at Rechlin, Göring, Milch, Udet and Jeschonnek, accompanied by a large staff of engineers and technical officers, met Hitler for an air display. This had been instigated by Milch, who was concerned that the Luftwaffe production programme could not be met because of the shortage of raw materials. Whilst Milch always tried to give an honest picture of the situation, Göring tailored his reports to make it seem that everything was proceeding without a hitch. At Rechlin, where Udet was in charge, Göring and Udet had got their heads together and agreed to divert Hitler's attention to other matters. Göring, who was himself baffled easily by science, gave his associates to understand that Hitler knew nothing about aircraft but was very interested in weapons. The purpose of this was to ensure that discussions about squadron problems could be avoided.

The air show made a lasting impression on spectators. Milch managed to make Hitler aware that everything he was seeing was in the experimental stage, but nobody told him that after the successful conclusion of all tests it would be two to three years before the squadrons got the aircraft. As soon as Hitler showed interest in something, or thought such and such a development was important, Göring gave him a promise to ensure its delivery to the forces as soon as possible.

Undoubtedly the most impressive display was the maiden flight of the He 176, the world's first rocket-powered aircraft. Although it was only in the air a few minutes, the aircraft reached a speed of 1,000kph—a phenomenal achievment for the time. The He 100 seemed superior to the Mc 109 but Göring and Udet had already decided in favour of the latter, leaving Heinkel to specialise in bombers. An overladen He 111 was seen taking off with the assistance of two rockets. In order to carry out its task as the standard bomber, it usually flew overloaded either with additional fuel tanks for longer range or with more bombs for greater effect.

Relying on Hitler's assurances, Göring, Milch and Udet were not expecting war until 1943; the show was planned with this in mind. Nevertheless, on the return journey I reminded Hitler that what he had seen was music for the distant future: I suggested that he should invite Luftwaffe technical experts—especially Milch—to an armaments conference. He was very much in favour. However, because of political developments it never took place and the Rechlin show made a false impression on Hitler.

The bottleneck was caused by the lack of raw materials. This was never discussed. It was unforgivable that Göring and his close associates never drew the necessary conclusions. The successful campaigns of 1939 and 1940 cast a dark shadow over the realities. Two years on, after the first crisis of the Russian campaign, the fatal errors were recognised at last.

The Polish Question and the Path to War
The 1919 Treaty of Versailles had ceded the German city of Danzig to Poland. The province of East Prussia was an enclave to which access from the Reich could only be guaranteed by sea. Hitler proposed that Danzig be returned to Germany and that an ex-territorial land or rail link be established across Poland to link the Reich and East Prussia. In Germany, this 'Corridor Question' was much discussed and even opposition circles sympathised with it. Certainly there was more understanding than there had been for the Czech question.

There was in existence a non-aggression pact between Germany and Poland, the fifth anniversary of which fell on 6 January 1939. The day previously, Ribbentrop opened talks on the questions with Polish Foreign Minister Beck at Obersalzberg. At the end of January Ribbentrop returned from the reciprocal meeting in Warsaw empty-handed.

At the end of March, after the resolution of the Czech and Memel problems, Ribbentrop had comprehensive talks with the Polish ambassador Lipski. The latter was shocked at recent events and travelled reluctantly to Warsaw with Ribbentrop's fresh approach. The next we heard was reports from London that the Poles had requested a closer relationship with Britain. On 31 March, when British Prime Minister Chamberlain spoke on the subject in the Commons, Poland delivered a brusque rejection of Germany's request for more talks. Hitler concluded that the Poles would only adopt such a stance if they had the written backing of the British.

On 11 April. in the Instruction for the 'Unified Wehrmacht Preparations for War 1939–1940', there occurred the first mention of 'Fall Weiss' (Case White), the cover name for military operations against Poland.

A provocative and undiplomatic letter from Roosevelt, published in Washington before its arrival in Germany, demanded Hitler's assurance that he would not attack about thirty named European nations and suggested negotiations about disarmament. This was a sore point with Hitler, for the disarmament question had been the strongest argument in his political battle to revise the Versailles Treaty. For him, the League of Nations was an institution formed by the victor states of World War I to supervise the disarmament of Germany. The victor states, notably Britain and France, had not disarmed, but actually re-armed. It seemed to him that the Western democracies wanted Germany to remain a pariah for ever. He denigrated Roosevelt's 'lying politics', which on the one hand condemned totalitarianism and on the other sought closer ties with the USSR.

Hitler's Reichstag speech of 28 April, generally considered one of his best ever, gave Roosevelt his answer in 21 points and reaped storming applause. As to the reality of foreign policy, Hitler declared that, by their recent negotiations with Britain, the Poles had acted in breach of the 1934 German-Polish treaty, which they had accordingly abrogated.

In a conversation with his military advisers at the end of May Hitler stated that Poland would always side with our enemies whilst Britain was the driving force against Germany. In order to isolate Poland and hold off the British, it was decided in June to investigate the possibility of an accommodation with the USSR. Favourable signals had been received from Moscow some time previously. Preparations to invade Poland were initiated in July, but to disguise his intentions Hitler kept to his normal social programme and attended the Bayreuth Festival that month as usual.

On 12 August 1939 Hitler ordered the Wehrmacht to move up to the Polish border and set Saturday 26 August as X-Day. At that time reports of Polish excesses against the German minorities in the former Reich provinces of West Prussia and Upper Silesia were appearing in the Press almost daily. They were confirmed by our embassies in Warsaw and German consulates elsewhere in Poland. As these advices were sober and devoid of propaganda, the situation was obviously alarming. Hitler spoke frequently to his private circle about the 'untenable' conditions and the stream of refugees which, according to the registration authorities, already exceeded 70,000. There was no possibility that the NSDAP foreign organisation had worked as *agent provocateur* as in Austria and the Sudetenland, for Germans were being subjected to something which resembled a reign of terror irrespective of their politics or religion. To Hitler this implied Poland's readiness to fight. It could only be understood in terms of Polish chauvinism, for Poland was isolated.

On 19 August the Russo-German economic treaty was signed. As it was appearing more likely that Britain would consider a German invasion of Poland as a cause for war, Ribbentrop convinced Hitler that a non-aggression pact with the Soviet Union would be the last chance to forestall British intervention and returned to Moscow for that purpose on 23 August.

At midday on 22 August, in the Berghof, Hitler addressed senior Wehrmacht commanders. He spoke for nearly two hours using a prompt of handwritten headings. His primary purpose was to win the confidence of the generals for his decision to invade Poland. In the first part of his speech he explained his judgement of the factors likely to determine the response of the individual European nations. Immediately before the midday break, he announced Ribbentrop's mission to Moscow. The astonishment and relief were almost tangible. The pact was received favourably by those officers who in the Reichswehr period had worked in co-operation with the Red Army. I knew that several generals were opposed to Hitler and his policy of war, but although Hitler had glossed over certain matters, such as the influence of the USA on various European states, there were no questions: the pact with the USSR had left the sceptics speechless.

Before lunch on 23 August Hitler received British ambassador Henderson with a letter from Prime Minister Chamberlain. A reply was dictated after a long discussion and handed to Henderson. This talk seemed to have incensed Hitler. He accused the British Government of having handed Poland a blank cheque in April to resist his moderated demands in respect of Danzig and the Polish Corridor. Since then the outcry against Volksdeutsche in Poland had increased steadily. The Poles would never have done that without the encouragement of Britain. The British preferred another war against Germany to a revision of the Versailles Treaty whilst he, Hitler, had done nothing to harm Britain's interests.

On the Obersalzberg a gloriously warm summer's day was drawing to a close. The terrace doors were wide open and Hitler spent his time in company in the open. During this waiting period he drew me into conversation while we walked the terrace. This encounter with him has remained one of the most memorable for me because of an unusual celestial phenomenon. Hitler had posed a general question about the strength and armament of the Polish Air Force and if it would be in a position to bomb Berlin. It was no more than 150km from the Polish border to the

Reich capital, but I told him it was out of the question that a Polish bomber force would be able to fly an offensive against German cities following the surprise attack. As we strolled up and down, the eerie turquoise-coloured sky to the north turned first violet and then blood-red. At first we thought there must be a serious fire behind the Untersberg mountain, but then the glow covered the whole northern sky in the manner of the Northern Lights. Such an occurrence is exceptionally rare in southern Germany. I was very moved and told Hitler that it augured a bloody war. He responded that if it must be so, then the sooner the better; the more time went by, the bloodier it would be. (I recounted this conversation to Speer in 1967 but later he attributed my remark erroneously to Hitler in his book *Erinnerungen*.[2])

Shortly afterwards Ribbentrop telephoned Hitler with the information that Stalin wanted the Baltic States of Lithuania, Estonia and Latvia. Hitler threw a cursory glance at the map provided for him and authorised Ribbentrop to concede them. At about two o'clock next morning, Ribbentrop advised that the treaty was signed. Hitler congratulated him and remarked to us, 'That will explode in their faces.' The public in Germany and worldwide reacted with surprise, astonishment, dismay, disbelief and condemnation.

On 24 August only 36 hours separated us from war. After the talk the previous day, Hitler was not sure that Britain would remain neutral even though Henderson knew about Ribbentrop's mission and implied that the British Government was impressed. So the mood that evening tended to be pessimistic. Hitler saw the coming military campaign against Poland, of the success of which he was absolutely convinced, as the only way out of the political cul-de-sac.

On the morning of 25 August I consulted the Luftwaffe General Staff about the mobilisation preparations, operational squadrons and objectives before joining talks at the Führer HQ Adjutantur regarding our arrangements for the coming days.

Hitler had finally advised Mussolini of tomorrow's invasion of Poland. Several times previously the Italians had expressed their annoyance that Hitler always notified his allies of events *post festum*, but Hitler preferred their resentment to the greater evil of risking their loquacity.

The previous evening Chamberlain and Foreign Minister Lord Halifax had made parliamentary speeches which had led to accusations in the British newspapers that Hitler wanted to conquer the world. At lunchtime Hitler summoned the British ambassador to protest and declared his wish to resolve the German-Polish question. After this he would be ready for an extensive accommodation with Britain.

Late on the afternoon of 25 August, Britain announced ratification of the Anglo-Polish mutual assistance treaty of 6 April and Italian Foreign Minister Attolico delivered Mussolini's note stating that Italy was not prepared for war. Ribbentrop immediately suggested to Hitler that the attack order be withdrawn to consider the implications. Keitel was sent for and Hitler ordered him to stop the invasion.

Hitler had been dealt a low blow. His plan had been overturned by a combination of factors beyond his control. When he appeared next morning, he had already read the foreign news reports. Now he saw a close connection between the two events of the previous day. Mussolini's stance must have been engineered by London, where his ambassador there, Count Grandi, although a member of the Fascist Grand Council in Rome, was a dyed-in-the-wool anglophile monarchist.

Harsh words followed, although Mussolini's loyalty was not questioned. Hitler attributed guilt to monarchist circles within the Italian Army and diplomatic corps, whose anti-German and pro-British threads intertwined at court. Yet, even in Reich Chancellery chambers, Ribbentrop's staff spoke out for the Italian policy in the hope of dissuading Hitler from war.

On the evening of 28 August the British ambassador delivered a memorandum implying that Poland was prepared to enter into direct talks with Germany. Hitler accepted the proposal on the 29th and requested that a Polish plenipotentiary be sent to Berlin the next day. Henderson interpreted this deadline as an ultimatum and became so excited that Ribbentrop had to intervene to calm him down. Accordingly Hitler remained prepared for bilateral discussions with Poland provided that Britain did not take part. The short deadline had a purely military basis. Hitler had been advised by his generals not to delay X-Day beyond 2 September because of the weather situation, the pre-condition for rapid operations being the use of the Luftwaffe. This gave Hitler only four days, and for this reason the Polish negotiator had to come at once.

The last exchange of notes with Britain seemed to clear the way for negotiations with Poland. Hitler emphasised that the only matters in dispute were Danzig, the Polish Corridor and the treatment of the

German minority. In the Führer Residence our impression that the danger of war was past was reinforced when the Reichstag deputies, recalled to Berlin on 26 August, were sent home next day after hearing a short speech in the Chancellery in which Hitler stressed his heartfelt wish to solve the Polish question without bloodshed. He had, however, stated his readiness to fight if Britain continued to oppose the right of the German people to revise the Versailles Treaty.

On 30 August Ribbentrop and Göring came several times to the Chancellery to help formulate the proposals for the Polish emissary. Hitler himself dictated the memorandum, which tabled sixteen points. I thought that these were not excessive. The city of Danzig would return to the Reich. The proposal for a referendum in the Polish Corridor was new: depending on its outcome, Hitler suggested an ex-territorial road and rail link between the Reich and East Prussia.

Hitler was very doubtful that a Polish negotiator would come, and he was right. Instead of a sending a plenipotentiary, Poland mobilised. Hitler sent for Brauchitsch and Keitel that afternoon and set X-hour for 0445 on Friday 1 September.

Just before midnight on 30 August Henderson called on Ribbentrop with a fresh memorandum and a verbal explanation. The British Government had not been able to recommend that Poland send a plenipotentiary to Berlin, but suggested instead that Ribbentrop should summon Lipski, the Polish ambassador, and give him the sixteen points in order to set up talks. Ribbentrop declined.

By the early hours of 31 August Hitler seemed to have made his decision. Initially impassive, he now broke into a tirade against Britain. The ratification of the Anglo-Polish treaty on 25 August was proof that Britain was engineering war in Europe. He doubted the assertion in the British memorandum of the 28th that London possessed the Polish Government's promise of willingness to negotiate with the German Government. That no plenipotentiary came on the 30th proved the lie. Britain's motive was delay because the Poles had no intention of entering talks.

As if to prove the point, Lipski called on Ribbentrop just after six in the evening of 31 August and said that the previous evening Britain had told his government about the possibility of direct talks between Germany and Poland. Warsaw would supply London with an answer within a few hours. When this report reached Hitler he reacted angrily; two days ago he had delivered to Henderson an offer of direct talks with a Polish plenipotentiary and this was the first the Poles had heard of it. Their behaviour was further proof that they wanted war. For these reasons Hitler considered it pointless to continue negotiations. British diplomacy bore the same hallmarks as in 1914 when all British notes had the single purpose of absolving London from blame in the event of war.

There now followed an unforgettable scene. Hitler stood in a circle of people which included Ribbentrop and Göring. Göring said that he did not believe that the British would declare war. Hitler clapped him on the shoulder and replied, 'My dear Göring, if the British ratify a treaty one day, they don't break it the next.' Hitler believed that Britain would honour her pact with Poland. It was Britain's centuries-old political tradition that her schemes proceeded under a pretence of freedom and human rights. Hitler's offer to Poland had been honourable, for his mission was against the Soviets. All other struggles served only this single goal— to clear the way for war against Bolshevism. That must interest all Europe, and especially Britain, which had an Empire at stake.

On 31 August, in the Chancellery, field grey uniforms were more in evidence than previously. In a short conference with Brauchitsch and Keitel that morning, Hitler signed 'Instruction No 1 for Warfare'. Diplomatic activity continued all day. From Italy came encouragement for a conference, as at Munich. That evening, German radio broadcast a summary of events of the preceding three days, including the sixteen-point proposal. The bulletin ended with the statement that the Polish Government had failed to respond to Germany's 'loyal, fair and admissible' demands. Whoever had ears should have known from that what it presaged for the morrow.

In the early morning of 1 September 1939 there was broadcast to the Wehrmacht, the German people and the world a proclamation by the Führer and Reich Chancellor that he had ordered the Wehrmacht to attack Poland. Next came Hitler's Reichstag speech, in which he wore for the first time the field grey tunic tailored for him without his knowledge by his SS aides. Previously he had always worn a brown jacket with swastika armband. Now he wore the field grey tunic with SS eagle high on the left sleeve—a garment which, as he said in his Reichstag speech, he 'would not cast aside until after victory'.

The Reichstag gave Hitler a storming reception, the shouts of *Heil!* being far more than usual, and spontaneous applause broke out continually during his speech.

31

All negotiations by the German Government against Versailles since 1919, and especially for the Polish Corridor, were popular in Germany, but as the day wore on and it became clear that Hitler had set in train a full-scale war, the mood sobered and the question of how Britain and France would react preoccupied everybody. Nevertheless Hitler was greeted jubilantly on his journey to and from the Reichstag, and on the Wilhelmsplatz an enormous crowd had gathered.

In the rooms of the Reich Chancellery the flow of visitors and the disquiet grew steadily. The latest reports of the foreign Press agencies were awaited avidly. All discussion centred on whether Britain would declare war. The Party functionaries were sure that Britain was bluffing again, otherwise Hitler would not have invaded Poland. They had no idea that he knew that he risked war with Britain when he gave the order, in the depths of his being hoping against hope that Britain would step back from the brink.

The first reports from the front spoke of victories. These fortified Hitler against the warnings and threats uttered that day from London and Paris. In the evening of 1 September the British and French ambassadors each delivered a note in which their governments declared themselves ready to fulfil their treaty obligations to Poland in the event that German troops were not withdrawn from Polish territory. The situation was becoming ever clearer and more grave. September 2 passed with reports of further military successes. Mussolini made the last attempt for a conference to end hostilities, but it was already too late.

At nine on the morning of 3 September, Henderson delivered to the Foreign Office an ultimatum stating that Britain would consider herself at war with Germany if by 11 o'clock the German Government had not given a satisfactory undertaking to cease hostilities and withdraw its troops from Poland. A few hours later the French ambassador handed in an ultimatum in similar terms. These were the declarations of war.

Chief Interpreter Schmidt, a member of Ribbentrop's ministerial office, proceeded immediately to the Chancellery, where Hitler and Ribbentrop were strolling on the winter garden. They knew already that Henderson wanted to present a note, and Ribbentrop had absented himself from his office because he knew that it could only be the declaration of war. Contrary to the description in Schmidt's book *Statist auf diplomatischer Bühne* (An Extra on the Diplomatic Stage), Hitler and Ribbentrop were standing together when he handed them the note; Göring did not arrive until later. I watched the scene through the glass doors. I had the impression that both were more disappointed than surprised. Perplexed dismay descended on the waiting guests and weighed down on everybody.

During the morning of that fateful 3 September, when there was no going back, I accompanied Hitler in the winter garden. Bitterly he gave free rein to his thoughts on Britain's 'short-sighted attitude'. Pausing suddenly, he asked me if I had writing materials: a statement had to be written for the German people. Before I had time to suggest he summon a female secretary, he began, '*Parteigenossen und Parteigenossinnen* [Party members].' I interrupted and asked if this proclamation was only intended for Party members. He reflected for a moment and then said, 'Write "*An das deutsche Volk* [To the German people]".' Then he dictated at speed. I had great difficulty in keeping up as I could not take shorthand. He noticed this and paused occasionally so that I could scribble most of it down. Immediately afterwards I dictated the result to a secretary and presented him with the rough draft. Standing at the table in the smoking room, he started correcting it at once. I watched over his shoulder. Heinrich Hoffmann photographed this scene and I was not surprised when the picture, which was to cause me such grief postwar, appeared next day on the front page of the *Völkischer Beobachter*.

CHAPTER ONE

1939

What motivated Poland to take on the Wehrmacht in a one-sided war? They were under the illusion that Anglo-French forces would attack immediately in the West where—in comparison to the Eastern Front—the German Army was spread thinly. This would result, as they supposed, in German troops being transferred from the East to reinforce the Western Front. They also set great store on information from France implying that within the first three days of war a *coup* in Germany would eject Hitler and clear the way to Berlin for the Poles. The source of these reports was German resistance circles, to which both France and Poland attached undue importance. We did not learn of this until the discovery of Polish ministerial files some weeks later, supplemented in 1940 by State documents seized in France.

The Poles were not equipped for modern war. They had 36 infantry and two mountain divisions and one mountain, one motorised and eleven cavalry brigades, but lacked armour and artillery. Against them the German Army ranged more than 50 divisions, including six panzer and four motorised—a clear superiority. The Polish Air Force was not an independent arm and its 900 aircraft, roughly half modern and half obsolescent, were distributed amongst Army units. The military leadership was good, and some groups fought on doggedly in ignorance of the overall situation.

To the mass of the German people, the attack on Poland was no more than the means of rectifying the Versailles diktat. War began for Germany with the British and French declarations on 3 September 1939.

The FHQ

During the first three days of war the Führerhauptquartier (FHQ) came into being. Its infrastructure remained virtually unchanged from beginning to end. Hitler was accompanied by two personal ADCs, usually Brückner (SA) and Schaub (SS); two female secretaries; two manservants;

attendant physician Dr Karl Brandt, representing Professor von Hasselbach; four military ADCs, Schmundt, Puttkamer, Engel and myself; and three liaison officers, Bodenschatz (Luftwaffe), Wolff (SS) and Admiral Voss. The Wehrmacht High Command (OKW) controlled the military planning staff headed by Keitel: Jodl was head of the Wehrmacht Command Staff (WFSt) throughout the war.

The Polish Campaign
The relationship between Hitler and the Army High Command (OKH) was fluid. At the outbreak of war there existed a certain tension, primarily to do with personnel appointments and which had its origins in 1938. For example, OKH had given Blaskowitz the Eighth Army when Hitler considered him unqualified for anything greater than overseeing motorisation. In the case of Kluge, Hitler had allowed himself to be influenced by Göring, who had repeatedly clashed with Kluge about the latter's outspoken opinions and public remarks on military matters. But OKH prevailed against Hitler and Kluge was given command of the Fourth Army, whose task was to advance through a section of the Polish Corridor to reach the Vistula. Hitler quickly gained a good impression of Kluge and was very upset when he had to be replaced following a flying accident on 4 September.

The key to the Polish operation was Reichenau's Tenth Army. With his panzers and motorised divisions, he was instructed to spearhead the attack through Silesia towards Warsaw. In the preliminary discussions Hitler had suggested that he 'look neither right nor left' but 'look only forwards towards his goal'. To protect his flanks he had List's Fourteenth Army to the south and Blaskowitz's Eighth Army to the north. Blaskowitz was also intent on reaching Warsaw as soon as possible. Therefore Blaskowitz and Reichenau were both looking only forwards. When a Polish division broke out of the Posen area a dangerous situation threatened for some hours until General von Briesen's 30th Infantry Division made a left turn and stopped the thrust. Von Briesen was wounded during the engagement. Hitler reproached Blaskowitz sternly for his negligence. In the event the quick victories bridged all differences and prevented serious crises.

Hitler distanced himself from command during the Polish campaign. A train in sidings at Lower Pomerania and later Upper Silesia served as his HQ. He was confident of success and expected at any moment a sign from the Poles that they wanted to give in and negotiate surrender on fair *Restpolen* terms.[3] In his Reichstag speech of 1 September he had said that the purpose of the war was to resolve the 'questions of Danzig and the Polish Corridor'. This would bring about 'change in the relationship between Germany and Poland to assure peaceful coexistence'. Thus he was ready to negotiate.

For their part, the Poles fought on bravely in every sector but without prospect of success. They had almost no telephone links. The various fronts trusted blindly in London's promise of relief as soon as possible. On 17 September the Polish Government abandoned Warsaw and set up in Romania. This was the signal for Hitler to annexe to the Reich those parts of Poland which had been German possessions until 1918, and cede the area east of the Narew–Vistula–San line to the Soviets. The remainder would be run from Cracow by a General Government under Reichsleiter Hans Frank.

That same day Soviet forces swarmed through eastern Poland as far as the line agreed with Ribbentrop. As the German Army was already beyond this line in its advance eastwards there was a great deal of annoyance at having to give up the territory won. Hitler remarked frequently at this time that the British guarantees made to Poland in March and August 1939 were the best possible proof that Britian had engineered the war in order to get rid of him—and, as in 1914, they had done it in such a manner as to taint Germany with the guilt.

On 19 September Hitler took quarters in the Casino Hotel at Zoppot, from where he was driven that afternoon to Danzig. The jubilation and size of the crowds were unbelievable. After being welcomed in the Artus Hof by Gauleiter Forster, Hitler delivered a long, unscripted reply in which he announced the annexation of Danzig into the Reich. I had the impression that much of what he said was for British consumption, for example, 'For the warmongers, Poland was only a means to an end. This war was not about the existence of Poland, but about the removal of the German regime.' Or, 'If Poland chose war, then they chose it because others were "mongering" in it.' To his enemies in the West he said, 'I have no war aims as regards Britain and France,' and concluded, 'Since the aim of Britain is not just war against a regime, but war against the German people, against German women and children, our response will be the same. And at the end one thing will be certain. This Germany will never capitulate.'

The Battle for Warsaw

During our stay in Zoppot, Hitler concentrated his attention on the battle for Warsaw. He observed that the city's commander was still waiting for the assistance of the Western states. On 21 September he had accepted Hitler's offer to allow the evacuation of the entire diplomatic corps and all foreign nationals from the city. They were led north of Warsaw by representatives of the German Foreign Office and escorted to Königsberg.

Warsaw now prepared itself for the final battle. Diplomatic reports stated that very remarkable signals had been received from the West: the French were said to have made a substantial incursion into southern Germany and all work in the Ruhr had stopped. No doubt this was intended to give a little more backbone to the commander in his defence of the city. The artillery bombardment began on 21 September and the Luftwaffe was ordered to start air raids. On the 22nd Hitler was flown around the outskirts of Warsaw to observe the effects. In close vicinity to the spot where the former Army C-in-C Fritsch had been mortally wounded, he was informed of the general's death, and, although making no comment, was visibly affected. Driving along the highway that day I was appalled at the large number of refugees fleeing the area. Most were younger people and many Jews.

On 25 September Hitler flew again to the Warsaw theatre and from a good vantage point watched the attack ordered for that day by OKH. Many parts of the city were ablaze. It highlighted how useless resistance was. Two days later the city's commander surrendered, and the last Polish forces capitulated on 1 October on the Hela peninsula.

During the campaign the Luftwaffe developed a style of attack which remained decisive until the end of 1941. On the first two days of war the Polish airfields had been laid waste and the mass of aircraft destroyed, enabling the German Army to manouvre across Poland unmolested by air attack. The Luftwaffe supported the Army's advance with complete aerial supremacy and in this way there developed a close inter-service co-operation which was to be the foundation for the successes of the next two years.

Hitler's Style of Leadership

Service in our Adjutantur now reverted to a steady routine centred on the daily situation conferences with Jodl or the Army General Staff. These talks convened every day at twelve and usually lasted for up to two hours.

The evening discussions, mostly around six or seven, were on a lesser scale. Jodl would sum up the current situation and if, as in the quiet periods between campaigns in 1939 and 1941, there was nothing special to report, the adjutants of each branch of service would then deliver a brief closing summary. The morning update was central, for here Hitler discussed all events and measures and made known his thoughts and instructions regarding future operations. Until the autumn of 1941 it was rare for him to give a direct order. His preferred method was persuasion, so that his generals put his ideas into effect from conviction. This persuasion was also the reason for the often protracted conversations with Hitler. Even after December 1941, when Hitler took over command of the Army, he still attempted to win over his listeners by argument. Only in the final year of the war, when the possibilities of putting across his ideas were so limited, did he make more use of direct commands.

During the Polish campaign I had the opportunity to appreciate Hitler's sharp logic and extraordinary fine feel for military situations. He was very good at putting himself in the enemy's shoes and his military judgment was balanced and accurate, whereas in the political field he was something of a visionary, but prey to wishful thinking.

Hitler, Halder and Brauchitsch

After the fall of Poland the enthusiasm throughout the ranks divided the Army leadership. The OKH leaders Brauchitsch and Halder were isolated and could expect no support for their designs to have Hitler removed. Thus although both were inwardly opposed to Hitler's plans and ideas, they went along with him in the hope that somewhere along the way the opportunity to strike would present itself. But it never did.

In my conversations with Hitler from September 1939 onwards I noticed his anxiety to understand the thinking of the OKH generals. He knew that he had amongst them some—a few—enemies. He did not have this worry with the Luftwaffe or Navy. Under Brauchitsch the Army continued to follow its own path, and this Hitler wanted to change. He was unsuccessful, and in any case his criticism of the General Staff and Army officer corps was based on a false premise. Driven by his own will to succeed, he expected too much of them and was disappointed and surprised by their 'mediocre quality', as he once expressed it to me.

Following the victory over Poland, I was often asked who advised Hitler on his war policies: people heard that there was an atmosphere of servility, nervousness and self-consciousness in his presence. I will not deny that an outsider who had made a report to Hitler once or twice might be under this impression. In the daily round of situation conferences there was a more or less fixed agenda where it was only possible for the individual to put his viewpoint in respect of the particular matter under discussion. Hitler discussed special questions and problems in private talks with a limited personal circle. Early in the war many visitors calling to make reports, mostly older, inwardly antagonistic General Staff officers, were self-conscious and uncertain. At that time I knew nothing of a broad active opposition to Hitler, but it is understandable that an officer with a foot in two camps might sweat a little, particularly if Hitler went into details and asked a few searching questions which could not be answered, and then he would recount later to his personal circle how perfectly frightful it had been to be made to discuss military matters with a person like Hitler, who after all had had no General Staff training. I listened to this sort of thing several times, but Hitler's questions were really quite normal and not extraordinary at all. Generally they simply sought details omitted from a report but which Hitler considered important for the overall picture.

Decision for a Campaign in the West

During the Polish campaign, when he went to the command coach to receive Jodl's morning report, Hitler's first question would be. 'Anything on the Western Front?', and Jodl always reassured him that nothing whatever was happening on the Western Front. For some time Hitler had been considering plans for a swift campaign against France, and so it did not surprise me when Schmundt stated so openly on 8 September. The matter was discussed frequently with his military advisers: the date they had been given was October or November. Hitler did not think it likely that Britain or France would sue for peace after the fall of Poland, and he was convinced that Britain in particular would remain belligerent. Hitler's intention was to overwhelm France and thus convince Britain that the war against Germany was pointless.

On 26 September Hitler returned by train to Berlin and next afternoon summoned Göring, Raeder, Brauchitsch, Keitel, Jodl, Halder, Jeschonnek and Bodenschatz to the New Reich Chancellery. We military ADCs were also present at this conference, the purpose of which was to discuss the attack on France. OKH had made known its disfavour about this, and it was not surprising when Hitler launched into a comprehensive lecture. The victory over Poland had changed the world's opinion of Germany, he said. The great majority of neutral states trembled before us. The major powers saw in us a great danger. The Polish campaign had increased their fears and respect. Throughout the world there was no love for Germany. Britain would attempt to agitate further against us. Therefore we had to reckon with a continuation of the war. Time was not on our side. In six months Britain and France would be better placed than now. Britain would have raised many divisions, perhaps not combat-worthy, but at least suitable for resistance. The panzers and the Luftwaffe had been the key to our success in Poland. Today the West was poorly equipped in this respect. In six months it would probably be different. If they had had the weapons, they would have been able to help Poland. It was erroneous to delay our attack in the West. If we were forced into trench warfare, we would have to rely on the Luftwaffe and U-boats for victory. We could quickly make good our minimal losses in Poland. It was essential to transfer as many units as possible to the Western Front. The quality was not decisive—the attack was no more difficult than that against the Poles. The decisive factor was the weather during the first three or four days. Between 20 and 25 October the attack should be made with the objective of striking a death blow to the enemy. The war aim was to force Britain to her knees. These were Hitler's words. He was totally convinced that a swift attack in the West would be successful.

On 28 September Ribbentrop returned to Moscow for the signing of the 'German-Soviet Border and Friendship Treaty'. This border was the Bug River. The eastern Baltic states had been gifted to Russia. Hitler had given his assent without long deliberation, but had made public the 'General Political Declaration of the Reich Government and the Soviet Government', which contained the observation that 'it would be in the interests of all peoples to put an end to the present state of war between Germany on the one hand and Britain and France on the other . . . Should, however, the efforts of our two governments be unsuccessful, that very fact would determine the responsibility of Britain and France for the continuation of the war.' The German Press made a big thing of this declaration but Hitler doubted that it would budge Britain. The earliest possible attack on France remained his priority, while Poland would be the springboard for a future military adventure. Therefore the latter's road, rail and communications networks were to be maintained and the Polish economy could continue as before.

On 5 October Hitler flew to Warsaw, where he was met at the airfield by Brauchitsch, Blaskowitz and Reichenau and later took the salute at the march past of the Eighth Army. The parade lasted two hours. It was the only occasion when he did this in the capital city of a conquered nation. After visiting Belvedere Castle, the former seat of the late Marshal Pilsudski, he returned to Berlin. Next day he addressed the Reichstag, describing the course of the Polish campaign and highlighting the achievement and fighting spirit of the fighting forces, the quick victories and the few casualties. In conclusion he spoke extensively about the political situation in Europe. There was no reason for the war to be continued, he said. It solved no problem in the West. He made suggestions for humanitarian arrangements and suggested the abolition of certain weapons and the prohibition of air attacks against civilian targets. But one could detect his suspicion of Britain. At the end of his speech he left the decision in the hands of the British Government. Should his suspicions be confirmed, we would fight. Not for a second did he doubt that Germany would triumph. Finally he offered thanks to God 'for having blessed us so wonderfully in the first major struggle for our right' and prayed that 'He allow us and all others to find the right path where it falls not only to the German people, but to all Europe, to find a new happiness in peace.'

This speech was not without its effect on the mass of the people. They trusted in the Führer and believed—contrary to Hitler's thinking—that Britain and France would be sensible. Hitler never doubted Britain's commitment to war and concentrated his mental energies totally on the imminent attack in the West. On 9 October he issued to the Wehrmacht Directive No 6 ordering the preparation of an attack on the northern flank of the Western Front through the Luxemburg/Belgian and Dutch areas 'as powerfully and early as possible'. How serious Hitler was about the need to fight immediately can be seen from his discussion document of 10 October addressed to senior Wehrmacht commanders, in which he stated unequivocally that 'the German war aim must be the final military annihilation of the West'. Regarding the Soviet Union, he stated, 'No treaty or agreement can ensure for certain the lasting neutrality of Soviet Russia. For the present, reason militates against their abandoning this neutrality. In eight months, in a year, maybe in several years, this can change.' With these words he made known to his generals his attitude to the treaty with Soviet Russia.

As early as 10 September Hitler had been completely surprised when the Kriegsmarine C-in-C, Raeder, made plain the importance of Norway in a naval war, primarily with regard to protecting the iron ore shipments from the port of Narvik. Raeder considered the implications so serious that he recommended the occupation of Norway. Hitler asked Raeder to have the Naval War Office (SKL) send him the files, but the matter was not raised again until the outbreak of the Russo-Finnish War on 30 November.

In early October, at Raeder's suggestion, Hitler visited U-boat crews at Wilhelmshaven. Several submarines were in harbour there after having made their first war patrols. It was Raeder's intention that Hitler should gain a deeper understanding of the U-boat arm's main purpose—the war against enemy trade. The Führer der Uboote, Dönitz, outlined events to date in a brief address, and, after inspecting the crews, many of them still unkempt, Hitler invited the officers to give detailed accounts of their experiences. One of them was Schuhart, whose boat *U 29* had sunk the aircraft carrier *Courageous* on 17 September. Hitler returned to Berlin with an excellent impression. On 14 October the British Admiralty admitted the sinking of the battleship *Royal Oak* by a U-boat inside Scapa Flow—an audacious achievement about which Hitler was so enthusiastic that he summoned the commander and crew of *U 47* to the Chancellery, where he decorated Prien with the Knight's Cross.

Hitler's preoccupation was to be at the Channel by late autumn, after having broken the French will to fight. This would pre-empt whatever was being schemed in London and Paris. The revised date for the attack against France, Belgium and Holland was 12 November. He authorised Brauchitsch and Halder to proceed with the operational plan. By now he had fresh ideas, but time had run out for fundamental changes.

On 16 and 27 October OKH attempted to dissuade him. Brauchitsch and Halder asserted that the divisions which had been victorious in Poland were not sufficiently suitable for battle in the West. On 5 November Brauchitsch met Hitler alone and supplied him with a memorandum tabling current Army weaknesses. In the course of the ensuing conversation Hitler began to put the counter-argument so forcefully that Brauchitsch fell silent. Hitler pointed out that the troops were trained to the same standard as four weeks before; the weather might be unfavourable in the spring. The truth was that OKH did not want to fight; all this talk of working-up was for delay. Hitler was shocked and annoyed at Brauchitsch and even mentioned it to me. He made no secret that Brauchitsch and Halder would have to be replaced, but it could not be done now, shortly before a new offensive.

Assassination at the Bürgerbräukeller

On 7 November OKH asked for Hitler's confirmation of the 12th as X-Day. Before the main situation conference Dr Diesing, the senior Luftwaffe meteorologist, delivered a weather prognosis so miserable that Hitler was forced to postpone his decision to the 9th. This would follow his return from Munich, where he had a speech to make on the evening of the 8th. His speech at the Bürgerbräukeller had only one subject—Britain.

I was awoken that evening to receive a telephone call. A bomb had gone off at the Party meeting but Hitler had already left the cellar. The device had been concealed beneath the central pillar. So now we knew that Hitler had enemies who would go to any lengths to get rid of him. It was noticeable the following morning, on his return to the Chancellery, that the incident had affected him. He accepted our wishes of good luck calmly and declared it a miracle that he had been spared: it was a sure sign of the mission he had been given as head of the Reich. It was reported from Munich that eight people had been killed and over sixty injured. Hitler took a lively interest in the condition of the survivors and wounded. Three days later, when he went back to Munich for the Feldherrnhalle political ceremony, he visited the injured in hospital and was obviously moved when shown over the demolished cellar at the Bürgerbräukeller. The criminal investigation later showed that Georg Elser, a 36-year old cabinet maker arrested at the Swiss frontier, had probably acted alone.

Hitler's Thought on the Operational Plan

In the large situation room a relief map of the territory west of the German border had been pinned up, and throughout October Hitler spent a great deal of time contemplating this map and meditating on his offensive. After supper, when previously it had been his custom to watch a film, he would return to the situation room with the duty military ADCs for hour-long conversations about all aspects of the proposed invasion.

These conversations were little more than a soliloquy, and we ADCs were the sounding-board for his ideas.

He studied the roads, rivers and other obstructions to troop movements, and as the weeks went by it became increasingly clear to him that his main thrust must be through the Ardennes towards the Sedan–Rouen axis. On 30 October, while juggling an extra panzer and motorised division to the Arlon–Sedan line—no more than a tactical strengthening of von Rundstedt's Army Group B—he saw the advantage of amassing his panzers. When the weather situation caused a further postponement of X-Day, Hitler revised his plans completely. On 11 October OKH telexed Army Groups A and B advising them that the Führer had ordered the formation of a mobile armoured group which, using open stretches of country either side of Arlon, Tintigny and Florenville, would bear down on Sedan. In Directive No 8 of 20 November Hitler ordered the weight of the attack transferred from Army Group B to Army Group A. Jodl then discussed the document with the General Staff. As a rule the latter were not inclined to follow Hitler's directives too strictly, and the various points were translated into orders only slowly. In any case, the first operational plan was still in force and was being postponed at regular intervals for periods of from six to eight days. At this time Hitler was not aware of Manstein's ideas, which coincided very closely with his own.

In November the BBC broadcast a very aggressive speech by Churchill in which he likened Hitler to a criminal lunatic and promised that if Britain and France were defeated all Europe would be enslaved, leaving the United States to fight on alone. Churchill was looking to his future: he was not yet Prime Minister, but he knew that in due course the war would dictate that he receive the reins of power.

On 23 November, considering it necessary to elucidate his most recent understanding of the general situation, Hitler summoned Göring, Raeder, Brauchitsch, the Army Group and Army C-in-Cs, all with their senior commanders, together with their Navy and Luftwaffe counterparts. He began by reviewing the development of his own career from 1919 through 1923 until the seizure of power in 1933. Since then he had built up the Wehrmacht to strike, he said. First he had been compelled to find a solution in the East. The superiority of the Wehrmacht had brought a swift success in Poland. For the moment the Soviet Union was not dangerous, but Stalin would only observe our common treaty for as long as it suited him. We could only move against Russia once we were free in the West. The Russian armed forces would remain inferior for one to two years. Italy under Mussolini was a positive factor for us. His death would be dangerous for Germany. Italy would not enter the war until Germany began her offensive against France. The Italian court was anti-German. Hitler deemed the United States 'still no threat to us'; of Japan he was uncertain—it was not even known if she would be hostile to Britain. 'Time works for the enemy. The ratio of might can only deteriorate against us. I will attack and not capitulate. The fate of the Reich depends on me alone.'

British rearmament was beginning only now, he continued. Its first phase would not be complete for one to two years. The French fighting forces were far inferior to ours. Germany had superiority, and the millions of Germans now in the armed forces were outstanding. Everything lay in the hands of the military leaders, and behind the Army stood the greatest armaments industry in the world. It impressed him that the British were beginning to loom large: they were tough opponents. In six to eight months they would be in France with greatly increased forces. Holland and Belgium would be on their side. They were waiting only for mutual support before invading the Ruhr. The outcome of the war depended on who held the Ruhr. It was important for us to have better bases from which to strike. Flights over England were currently too costly in fuel. That could only be changed by occupying the Low Countries: 'It is a difficult decision for me. I must choose between victory and defeat. I choose victory.'

Hitler now declared his decision to attack France and Britain at the earliest opportunity. He dismissed Belgian and Dutch neutrality as 'meaningless'. He saw the military conditions as favourable. But it was a precondition that the higher leadership should give an example of fanatical determination. If the people's leaders had always had the courage which the simple rifleman had to have, there would never have been failure. 'It is for the nation a question of to be, or not to be. I implore you to pass on to your men the spirit of resolution. I will stand or fall in this struggle. I will not survive the defeat of my people. Outwardly no capitulation; inwardly no revolution.'

During the late afternoon Hitler had another serious talk with Brauchitsch. He considered it essential to win him over. The latter asked the Führer to relieve him of office if he was thought lacking. Hitler declined, and reminded Brauchitsch of the need for every soldier to remain at his post.

Developments at the End of the Year

After the evening meal Hitler took me into the large situation room, where we walked the length of the room together. He wanted to speak his thoughts aloud in order to detect errors in his planning. He repeated his criticism of Brauchitsch and Halder and condemned their negative attitude to the Western offensive. 'The 100 German divisions coming to readiness in the next few months are at present superior to those of Britain and France. In six months that can change,' Hitler said. This was his main concern, for he did not know the rate at which his two enemies were rearming. In spring 1940 he needed the Army free for a great operation in the East against Russia. This was the first I had heard of the idea. It seemed utopian, but apparently the plan had been long thought-out. And soon the Wehrmacht would be asked to fulfil it.

On 29 November diplomatic relations were broken off between Russia and Finland. Hitler shook his head: he considered it impossible that Finland could hold out against Soviet forces. Diplomats in Moscow and Helsinki were instructed to send regular detailed reports. He read everything the Press turned out on the subject, and watched cinema newsreels, trying to form a picture of what was going on, although the material supplied was scanty and allowed no conclusions to be drawn. Naturally his sympathies were with the Finns, but he was forced to remember how he was bound to neutrality by the non-aggression pact with Russia.

On 12 December there was an important conference, about which naval adjutant Puttkamer put me in the picture. In discussing the Scandinavian problem, Hitler and Raeder had agreed that support for Finland should not go through 'unreliable' Sweden. It was important that Russia had a show of German neutrality. Raeder also reported on his talks with the Norwegian fascist leader Vidkun Quisling. OKH considered control of the Norwegian ports indispensable. Hitler accepted this and agreed to talks with Quisling to form an impression of him. The two met a few days later in the Chancellery, but Hitler made no decision.

As 1939 drew to a close the situation in the West remained unclear. Hitler had not yet abandoned his plan to embark upon a winter offensive against France, but on 12 December X-Day was put back to 1 January 1940. On 27 December even the setting of a new date was deferred until 9 January.

Hitler spent Christmas with his troops in the West. On 23 December he visited a reconnaissance unit near Limburg/Lahn, passing the afternoon with the Grossdeutschland infantry regiment and the evening with the SS-Leibstandarte Adolf Hitler, where he made a short speech. The following day, 24 December, he lunched with a heavy battery in the Flak Zone before moving on to the Spicherer Höhen between the French and German lines, where he was shown—to his great interest—a trench complex. Hitler was hailed as the liberator of the former German territories in Poland and West Prussia. For the coming encounter in the West his forces were sure of victory and eager to move. Some of the higher staff on the Western Front would not have shared this confidence. Hitler exuded calmness and certainty; doubt simply did not enter into it. In the brief talk he made at each location he emphasised that the 1939 successes proved the superiority of the German Wehrmacht. The weather was very depressing, the thermometer usually hovering around 0°C, and a thin mist lay motionless over the whole landscape. Hitler recognised this and made a distinct attempt to raise the mood. It was dark when he returned to his railway coach. On Christmas Day he called in on the the newly re-formed Regiment List before his special train returned him to Berlin.

After receiving an update on the Army's plans on 27 December, he left Berlin in the company of Schmundt to spend a few days in Munich, followed by New Year at the Obersalzberg, where he looked forward to a quiet fortnight thinking about the Western Front.

CHAPTER TWO

1940

The New Year began quietly. The bad weather persisted; a thick mist continued to shroud the whole country. On 3 January Hitler read a long letter from Mussolini suggesting that Hitler take the lead in 'the restoration of the Polish State' and refrain from attacking in the West. The Italian leader also objected to the friendship with the Soviet Union, which remained Europe's greatest threat. I did not see Hitler's immediate reaction to this letter but I gathered that it annoyed him. He did not reply to it and, although he had not seen Mussolini since May 1938, saw no reason to meet him now. What the letter did prove to him was the Italian Government's bias towards Britain and France.

Early on 9 January Hitler requested a weather report. The meteorologist indicated the possibility of an improvement from the east: he could provide better details tomorrow. Hitler postponed his decision until then. A high-pressure system of unusual permamence was promised: on the 12th and 13th it would cloud over, but this would be followed by twelve to fourteen days of clear winter weather with temperatures of −10°C to −15°C over the European mainland. X-Day was now 17 January. Should the improvement not materialise the attack would be put off to the spring. There was a tense mood in the Chancellery. In the afternoon Brauchitsch and Halder came. On the 12th or 13th the Luftwaffe would soften up some airfields in the north of France.

January 11 was a black day. On a flight from Fliegerführer 220 (Münster) to a conference at Fliegerkorps I (Cologne) the pilot lost his bearings and, being low on fuel, made an emergency landing near Mecheln in Belgium. He had a courier aboard and this officer had in his attaché case a plan showing the troop deployments for X-Day. Hitler received the news impassively and deferred any action until it was known what documents had fallen into Belgian hands. The German military attaché in Brussels reported that all papers had been destroyed, but Hitler was sceptical. After a few days a new story suggested that the courier had been interrupted while trying to burn the documents: both he and the pilot had been captured and taken to a Belgian military barracks, where a second unsuccessful attempt was made to set the documents alight. The Belgians accordingly took possession of the plans, which they passed without further ado to the French General Staff. Hitler remained calm: as Luftwaffe chief, Göring ultimately bore responsibility for the mishap. But inwardly Hitler was fuming.

After dinner on 11 January, in conversation with the duty military ADCs, Hitler spoke frankly about the negligent manner in which the most secret files were handled by the Luftwaffe. The event prompted Hitler to issue immediately his 'Basic Order No 1', which stated that no aspect of a state secret was to be divulged unless absolutely essential on military grounds. It was also forbidden to 'pass on publications, orders and reports of significant importance' without due consideration. The order was to be hung in all military offices and orderly rooms.

The fog persisted: the Luftwaffe could not be guaranteed three consecutive days' flying weather and the enemy had a copy of the current troop deployment plan for the offensive in the West. For these reasons Hitler abandoned the attack for the time being. In any case, he had resolved to amass his panzers for a surprise thrust through the Ardennes to the Meuse between Dinant and Sedan, from where the force would stream out to the mouth of the Somme. The Mecheln affair had made up his mind for him, and he forced through his radical new idea despite all the obstacles OKH put in his way. In the Sportpalast on 24 January Hitler addressed 7,000 subalterns. It was in the previous year that he had initiated the custom of lecturing the most junior officers on the European situation. 'This Europe,' he told them, 'managed by the grace of Britain and France, refuses to grant us the right to exist. No matter what restrictions we become subject to, we will never satisfy France and Britain. . . . if this struggle for my people cannot be avoided, it is my will absolutely to carry it through in my lifetime.' He reaped a noticeably greater ovation from his young listeners than in the year before.

On 30 January he stood again on the podium at the Sportpalast. In peacetime the anniversary of the seizure of power had always been marked by a Hitler speech to the Reichstag, but this year he addressed the German people directly. He received a tremendous reception, and during his speech there was repeated evidence of enthusiasm. Of Britain he spoke sharply: 'Herr Churchill burns with impatience for the second phase. Through his middlemen—and personally too—he hopes that at last the bombing war will begin. And they cry to the heavens that this war will not of course stop short at women and children—when did Britain ever stop short at women and children!'[4]

Preparing for 'Weserübung'

The preparations for Operation 'Weserübung', the invasion of Norway and Denmark, came suddenly to the forefront when on 16 February an incident occurred inside Norwegian territorial waters which excited Hitler's interest and wrath. The German motor ship *Altmark* had been fired on and boarded in Jössingfjord by the British destroyer *Cossack*. The tanker had been supply ship to the pocket battleship *Admiral Graf Spee*, which had been scuttled off Montevideo in mid-December, and was carrying about 300 merchant seamen from sunken British steamers. On the final part of her voyage she had been attempting to break through to Germany by way of the Norwegian Indreled. Hitler asked why *Altmark* had not resisted.

On 21 February Hitler received General von Falkenhorst, whom Jodl had recommended as suited to command the battle in Norway. Hitler gave him the task of planning the invasion. As the greatest secrecy was necessary, no official documents such as maps could be made available to him. Therefore Falkenhorst bought a Baedeker's guide to Norway, retired to a hotel room for a few hours and presented Hitler with an outline plan the same afternoon. It was accepted: the terrain offered few variations.

Discussing the Operational Plan

Hitler's main interest remained the offensive in the West, despite the pressure for 'Weserübung'. The daily situation conferences with Keitel and Jodl often degenerated into involved conversations about the resistance to be expected on the French and Belgian borders. Hitler had had himself supplied with very detailed files about the frontier defences, individual forts and artificial obstructions and on the basis of these reports he made his own plans for the attack. His suggestions and way of thinking brought Halder, when he was drawn into the discussion, to the brink of despair. Halder's view was that all this was a matter for the commanders and men on the spot ,whereas Hitler argued the need for the most important individual operations on the opening few days to be planned minutely in advance. The controversy gave rise to endless argument.

A very important meeting took place between Hitler and Manstein, Rundstedt's Chief of Staff, in the Chancellery on 17 February. Around the first of the month, Hitler's senior ADC, Schmundt, had paid a visit to Army Group A, where, during a long talk with Manstein and his adjutant Trescow, Schmundt had realised that the Army Group had very definite ideas, at variance with those of OKH, as to how the Western campaign should be conducted. Since the autumn Manstein had sent papers to the General Staff on several occasions. Halder had rejected them with the assurance that the operation would be conducted in accordance with the OKH plan, and when Manstein persisted, Halder had him appointed commander of the new XXXVIII Korps away from the front. This measure had caused some raised eyebrows, since it was unusual to replace an Army Group commander between campaigns. The OKH had said nothing of Manstein's opinions to Hitler. Schmundt was astonished at the similarity of views between Hitler and Manstein, and when he spoke to Hitler on his return he found himself pushing at an open door.

Halder's attitude did not surprise Hitler and confirmed his suspicions. If only he had heard of Manstein's ideas earlier, while he, Hitler, was still toying with the concept! Instead, only a chance conversation on the occasion of Manstein's removal had brought it to light.

Hitler pored over Manstein's plan. It coincided precisely with Hitler's own: the weight of the attack would fall to Army Group A with the massed panzers and motorised divisions. At once he ordered OKH to prepare the new plan.

After Manstein had left, Hitler spoke harshly to Schmundt against Brauchitsch and Halder. Both wanted to sabotage his plans for the Western offensive: already they had made the task extraordinarily difficult for him, he said. He did not want a change at OKH yet, but once the French were beaten, then he would sort them out.

Fritz Todt

Shortly afterwards, Hitler's dissatisfaction with OKH received a fresh stimulus. He had heard complaints from various sources about the supply of weapons and ammunition to the Army. The fault must lie with OKH, he believed: an aged staff set in its bureaucratic ways was responsible. Therefore he considered it necessary to make a change. His antipathy towards OKH motivated him to appoint a civilian minister to oversee the new Reich Ministry for Armaments. Sweeping powers would revolutionise all centres into achieving the highest output. When the General Inspector of German Roadbuilding, Dr Fritz Todt, received the portfolio on 17 March it hit the Army like a bomb and Todt had a big struggle on his hands to create and develop his office. In fact he needed more than a year to establish the lines of communication to the various outposts of his large empire.

On 24 February we drove to Munich, where that evening Hitler addressed old Party comrades in the Hofbräuhaus on the twentieth anniversary of the proclamation of the Party programme. His speech stood in the long shadow of the impending battle in the West, but he spoke frankly of the strong resistance which Britain would offer and also mentioned the influence of the Jews.

The Visit of Sumner Welles

From the beginning of March the US Under-Secretary of State Sumner Welles, who, as President Roosevelt's special envoy, was touring the capitals of Europe, spoke with Göring, Ribbentrop and Hess in Berlin. Hitler had prepared a guideline calling for the greatest caution in conversation. Sumner Welles should do the talking. The relationship between Germany and the United States was not good. If he had been sent with the intention of bringing about a better diplomatic climate, then that would be in the interests of the two peoples. Hitler wanted to emphasise the good relationship he had with Russia. He had made his last offer of peace to Britain and France in October and in return had reaped only scorn. Not until the Anglo-French will to destroy Germany had been broken could one build a Europe at peace. The Reich was determined to end the war victoriously. Hitler received the US special envoy on 2 and 4 March in the presence of Ribbentrop, Meissner, head of the Chancellery, and the American chargé d'affaires Alexander C. Kirk.

On 8 March Hitler dictated a very long letter to Mussolini explaining his stance on various questions. It was important for him to keep Italy on his side whilst Sumner was travelling through Europe. Ribbentrop delivered the letter in Rome on 10 March and satisfied himself that Sumner Welles had not succeeded in influencing Mussolini.

The Duce placed great value on talks with Hitler at the Brenner on 18 March. In the morning situation conference next day Hitler gave Göring,

Keitel and Jodl an almost rapturous account of the meeting. He was especially pleased that Mussolini wanted to keep his eggs in the German basket and was ready to commit his forces in the battle against France, although on this latter point Hitler seemed somewhat unconvinced.

Hitler spent Easter at the Obersalzberg. I was duty ADC and flew from Tempelhof with my wife to the Ainring airfield near Salzburg. We spent four very pleasant and relaxed days. Since the outbreak of war Hitler had put a stop to his evening film show and now he spent the evenings with guests around the fireplace at the Berghof great hall. The main topics were Mussolini and Hitler's architectural plans for Berlin and Munich. On Easter Monday he had a long talk with Dr Todt about armaments and the new Ministry. I was drawn into the conversation on several occasions. His major concern was the OKH. He spent one whole evening discussing plans for field weapons. He considered an anti-tank weapon as a variant of the 8.8cm flak gun as most important. The production of panzers and panzer guns with long barrels occupied him intensely. These conversations often lasted two to three hours while his guests watched films in the skittle alley.

'Weserübung'

Hitler issued the Directive for 'Weserübung' on 1 March. He knew that the British were preparing to occupy Norway and was anxious to get there first. On 5 March he assembled the senior Wehrmacht commanders for a conference at which Göring learned the details for the first time. He was obviously piqued and attempted—in vain—to get himself involved in the planning stage. He was certainly disappointed if not actually offended that Hitler had not entrusted the mission to him.

On 1 and 2 April, after discussing the operation with Falkenhorst, Göring and Raeder, Hitler set 9 April as the date for the occupation. On the 3rd the first transport steamers set out for the Norwegian coast. Hitler was on tenterhooks in case the British invaded first. The large scale Kriegsmarine operation began on the night of 6 April. By 8 April most naval surface units which could float were at sea with troops aboard and heading for Norway.

On the morning of 8 April the French and British Governments delivered notes to the Norwegian Foreign Ministry advising that they had begun to lay minefields in Norwegian coastal waters. There was great indignation in Oslo. However, this helped justify the measures Hitler had set in train and so he welcomed it. Next morning German ambassadors visited the Foreign Offices in Oslo and Copenhagen and presented demands that the occupation of the two nations respectively be acknowledged. The Danes complied. The German demand to Norway also stated that Quisling would take over the government in Oslo. The king of Norway and his ministers would not bend.

The Luftwaffe occupied the airfields at Oslo and Stavanger without difficulty. The invasion of the principal ports from the sea had mixed success. Three cruisers were sunk. There was a disaster at Narvik, where, after disembarking 2,000 mountain troops under General Dietl's command, ten German destroyers were bottled up in Narvik Fjord by a superior British naval force. All were sunk.

Falkenhorst's Gebirgsjäger (mountain troops) set out from Oslo for Trondheim but were held up by weather and stubborn resistance. The situation was very worrying for Hitler. The German Army stood poised west of the Rhine awaiting the order to strike. Hitler was extremely impatient: valuable days for his French campaign were being lost. Nervous and at a loss what to do next, he was inclined to evacuate the area around Narvik and if necessary even abandon Trondheim. If the weather over mainland Europe had improved and a stable system of high pressure had set in, presumably he would have gone ahead in the West at once.

His main conversational partner was Jodl, who knew both Narvik and Dietl. The latter was an energetic leader who would succeed in the inhospitable terrain if anybody could. On 14 April a British force stood 160km north of Trondheim and on the 17th they made landings at Andalsnes, 250km south of the port. Jodl took stock of the situation very calmly. In his opinion the British had no chance.

On 22 April Jodl sent his Army General Staff Officer, von Lossberg, to Norway. At the same time Schmundt decided to fly to Oslo, since he distrusted Lossberg. They were both back in Berlin by the 24th. Hitler spoke adversely about Lossberg, who was arrogant and had found out practically nothing. Schmundt knew his chief better. His detailed report about the fighting on the road between Oslo and Trondheim put Hitler's mind at rest. On the narrow highway it was difficult to fight effectively. One just kept on hammering away patiently. There was no doubt that this would eventually succeed. The intervention of the Luftwaffe would be decisive, but the weather was keeping them on the ground.

The two British groups had no air support or useful AA weapons. Eventually both were battered by the Luftwaffe operating from Trondheim and suffered heavy losses before pulling out in the first week of May. The stragglers were mopped up as far as Narvik.

Meanwhile the British strengthened their forces elsewhere. Their objective was to cut off the iron ore supply line. It was difficult to reinforce Dietl and air support from Trondheim was not available, but Dietl nevertheless remained confident and worked day and night at building up his defences. Ultimately the beginning of the Western offensive caused enemy troop withdrawals and the siege petered out.

Once the campaign in the West was in full swing Hitler took little further interest in the fighting in Norway. On 19 April, against OKH advice, he had sent Josef Terboven, Gauleiter of Essen, to Norway to head the administration and was evidently relieved on 30 April to be informed by Jodl that communication between Oslo and Trondheim had been restored.

On 10 June Hitler inserted into the draft OKW final report on the battle for Norway, and especially Narvik, the phrase 'In a two-month long battle, Austrian mountain troops, Luftwaffe detachments and our destroyer crews gave for all time proof of their glorious soldierly qualities', and on the 13th he sent an order of the day to his soldiers in Norway thanking the commanders and men for their bravery and self-sacrifice by means of which they had helped 'to save the Reich from a great danger'.

Norway was of great importance for the continuation of the war against Britain. The battle had been a difficult one, and without it the victorious advance through France could not have been achieved so swiftly. Hitler had dreams of a large-scale development of the port of Trondheim, which would become the most northern German city.

The Norwegian campaign highlighted Jodl's qualities. He had made his views known to Hitler quite frankly and supported him ably during the period of crisis. On the conclusion of fighting, the Führer recognised and praised his role. Hitler valued Jodl as a faithful and devoted staff officer whose suggestions he often followed in the course of the war.

During the battle for Norway Hitler had concentrated his energies mainly on planning the French campaign and once summoned Army commanders to talks in the Chancellery. On account of his grave suspicions of Brauchitsch and Halder, he came close to ejecting the OKH leadership on several occasions. Only the approach of the great task ahead held him back. Brauchitsch and Halder had forecast heavy fighting in France which could last for years. Whether this was actually their belief or a ploy to deter Hitler from attacking I cannot say. Hitler knew that neither could be trusted and inclined to the opinions of Army Group commanders Leeb, Rundstedt and Bock, who wanted to attack immediately.

Attack in the West

On 1 May Hitler set X-Day for the 5th. On 2 May he held a conference with Göring and the Luftwaffe leadership about the proposed landings in 'Fortress Holland'. General Student, with whom Hitler had previously discussed the operations against The Hague and the Scheldt estuary, and Graf Sponeck, commanding the Luftlandedivision drops on The Hague and Rotterdam, also took part. Hitler spoke at length to those officers charged with special operations; as what mattered most to him were the element of surprise and quick successes, he laid special stress on these aspects.

On 3 May the success in Norway and his optimistic view of the French campaign gave Hitler the necessary impetus for his speech in the Sportpalast to 6,000 senior cadets. At the end of it they knew exactly what was required of them.

On the 4th he delayed X-Day until 7 May and finally at Göring's request until 10 May, but this would be the last postponement, he added. On 9 May Hitler dictated a proclamation to his soldiers on the Western Front which ended with the sentence: 'The battle which begins today will decide the fate of the German nation for the next thousand years. Now do your duty. The German people gives you their blessing.' The nearer the fatal hour approached the calmer and more optimistic Hitler became. It seemed to me that he had shed the doubts which had assailed him during the previous six months and was content to allow events to take their course. He was of the opinion that France would give in after about six weeks. It was in fact important that they should do so since he expected that a quick success would persuade Britain to settle; it would be unimaginable for her to risk losing the Empire; therefore, after the German victory in France, she would sue for peace.

On 9 May the day at last dawned when Hitler could take up residence in his new Führer HQ at the front. Speer had had a castle between Bad

Nauheim and Usingen refurbished but it failed to meet with the Führer's approval and he had commissioned Todt and Schmundt to locate and refit a new FHQ in the Eifel area further north. It should be as simple as possible. Eventually Todt found a flak emplacement near Münstereifel which would serve after a few modifications.

Just before five that afternoon Hitler's special train stood in Berlin-Finkenkrug station, on the main line to Hamburg, a few kilometres west of Staaken airport. He drove there escorted only by plain-clothes detectives and SD men. All other members of the entourage had to get to the station surreptitiously. The train left punctually and set off towards Hamburg. Hitler had announced that we would be visiting troops in Denmark and Norway. I doubt that anybody was taken in by this, for everyone had his private 'source'. A long stop was made at Hagenow-Land to take in telephone messages, the tracks were switched and the train headed for Hanover. The change of direction escaped nobody and the destination was soon clear. That evening we stopped briefly at Burgdorf near Hanover, where I collected the latest weather forecast. It was satisfactory: Hitler would give his definitive order to open the Western Front next morning.

During the journey Hitler was in sparkling mood, completely confident of victory and devoid of any niggling doubts. The atmosphere at dinner in the buffet car was lively, and he expressed the hope that the preparations in which he had involved himself personally would all go well. In particular he mentioned the Belgian fort at Eben Emael. It was already dark when our train pulled into a small station near Euskirchen. Three-axled Mercedes were waiting to convey us to the well-camouflaged Führer HQ Felsennest, a half-hour's drive away.

Hitler shared his bunker with Schaub, Keitel and a manservant. A second bunker accommodated Jodl, the three military adjutants, Keitel's ADC and Dr Brandt. There was additionally a dining bunker and a barracks on a slope a short way off. The barracks had been converted into a situation conference room with quarters for Puttkamer, Jodl's ADC and a sergeant-writer. The dining bunker contained a long table with twenty places. Everybody ate here. A map of the entire area to be conquered hung on the long wall. The remainder of the retinue and Press officials lodged in a nearby village, where some houses had been requisitioned.

X-Day began quietly and Hitler kept to his bed through the morning. Towards midday the first sparse reports came in. The bridge at Maastricht had been damaged but was being quickly repaired. The bridges over the Albert Canal had mostly been taken intact. The glider landings on Eben Emael had gone off well. Otherwise there was nothing. Later it was reported that the Belgian and Dutch military had expected the attack on 10 May: the date had been betrayed. Nevertheless resistance everywhere was slight. In some places the odd bridge had been demolished. Various artificial obstacles held up the initial advance. Elsewhere the invasion went ahead unhindered. Morale was excellent. Our troops were confident of victory. What the Belgian and Dutch were offering amounted only to delaying tactics. The French Army was in a difficult position: they had expected the attack from the north through Belgium and were having to manoeuvre awkwardly to engage. On the whole the opposition was no match for our panzers and Luftwaffe—this was obvious during the first ten days.

The Dutch Army capitulated on 14 May. Owing to a signals breakdown the planned air attack on Rotterdam could not be aborted and went ahead after the surrender had been accepted. The city received appalling damage, with heavy casualties amongst the civilian population. Belgium gave in on 24 May, the instrument of unconditional surrender being signed four days later. The Belgian king elected to remain with his people.

A deplorable bulletin was issued following an accidental calamity on 10 May. The town of Freiburg-im-Breisgau was bombed. People had been killed and property seriously damaged. The official investigation found that German aircraft were responsible: a squadron had orders to attack a French town west of the Rhine, but two machines had gone astray and attacked Freiburg in error. Hitler was informed and ordered that the matter be kept quiet. Unfortunately the Propaganda Ministry got hold of it and turned the affair into an Allied terror raid.

The German main thrust rumbled down through difficult terrain and by 12 May had reached the Meuse at Dinant. On the 20th the spearhead of Guderian's 19th Army Corps was at Amiens and Abbéville on the Somme estuary—a spectacular success. Eben Emael had surrendered on the 11th: a special type of explosive had been used for the first time to crack the nut. Hitler invited the victorious team to FHQ, where the two commanders were decorated with the Knight's Cross, after which they described to him the proceedings in depth.

On 14 May I wrote to my uncle, Otto von Below: 'The first four to five days of this campaign have been more successful than the Führer,

Army or Luftwaffe could have dreamed. Everywhere our bombers have been uncannily successful against the enemy air forces and armies. The enemy air force is already down to 60 per cent of his starting numbers. Our massed motorised units have not been attacked at all. The crossings and bridgeheads on the Meuse at Dinant and Sedan were quickly secured. British troops and parts of the French Army have moved into the Brussels–Ghent–Courtrai area, having failed to divine our intentions or identify the main thrust. The Army is poised to strike its surprise blow. I suggested it to you at Christmas. We have reached the starting point.'

Dunkirk

On 19 May the French Government nominated General Weygand, who was in Syria, as successor to Gamelin. His appointment gave rise to a surge of hope throughout France. In the Great War Weygand had been Foch's right-hand man. He was proven and enjoyed great confidence. However, when he saw the confused situation he was supposed to solve, particularly in northern France, he must have known at once that it was already too late. The panzers of Guderian and Reinhardt on the Somme estuary rolled forwards on 23 May, passed through Boulogne and Calais and pressed on towards the the the Belgian frontier. Next day they received Hitler's instruction to halt on the line Gravelines–St Omer–Béthune. This order caused uproar. Brauchitsch and Halder arrived at FHQ to protest. Hitler knew that the entire British Expeditionary Force, about 300,000 men, was bottled up in an area stretching from Dunkirk to as far back as Lille: it was their intention to evacuate to England through the port of Dunkirk. However Hitler rejected the plea of the two generals. He expected the British to put up a stubborn and protracted resistance . He was concerned that German motorised forces would get bogged down there for days on end when he needed them immediately on a new front facing south. He wanted to conclude the fighting as soon as possible and thus prevent fresh resistance developing in the south of France. On 24 May he did not have intelligence as to what enemy forces were present in France, and in particular he was worried that the British might land fresh divisions though the port of Bordeaux and set up a new front there.

Hitler's decision on Dunkirk was strongly influenced by Göring, who saw the chance for his airmen to strike a decisive blow against Britain. He persuaded a sceptical Hitler that the Luftwaffe could prevent the withdrawal of the BEF. Hitler relied on this promise, although I must say he did not appear altogether convinced by it. However, it suited his plans, and, undoubtedly strengthened by Göring's assurance, on 24 May he flew to Army Group A in order to discuss the next step with Rundstedt. The Dunkirk situation was deliberated upon at great length. Hitler's conviction was for a swift drive towards southern France. The British Army had no relevance for him. Halder wanted to go into the Dunkirk cauldron with all available forces and annihilate the BEF. Hitler thought this would take several days and hold back the thrust towards southern France for too long. In the end he left the decision to Rundstedt, who decided upon the quickest possible resumption of the offensive. Accordingly, the forces on the Somme and Aisne were regrouped. Bock's Army Group B led from the coast down to about Bethel, Rundstedt's Army Group A made eastwards for the Saar, and Leeb's Army Group C remained where it was. The attack of 5 June in which the Panzer Korps of Hoth and Manstein had particular success brought the whole front into motion.

Marshal Pétain was appointed French head of state, but despite French optimism Hitler doubted that Pétain would succeed in setting up a resistance. In a letter to my uncle on 29 May I wrote: 'The swift crossing of the Meuse came as such a surprise to the enemy that at first he offered no resistance. Our panzers and motorised divisions quickly overcame all obstructions and then raced for the Channel. Our infantry divisions marched to the west at an unheard-of pace and quickly erected an effective defensive front to the south. To their rear in the north the mouth of the bag was calmly pulled tight. The élite of the French divisions had been knocked out here: the British divisions, in a state of exhaustion, decamped to England, leaving their equipment behind. Fifty per cent of our divisions saw no action at all. The Führer himself is very stirred by this great success.'

For the beginning of the second phase of the offensive, Hitler transferred his FHQ to the southern corner of Belgium at Bruly de Pêche, in search of which Schmundt and Todt had feverishly scoured the countryside. I remember this FHQ well, for it was here that we received news of the French surrender.

Mussolini declared war on France on 10 June; his troops joined the fray next day. Hitler had been awaiting this development with some anxiety since it relieved him of a heavy additional burden in the Mediterranean. On 14 June Paris was declared an open city and surrendered without a fight. Verdun capitulated on the 15th. Hitler accepted the reports in silence: his vivid memories of the Great War affected him strongly. After heavy artillery and bombardment to soften up the defenders, the German First Army eventually breached the Maginot Line south of Saarbrücken on 16 June after two days of fierce fighting: a second breakthrough in the southern sector the same day enabled the Seventh Army to cross the Rhine into France. Some Maginot forts continued to fight for a few days after the French surrender until ordered to desist by a high French military commission.

Victory and Armistice

On 18 June Hitler conceded the French request for an armistice. Overwhelmed by emotion, he advised the French Government through the Foreign Office that he would first have to consult the Italians, and he flew the same day to Munich to meet Mussolini. Hitler was not enchanted at having to hail him as a comrade-in-arms of equal status. Mussolini was in high spirits and promised great successes in the future. Two days later the French Armistice Commission convened in Tours. The negotiations were set to begin at eleven in the morning of 21 June at Compiègne, precisely where, on 11 November 1918, the Armistice documenting the German defeat had been signed by Erzberger, Marshal Foch and Admiral Wemyss. Hitler had dreamed this fantasy many times and was now gloriously fulfilled in this role by history. In the woods at Compiègne the railway coach in which the 1918 ceremony had taken place was pushed from its shed into a clearing in the open. Nominated to take part at the first negotiations were the C-in-Cs of the three Wehrmacht branches of service, plus Keitel, Hess and Ribbentrop. The French delegation was delayed and the negotiations did not begin until three in the afternoon. Hitler strode to the historic coach alone, inspected the paraded honour battalion and then boarded. After a few minutes the French Armistice Commission led by General Huntziger arrived and climbed aboard the car immediately. Once Keitel had read the preamble to the Armistice Commission, Hitler and his retinue departed. Keitel chaired the negotiations, which concluded next day. The Armistice came into effect at 0135 hours on 25 June simultaneously with its announcement by German radio. At the time we were gathered about Hitler in the dining room at FHQ and listened to the bulletin in silence. On its completion, just outside the window a bugler of the Führer's escort battalion blew *Das Ganze Halt*. It was a deeply moving moment and the mood remained sombre for some time. We found it difficult to reconcile jubilation and gravity.

In France the tension snapped. The masses of refugees on the highways returned home. Hitler made a number of journeys through occupied France. Following the transfer of FHQ to Bruly de Pêche he had visited several Great War battlefields, Vimy Ridge, Loretto Point and the Memorial to the Fallen at Langemarck; now he drove with Great War comrades to former trenches near Reims where they had served. On 28 June Hitler flew to Paris for an unofficial early morning tour and saw the Arc de Triomphe, the Opera House and Napoleon's tomb at the Invalides. At the last he expressed the desire that the sarcophagus of Napoleon's son, the Duke of Reichstadt, should be brought to Paris from Vienna. At the Opera House, in the company of Speer, sculptor Breker and architect Gieder, he explained how it should be done and enlightened his listeners on many points concerning the construction and refurbishment of the monument.

On 29 June Hitler transferred his FHQ to the Black Forest near Kniebis, where Schmundt had had a flak emplacement converted for the purpose. It was noticeable how a great millstone had been lifted from Hitler's neck. He had a wide range of interests and for a while could involve himself in matters not immediately connected with the war. The proximity of the former French department of Alsace, which was now part of the Gau of Baden, tempted Hitler to spend a few days there sightseeing. Accompanied by Chancellery officials Lammers and Meissner, he visited the cathedral and old quarter of Strasbourg and next day inspected sections of the Maginot Line from the Alsace side. Meissner originated from Alsace and supplied a stream of anecdotes for the Führer's benefit.

In his Black Forest HQ he sat in deep contemplation of his enemy Great Britain. He did not imagine for one moment that Churchill would be ready for peace negotiations, and as if in confirmation there occurred an event on 3 July characteristic of Churchill's attitude when a British naval force appeared off Mers-el-Kébir near the French North African port of Oran and demanded the surrender of the French fleet units based there. When the French admiral refused, the Royal Navy opened fire and sank them.

Hitler stated that in the next Reichstag session he would make a fresh offer to Britain even though he did not think it likely to be successful. He wished that Britain would terminate this war in the West because the coming conflict against the Soviet Union was unavoidable and he did not want an enemy at front and rear.

At his Belgian FHQ he had got Brauchitsch to agree the disbandment of twenty infantry divisions and the formation of ten new panzer divisions. The French campaign had brought to light a number of serious questions for discussion, particularly the Waffen-SS losses. A dashing, light-headed and inexperienced leadership had cost the few SS units in the field exceptionally high casualties. Death-defying and admirable, yes, but irresponsible. Hitler wanted this prevented in future. But what amazed the Great War veterans more than anything was the failure of the French Army and its generals. It had surprised even Hitler, although the Führer had never doubted that victory would be his.

Continuation of the War Against Britain

Brauchitsch and Hitler had had their first conversations on the subject of Britain at Bruly de Pêche. As I remember, Brauchitsch mentioned almost casually that if Britain were still not prepared to sue for peace it would probably be necessary to invade as soon as possible. Hitler agreed, but preferred to see how things turned out in the short run. Britain's war policies, he said, amounted to an expression of Churchill's personal ambitions. These could only be realised through war. Accordingly Churchill had been beavering away since the mid-1930s in the hope of engineering a war and had now found an ally in his endeavour—Roosevelt. 'I have certainly surprised Britain,' Hitler said, 'and Roosevelt cannot yet join in as much as he would like. In America such a programme runs more slowly.' But Churchill had organised feeling against Germany in the English-speaking world with allegations that Hitler wanted war with the West. If a German invasion of Britain succeeded, it would then be at least questionable whether Britain would be able to carry on the fight from her outposts of Empire as Churchill was now promising in Parliament.

Deep in the Black Forest, at the conclusion of a difficult but victorious operation, Hitler had harsh things to say about the OKH. Fritsch and Beck had made repeated attempts to prevent him beginning a war. Their method had been to sabotage rearmament and argue French superiority. He had never believed this and now he had proof of his correct judgement of the French forces. As Brauchitsch and Halder followed in the footsteps of Fritsch and Beck, it was only right that he should be suspicious of their advice.

Hitler also dealt harshly with the members of former ruling houses who had fought at the front. This was provoked by the death in action of Prince William of Prussia at the end of May. Hitler had received the report with annoyance and after some thought ordered that all princes were to be withdrawn from the front line and given service out of harm's way. In general this order was not well received since those affected by it felt discriminated against. The real reason was that acts of bravery by the nobility becoming generally known might foster a return to the monarchical spirit in Germany. A more radical solution—in the shape of numerous dismissals—was only forthcoming after the events of 20 July 1944.

At three in the afternoon of 6 July, Hitler's train pulled into Berlin's Anhalter terminus, where the entire Reich Government awaited the Führer on the platform. Göring spoke a few over-emotional words of welcome before Hitler inspected an honour guard and was then conveyed to the Chancellery standing in the back of a Mercedes limousine driven at a walking pace, amidst scenes of unbelievable jubilation and acclaim. Countless thousands had filled the Wilhelm-Platz and Hitler was induced to step out on the balcony several times that afternoon to acknowledge the crowd's delirium.

The Chancellery soon swarmed with visitors—ministers, Reichsleiters and Gauleiters. No generals attended. Throughout that afternoon an air of anxiety prevailed which did not disperse until evening. After the victorious campaign, in Berlin I noticed amongst the so-called educated circles a very pessimistic atmosphere. The campaign in the West left in its wake an odd mixture—fear, condemnation of its folly and a reluctant admiration.

Hitler's life in Berlin now resumed its usual course. His day would begin at noon with Jodl's situation report. This would lead to further military discussions, usually with the three Wehrmacht C-in-Cs. After lunch there would normally be a number of civilian appointments until Jodl's evening situation report. Hitler would spend the evening in the circle of his companions-at-table. The film show had been discontinued, but the Propaganda Ministry would often send over the latest pre-release cinema newsreels which Hitler watched without a sound track, commentary being read to him from a script by an orderly officer. Hitler would frequently require changes to the text. The remainder of the evening would then be spent before the fireplace in conversation with his intimate circle.

During the course of 1940 I noticed how Hitler would deliberate and seek exhaustive counsel before making a crucial decision. After he had given an order he could no longer be argued out of it. He looked for special qualities in his advisers and made particular efforts to know new generals. Over the years I had the opportunity to recommend to Hitler a number of able front line officers without General Staff training. These included Hube and Rommel, whom I knew from my infantry training days between 1929 and 1933. Both fulfilled Hitler's expectations of them.

Planning 'Seelöwe'

On 7 July the Italian Foreign Minister Count Ciano arrived in Berlin and was received at once by Hitler. The meeting was not an easy one, for Ciano wanted to talk about Mussolini's territorial demands upon Malta, Egypt and Somalia. Hitler evaded this with a description of his success in France and announced that Britain was to be attacked next 'with fire and sword'. These words were for London's benefit, for Hitler knew that Ciano's intermediaries would leak the content of the conversation to the British. Probably for the same reason, he invited Ciano on a short tour of northern France to ensure that he saw the extent of German domination there.

In Munich on 10 July, before lunch, Hitler entertained Hungary's President, Count Teleki, and Foreign Minister, Count Csaky. Both were only interested in advancing their claims to the Siebenbürgen area of Russia. Hitler declined to discuss this matter. That evening we drove up to Obersalzberg, where Raeder arrived next day. He wanted to ascertain Hitler's intentions towards Britain. Hitler replied that he was deferring his decision until he had sounded the effect from London of his impending speech to the Reichstag. Raeder was not in favour of an invasion of England: he was of the opinion that the U-boat war and air attacks on large cities such as London and Liverpool would eventually bring Britain round. They both agreed that an invasion of Britain should be the last resort; in any case, German air superiority over the Channel and southern England was the essential precondition.

For about an hour on 13 July Ribbentrop discussed with Hitler the problem of invading Britain. I recognised from the way he spoke that

Hitler was not keen on the operation, but nevertheless he gave the order for plans to be prepared at once. His understanding of the situation was that Britain was hoping for Russia's intervention on her side. A collapse of the British Empire did not lie in Germany's interests but would be advantageous only for the United States or Japan. Hitler preferred to lengthen the front against Britain by co-opting Spain into the European set-up. Ribbentrop must plan for a trip to Madrid.

The OKW prepared Directive No 16, 'Regarding the Preparations for an Invasion of England', and supplied it to Hitler for his signature on 16 July. The operation had the cover-name 'Seelöwe'—Sea-Lion. The first sentence stated: 'As Britain, despite her hopeless military situation, has still made no sign of her preparedness for an understanding, I have decided to prepare, and if necessary carry out, an invasion of England.' Hitler signed it and the same day convened a sitting of the Reichstag for 19 July.

From Obersalzberg on 14 July Hitler made a short excursion to the steel works at Linz and the panzer factory at Wels. During his inspection he ordered an immediate expansion of production—a clear indication (together with his special interest in long, heavy gun barrels on the new panzer models) that he had the expansion of his military objectives in mind.

Promotions

Over the next four days he worked on his draft speech to the Reichstag and wrestled with the thorny problem of whom to promote. The elevation of the Army C-in-C, Brauchitsch, to field marshal was widely expected but in his opinion unjustified. On the other hand, he wanted the Army to receive some form of special distinction. His solution was the simultaneous promotion of the three Army Group C-in-Cs Rundstedt, Leeb and Bock and of the Army commanders Kluge, List, Reichenau and Witzleben.

Hitler wanted the senior commanders of Air Fleets 2 and 3, Kesselring and Sperrle, promoted to field marshal. Göring demanded the inclusion of Milch as well. Hitler's poor relationship with Milch had nothing to do with his omission: if he promoted Milch he would also have to promote Keitel to field marshal in order that the the OKW C-in-C should not be outranked by the Secretary of State for Aviation. Keitel's promotion would not be recognised by the Army, but even so he could not be passed over. The question was much discussed between Hitler, Schmundt and Keitel.

Reichstag Sitting, 19 July

The Reichstag sitting had been tabled for seven on the evening of 19 July in the Kroll Opera House. The seats of the six deputies killed in action were left empty and marked by a simple laurel wreath. The front row of the auditorium was filled by Wehrmacht senior commanders. Everywhere the uniforms of the Wehrmacht branches dominated. Hitler was given a rapturous reception. Göring opened the session with a dedication to the fallen, after which Hitler embarked upon a long speech. Following his explanation of 'the inherently necessary revision' of the Versailles Treaty he criticised 'international Jewish racial poison', for which 'the war was a welcome means to bring affairs to a better prosperity'. The files of the Allied Supreme War Council discovered at La Charité in France had given a picture of Allied plans. When he had made his peace offer, he had been insulted and offended by Chamberlain and the British warmongers Churchill and Eden. He described the Norwegian campaign as 'the bravest operation in German war history', and of the offensive in the West he observed that the welding together of the entire Wehrmacht had resulted in the 'total annihilation of those Anglo-French forces present'. He went on to portray the operations and successes of the Army and Luftwaffe armies and groups involved and, emphasising the role of the commanding generals, announced the list of promotions with especial reference to Göring, who had been made Reichsmarschall and awarded the Grand Cross of the Iron Cross. Other promotions to Generaloberst included Halder, while Jodl and Jeschonnek became full generals.

Speaking of his alliance with Italy, Hitler offered his personal thanks to Mussolini. He exaggerated somewhat the involvement of Italian units. There followed a rather casual remark for Britain—'I see no reason which would compel the continuation of this war'—and he rounded off his speech by offering thanks to 'the Grace of Providence' which had allowed 'this work to succeed'.

I was disappointed by the Reichstag speech. Judging by his remarks about Britain beforehand, I was expecting something much more substantial. I wondered if his attitude towards the conflict with Britain had changed: what he had said lacked any concrete suggestion. About an hour after it finished the Press reported the first response from Britain—a short but clear refusal of any idea of reconciliation. Further icy words from London followed overnight and confirmed Hitler in his assumptions.

On 21 July, in the Chancellery, he met the Wehrmacht C-in-Cs. It was still a puzzle to him what Britain was up to: if she were bent on continuing the war, then her politicians were either hoping for a change in the US attitude or for some sort of accommodation with the Soviets. He considered the idea of invading Britain very risky. Stalin had been in contact with London and expressed his interest in holding the political situation in Europe in suspense. Russia must be watching very closely. An attack on Russia had to be planned for, and, in the greatest secrecy, the General Staff would be asked for their thoughts so as to determine the size of the project, its likely duration and its objectives.

After this Hitler went off to the Bayreuth Festival, where on 23 July he attended a performance of *Götterdämmerung*. This was his only visit of the war to the Wagner Festival: the event was kept going mainly for armaments workers and wounded soldiers.

Over the next few days he received a series of official visitors both at Obersalzberg and in Berlin. The Presidents of Romania, Bulgaria and Slovakia called in to argue for various territorial adjustments. The Balkan question was beginning to loom large, but Hitler chose to make no decisions at this stage, his mind being fixed on events in the Russian arena. He had the newsreels of the Russo-Finnish War screened again to see if he had overlooked something about Red Army motorisation, armament and striking power six months previously.

The Wehrmacht C-in-Cs and the Chiefs of the General Staff attended a meeting on 31 July at which Raeder reported on the current preparations for 'Sea-Lion'. He was considering a date between 19 and 26 September, although a postponement to the spring of 1941 was preferable. Hitler would not entertain this and decided upon 15 September. Whether the invasion could proceed on that day depended on the Luftwaffe, he said. In the next few days they would be stepping up their attacks on English fighter airfields, ports and naval targets. If these were successful, then we would go ahead; otherwise the date would be put back to 1941.

Hitler also spoke about the Soviet Union, which recently had established new links with London. He thought it likely that Russia would attack from the autumn of 1941 onwards. If she were crushed beforehand, however, a great hope for Britain would be lost. Hitler stated that his decision to invade the Soviet Union in the spring of 1941 was final. Halder was given the job of examing the fundamental questions.

Air War over Britain

The following day Hitler signed Directive No 17, 'The Prosecution of the Air and Naval War against Britain', promising, 'In order to create the conditions to defeat Britain, I intend to carry out the air and naval war against the British homeland more keenly than previously.' The Luftwaffe must 'cut down the British Air Force as soon as possible with all means at their disposal'. The date for 'sharpening the air war' was 5 August. This instruction was necessary. I had observed that the Luftwaffe formations in the most northern area of France had been arranged in battle order and readied for the aerial assault on Britain, but no indication had been supplied as to when the operation was supposed to begin, if at all. Jeschonnek told me that he had given the operational orders to Göring a few days previously and as far as he knew Göring had put them in a safe. He had had a number of conversations with Göring in the last four weeks, primarily about bombing England, and the Reichsmarschall seemed to have the impression that nothing further would come of it. He was thinking only about 1941 and the coming attack on the Soviet Union. Directive No 17 took him by surprise, and he had to inform the Air Fleets immediately.

On 5 July the weather was unfavourable and it was not until the 8th that the first fighter attacks could be made. Göring went to Cap Gris Nez to direct operations personally. In the first few days our fighters claimed to have inflicted heavy losses on the RAF over Kent and the Channel. These successes were difficult to substantiate. The daily reported figures were amazingly high. On 11 August we had destroyed 90 British aircraft for 21 of our own, on the 12th 92 for 24 and on the 13th 132 for 28. Göring reported this fantastic success rate to Hitler: he calculated that the British must already be scraping the bottom of the barrel for aircraft. But Hitler seemed unimpressed. In September, at his request, I asked the Luftwaffe General Staff for the British fighter strength. According to them the RAF had 600 fighters in front-line squadrons and 600 older types in reserve. I presented these statistics to Hitler, who discussed them with Göring at the next opportunity. Göring was appalled and asked me where I had got them. When I told him he rang the Luftwaffe General Staff at once and was given the same figures but told Hitler that the information was wrong. This was not the end of the affair. Göring ordered the General Staff to show statistical material intended for the Führer to himself before despatch. It was not long before Hitler asked me for some other aircraft figures. It was towards midnight. I rang Göring, who had retired for the night. Testily he referred me to the duty officer at General Staff. Next day Bodenschatz told me that I had annoyed Göring. Apparently the instruction had now been rescinded. Göring never spoke to me about this, however, nor showed me any irritation.

During August the RAF made their first air attacks on Berlin. They caused little damage but were a nuisance because they drove us for a few hours each night into the cellar. The raids were so relatively innocuous that Hitler interpreted them as a calculated insult and told Göring to take counter-measures. This was the motivation for the air raids on London, and Göring went at once to northern France to explain what was required to Sperrle, Kesselring and the bomber commodores. The attacks on the British capital began on 7 September. Whereas this escalation of the Battle of Britain caused substantial damage to property and losses amongst the civilian populations of London and other cities, the objective of the bomber war was not achieved. The weather did not permit heavy raids to be made every night. The British fighter and anti-aircraft defences grew steadily stronger: sometimes the fighters were up in such numbers as to divert a formation from its target or frustrate the odd attack altogether. The fighting strength of the German groups declined little by little. Demand for replacements outstripped supply. Most effective were the 'terror raids' against London, and on 14 November the night attack on Coventry. Elsewhere in southern England the raids had little more than a nuisance value, although in some there were serious civilian casualties. They had no influence on the determination of the British Government. If it had been possible to keep bombing one city night after night, week in week out, I suppose this might have had some effect, but we did not have the necessary strength to do it. It was found impossible to achieve a military victory by air attack alone. Hitler was one of the first in the German leadership to recognise that the air war against England had neither achieved its objective nor was likely to. Nobody was party to his frequent conversations with Göring at this time, but from his observations I took it that he did not share Göring's continuing optimism about the bombing of Britain. If the fighting across the Channel was not successful and the RAF remained viable, Hitler would have to seek an alternative solution. He knew that very well.

Whilst the battle over the Channel was raging in August, there was no outward indication that Berlin was a city at war—provided one overlooked the few British nuisance raids. On 14 August Hitler received Göring and the Army field marshals and presented then with field marshals' batons in his study in the new Reich Chancellery. Thanking them for their services to date, he emphasised the obligations which the rank imposed upon them. The three Luftwaffe field marshals were away at the Channel coast. On 4 September he granted batons to Kesselring, Sperrle and Milch and that same afternoon opened the 1940/41 Winter Relief Programme with a speech in the Sportpalast, thanking the German people for their forbearance during one year of war and calling upon them to give the world 'a demonstration of our indissoluble sense of community'.

On 30 August the Second Arbitration of Vienna ordered Romania to cede half of the Siebenbürgen to Hungary. This decision forced King Carol II to abdicate in favour of his son Michael. General Antonescu, a fervent nationalist, took over the government on 6 September; shortly he would ally Romania on the side of Germany. Although Romania still had to hand over southern Dobrudscha to Bulgaria in compliance with the terms of a mutual treaty, Hitler was of the opinion that the Balkan border disputes were now resolved. He mentioned this situation quite frequently since he intended to obtain control of the Romanian oilfields at Ploesti. He had despatched a brigade to Romania to secure the area, but the British controlled the eastern Mediterranean and might have an interest in the oilfields too—a suspicion which caused him some discomfort in the coming months.

The Question of 'Seelöwe'

On 13 September, after dining with the Wehrmacht C-in-Cs and their Chiefs of Staff, Hitler discussed with them certain technical questions, particularly tanks and anti-tank weapons. Next day the theme was 'Sea-Lion'. Nobody believed in the operation any longer, but Hitler commended a successful 'Sea-Lion' as the best current solution for victory against Great Britain; the advance plans for the landings had been finished and now only four to five days of calm weather were required. This was necessary to assist the Channel crossing of the small naval units, which had only limited seaworthiness. For the time being the Luftwaffe was engaging RAF fighters from dawn to dusk. However, the weather situation was very unstable. Hitler stated that he was not calling off the operation at present: the British had to be left in uncertainty. He opposed a Luftwaffe request for a free hand to bomb residential districts on the grounds that attacks on military targets were more important. Bombing to cause mass panic should be undertaken only in the last resort; the danger of British retaliation against German cities was too great.

I had the impression from this statement that Hitler had even given up hope of a successful invasion of England in the spring of 1941. It was in the autumn of 1940 that he shrank back in the face of the imponderable—an improvised crossing of the English Channel.

On 22 and 24 September, respectively, Mölders and Galland were invited to meet Hitler to mark their 40th aerial victories. At his request they spoke frankly about the air war. From this Hitler realised that the RAF was stronger than the Luftwaffe Staff had admitted. Additionally, the weather had been so changeable that it had not been possible for aircraft to get up any four days in succession. There was nothing to choose between British and German pilots, but the former had the incomparable advantage of flying over their own territory. If a British pilot had to bale out, he was available immediately for a fresh mission. German pilots were lost to the Luftwaffe. This conversation impressed Hitler deeply and reinforced his intention not to risk 'Sea-Lion' unless he held all the cards.

From Hitler's comments at the situation conference after a private talk with Raeder on 26 September, I inferred that Raeder was against war with the USSR and in favour of an operation in the eastern Mediterranean from Egypt through Palestine and Lebanon as far as Turkey. Hitler replied that, whereas he could see the reasoning for this, he would have to sound out the Spanish first. The most important place in the Mediterrean was Gibraltar. Once Gibraltar was in German or Spanish hands, one could then look more closely at the eastern end of the Mediterranean.

On 27 September Hitler attended the ceremonial signing of the tripartite pact involving Germany, Japan and Italy, and after the formalities dined with the guests in his apartment. He was keen for this treaty signing to come to the world's attention, especially in the USA and USSR. He considered the Japanese forces to be the most important military factor in the Pacific. All his efforts in these autumn months of 1940 were directed towards welding a powerful and effective alliance against Britain. Ribbentrop was asked to draft a letter to Franco to get him interested in the idea of the common front. Ribbentrop saw the arrangement as beneficial for the stable political relationship with the Soviet Union that was his personal desire, but Hitler told him he was not optimistic: Russian machinations in recent weeks in Romania, together with the radical sovietisation of the Balkan States,[5] had made him very doubtful. I noticed again and again how he dwelt on the problem of Russia. As Luftwaffe ADC these were difficult weeks for me. Our bomber squadrons flew the Channel to bomb targets in England every night when the weather permitted, while in Berlin all the Führer could think of was how he could overcome the Soviets in the shortest possible time. He had not yet answered my question as to his intentions since he had not yet made his decision, but as the weeks went by it was obvious that the Russian question was going to be answered soon.

On 4 October Hitler met the Duce at the Brenner pass. I could find out little about this conversation except that the Führer spoke more about France than Britain. Apparently he wanted to discourage the Duce from invading anywhere new. From the Brenner we drove to Obersalzberg, and we did not return to Berlin until the 8th. It was in this period that Hitler agreed to postpone 'Sea-Lion'. Although he expressly reserved to himself the final decision regarding the invasion of England, henceforth nobody in the Wehrmacht believed it possible and thus 'Sea-Lion' sank without trace.

Domestic Dramas
Hitler was again at Obersalzberg from 16 to 21 October His guests included the Italian crown princess, a sister of the King of Belgium. She made an impassioned plea for her brother. There was an unsettling domestic drama during her stay. Hitler's house manager Willy Kannenberg wanted to complain to Hitler about several young SS orderly officers. Apparently it involved a string of mostly trivial incidents. Hitler's senior personal ADC, Wilhelm Brückner, had got wind of it and attempted to persuade Kannenberg not to bother the Führer with these trifles. His efforts were in vain and Kannenberg got his hearing, with the result that Hauptsturmführer Wünsche was sent back at once to the Leibstandarte. Brückner took Wünsche under his wing, criticised Kannenberg and was dismissed immediately from Hitler's service for his trouble. Schmundt intervened unsuccessfully on Brückner's behalf. Eventually all that could be done was to get Brückner accepted into the Army as a Hauptmann in occupied France. His departure signified a real change in Hitler's circle. In the military Adjutantur his authority was widely acknowledged. Since

no replacement was appointed we assumed that one day he would be re-employed, but he never returned. Both Martin Bormann and Eva Braun were obviously glad to see the back of him, and so perhaps that explained it.

Meetings with Pétain, Laval, Franco

On 21st October Hitler set off for France to have separate meetings with Franco, Pétain and Laval which he thought promised a greater understanding between the three nations during the war. Next morning I boarded the special train at Aachen, arriving that afternoon at Montoire, a small station in unoccupied France. Here Hitler received the French representative, Prime Minister Laval, in the presence of Ribbentrop, who had come down from Berlin in his own train. Virtually nothing about these talks was made known. On the 23rd our train moved out of Hendaye station as far as the Spanish border stop where the meeting with Franco was to be held. Franco's train was an hour late and Hitler passed the time strolling the platform in bright sunshine with Ribbentrop. The Caudillo was accompanied by his Foreign Minister, Serrano Suñer. The conference was supposed to conclude with an early luncheon in the German dining car, but it dragged on instead for more than two hours. It was almost dark when Franco took his leave. Hitler's train retired for the night to the security of the railway tunnel at Montoire.

At dinner Hitler spoke about the talks. He was very dissatisfied with the outcome. He had offered Franco an alliance and suggested a joint operation to conquer Gibraltar. For the future in this war he expected no less than brotherhood-in-arms. Franco had received these suggestions more or less impassively; he had given no firm agreement other than an assurance to communicate his position on all aspects within a few days. Hitler expected a clear refusal.

Towards dusk next day the Vichy head of state, Marshal Pétain, arrived at Montoire station. Hitler walked towards him on the platform and led him into a saloon car. The purpose of the talks was to see if France could be induced to participate in the war against Britain. Laval had been offish; Pétain was taciturn and dismissive. He gave no answer throughout, but his manner said it all. Despite his disappointment, Hitler paid the elderly head of state due respect on his departure.

The return to Berlin from Montoire was a lengthy procedure because travel was restricted to daylight hours for security reasons. Hitler had a number of talks with Keitel and Jodl. He was now more convinced than ever that Russia would be in the position to attack Germany in 1942 and he confirmed that the war against Russia would have to begin in 1941, the period in mind being May to September, when it would be still quiet in the West. By 1942 he must have his hands free again to grapple with Britain. This statement came as no surprise to me. In recent weeks I had heard him speak along these lines on several occasions.

During our return a letter from Mussolini was delivered aboard. He wrote about an intended invasion of Greece. Once across the German border, a report from the embassy in Rome confirmed the Italian intention. Hitler believed there was still time to talk Mussolini out of the idea and he had Rome contacted immediately to arrange a meeting with the Duce in Florence for the morning of 28 October. Thus we travelled from Aachen to Florence via Munich, arriving at our destination at eleven. Mussolini greeted his visitor at once with the news that Italian troops had crossed the border into Greece that morning. He effused optimism and, certain of victory, was even now awaiting the first reports of successes. Hitler seemed composed and did not betray to Mussolini how gravely he judged this adventure. The conversation followed its usual very friendly course and Hitler gave no hint of his annoyance. Mussolini presented him with Hans Makart's painting *The Plague in Florence*. Hitler knew that this picture was owned by the Italian state and had once confided to his private circle his wish to purchase it. The gift should have been a joy to receive, but not in the circumstances.

Russia, Britain, the Balkans, Gibraltar

At six that evening Hitler boarded his train for Berlin, where, on his arrival, he had a series of talks with the OKW, Brauchitsch and Halder. He still considered the capture of Gibraltar from landwards extremely urgent. This was to be a matter of special importance for the planning staff. Naturally it depended on Franco's agreement.

The embroilment of the Italians in Libya was a worry. They did not need German assistance in North Africa, but Hitler was anxious in case the British should gain a strong foothold there. OKH had sent General von Thoma to reconnoitre, and on 3 November he submitted to Hitler a sober and concise report of his findings that a German action in North Africa was pointless and had no prospect of success. Thoma highlighted the difficulties of supply through Italy and the Mediterranean.

At the beginning of November, before the visit of Russian Foreign Minister Molotov, Hitler remained indecisive, casting a baleful eye at the British in Egypt, from where they were well able to venture towards the Balkans or Libya. In the Balkans were the Ploesti oilfields upon which he had designs.

Hitler stayed over in Munich for the Party anniversary of 9 November after speaking the previous evening in the Löwenbräukeller. His words were full of portent and he left no doubt but that this war had to be fought to its victorious conclusion. How this would be done he left open. The people should realise that the great struggle still lay ahead. As an example he quoted the continuing air war over Britain, which, in his own words, Churchill had brought upon himself by his pathetic air raids on Berlin that summer.

Hitler returned to Berlin in the morning of 10 November, the itinerary for the journey having been planned so as to avoid arriving in the capital during the usual hours of the British nuisance raids. In the large situation conference room the subject was Russia. Jodl said that the Army ought to be told something since it was only six months to May. Hitler replied that a decision about Russia would not be made until after Molotov's visit and ordered a directive to be drafted listing in a condensed form all Axis plans currently under consideration. On 12 November the Wehrmacht Planning Staff issued Directive No 18 tabulating Spain and Gibraltar, the Italian offensive against Egypt, the Balkans, the possible German occupation of Greece and the Soviet Union. Even the abandoned 'Sea-Lion' was mentioned. The most ominous was point 5, the Soviet Union, confirming that 'all verbally ordered preparations for the East' were to be carried through.

Directive No 19, Operation 'Felix', followed shortly afterwards. This contained detailed particulars for the stationing of German troops at readiness in Spain and Portugal so that an attack could be ordered on 10 January 1941. On 12 December, however, the directive was rescinded and all plans for the Iberian peninsula scrapped when Franco notified Hitler that he intended to remain neutral. Hitler had sent Admiral Canaris, head of the Foreign Abwehr section, to Madrid to explain Hitler's intentions. Hitler trusted Canaris and did not blame him for the failure of his mission. Personally I would have had my doubts about using using Canaris to elucidate policies on Spain: his position seemed questionable to me.

Molotov in Berlin

Molotov had his first talks with Hitler in the afternoon of 12 November. He had brought with him from Moscow clear and unequivocal questions touching on all problems which had developed in recent months between the Soviet Union and the Reich. Commencing with Finland, they covered Romania, Bulgaria and Turkey. Molotov gave Hitler to understand that these states belonged within the Soviet sphere of influence and had, so to speak, nothing to do with Germany. It was difficult for Hitler to skirt round all this in conversation. Next day Molotov pressed for specific answers to his questions but received nothing firm. In the evening of the 13th he had a long meeting with Ribbentrop, who believed sincerely in keeping the Non-Aggression Pact alive.

Hitler discussed the Kriegsmarine with Raeder next day. Raeder did not think that the Russians were planning for war with Germany in the next few years and suggested that if there were to be an attack against them—something he was very much against—then it should not be begun until after Britain was defeated. Hitler said he would think about it.

In the latter part of November Hitler spent a few days at the Obersalzberg on the occasion of a visit by the Bulgarian King, Boris, and raised the question of Russian guarantees to Bulgaria which could cause Germany great difficulties in the Balkans. Hitler wanted to win the monarch over to the Axis. King Boris took a negative stance on all questions, although he was very friendly and expressed his personal opinion quite frankly.

On 19 November the King of Belgium came to plead for the return of two million Belgian prisoners-of-war and to establish Hitler's vision of the future Belgian-German relationship.[6] He went away having achieved nothing.

The Romanian head of state, Marshal Antonescu, made his first official visit to Berlin on the 23rd, where he impressed Hitler with his charisma. He spoke at length on his country's problems and vilified neighbouring Hungary. The entry of Romania to the tripartite pact was celebrated in the Chancellery, followed by a banquet. Hitler said of Antonescu that he had found in a him a friend of Germany.

'Barbarossa'

A very significant measure had been undertaken in the autumn when Hitler despatched Todt, Schmundt and Engel to the east to look for a site for a Führer HQ. The most suitable spot suggested was a parcel of land near Rastenburg. Hitler ordered construction to be begun at once, with April 1941 as the deadline for completion. Specifications stipulated that it should be bomb-proof and have sufficient area to accommodate the entire HQ. This decision seemed to me to bring the Russian campaign a major step closer.

On 5 December Hitler discussed with Brauchitsch and Halder various aspects of the European situation, primarily Britain and Russia. Hitler said that the cessation of daylight attacks had saved the British fighter force. The attacks on British industry were minimal. However, whereas losses of material could only be made good by importing from the United States, this should not be overestimated: 'The RAF will be no stronger in 1941 than it is now. In the spring the Luftwaffe will be substantially stronger.' Regarding the Soviets, he was of the opinion that the Russian soldier was inferior and the Red armies leaderless. In an attack on the USSR the danger of forcing Russian armies back *en masse* must be avoided. The attacks must be organised so that the Red Army would be broken down into sections for its men to be rounded up. Attacks must be commenced from selected strongpoints, from where large encircling operations could be launched. Hitler expected that these great successes would culminate in a certain moment when total disorganisation would set in amongst the enemy forces. For Hitler everything was finalised.

On 10 December, in a speech to workers at a Berlin armaments factory but which was intended for all armaments workers throughout the Reich, Hitler emphasised that the most difficult days still lay ahead: eight days later he placed before the Wehrmacht C-in-Cs Directive No 21, Operation 'Barbarossa'.

When the new Japanese ambassador Oshima presented his credentials on 22 December, Hitler greeted him especially warmly. Oshima had been recalled to Japan when Hitler concluded the pact with the Soviet Union in 1939: the time now seemed ripe to return him to Berlin. It must have been rumoured that Hitler was revising his attitude towards Moscow.

This was Hitler's last official business in Berlin before the Christmas holidays. On 23 December we arrived in the special train at Calais, where Hitler visited the army and naval long-range batteries which regularly shelled the English coast. Hitler had taken a keen interest in this artillery since the summer. That afternoon he inspected Kriegsmarine units at

Boulogne and on Christmas Eve two fighter squadrons, where he spoke very appreciative words about their operations of recent weeks. That evening, in the special train, Hitler promoted Engel and myself to the rank of major in advance of seniority—for us both a very pleasant surprise. On Christmas Day he inspected a bomber squadron and that afternoon received in his train Admiral Darlan, the representative head of the French Government, who had been appointed as successor to Laval a few days earlier. The talks left Hitler dissatisfied and irritated. He criticised the removal of Laval, which he attributed to anti-German elements on Pétain's staff. I could discover no further details of this conversation.

On 26 December, after a morning with an infantry regiment, Hitler sped by train to Metz, where the SS-Leibstandarte Adolf Hitler were quartered. Amongst these men he was always in good spirits. In his speech he gave this feeling visible expression. The SS-Leibstandarte must always expect to be deployed to the hottest spots of the battle, he said: 'It is for you who are honoured to carry my name to stand at the forefront of the struggle.'

Next day in Berlin he had a long talk with Raeder, who spoke out very forcefully against war with Russia—which now looked very likely in the light of Directive No 21—before Britain was vanquished. Hitler replied that the blow against Russia would also hit Britain severely. Escalating Russian rearmament, which would put Russia into a position to attack Germany some time in 1942, had made it a necessity.

Priorities in Armaments

Raeder made a request for increased U-boat production. At present only twelve to eighteen boats per month were coming off the slips. In the light of the decision for war with Russia, this exposed a serious dilemma. Hitler had ordered Todt to give priority, with all the means at his disposal, to armaments for the Army with a view to war in 1941; Kriegsmarine requirements had been deferred. Once Russia had been defeated, the whole question could be reviewed. I discussed this with Jeschonnek, who had been following the development with the greatest concern. Luftwaffe losses resulting from the Battle of Britain in recent months had risen constantly. The current production scarcely covered these losses. It was not possible to form new bomber groups because the production of the Ju 88 was still posing difficulties.

I gave Hitler a note of Luftwaffe aircraft numbers and requested him to discuss the matter with Göring: I saw a big question mark here for the future. Hitler admitted that maintaining the Luftwaffe was important, but he needed all available production capacity for the Army for the spring of 1941. The matter could be looked at again after the summer. However, he would speak to Göring about it. I was very disturbed by this answer. I knew that the RAF was becoming much stronger and saw in this impending two-front war a great danger for the Reich. Jeschonnek agreed and had a very serious talk with Göring but did not succeed in getting Dr Todt's orders amended. Göring had given in to Hitler against his better judgement.

Critical Voices

During that winter of 1940 I began to hear more frequently in leading military and civilian circles adverse opinions being uttered about the direction of affairs. These opinions varied between harmless criticism of the leadership to pure defeatism, such as 'We cannot win the war'. Hitler himself was criticised for being too emotional and taking what the British did and said too personally. Now he was going to embark on a two-front war without production capacity and raw materials in sufficient quantities.

Such critical voices were in the minority, but one could not ignore them, for the sentiment was stated soberly and emphatically. Not that I was convinced by it at all. Despite some reservations, my personal view was that Hitler calculated every step in a cautious manner so that there was no possibility of a catastrophe. In my opinion these mostly highly placed critics and doubters were guilty of a basic error of assumption. They looked down contemptuously on Hitler, withheld their positive co-operation or in some cases worked against him from within on the premise that that would in some way help to uproot him. They failed to see that the people were behind Hitler, and this fortified him. Negative opposition seemed to me to be a false path after I had seen how one could talk to Hitler and convince him of an error if the argument had some substance and was presented properly. Frequently I looked on as generals and such like would fail to adopt the right approach to Hitler. He had heard the opposition to his plans within the Army before the Polish and French campaigns and had then been vindicated. Afterwards he was inclined to condemn senior officers' criticisms as defeatism. He said to me, 'When a man selects the career of a military officer, I cannot understand why it should not be his most cherished wish to practise at least once his chosen vocation. Prussian officers always had this outlook. If a soldier, a general, sets out to deter me from war by faulty planning and delays in armaments, that is sabotage. What we should have is the situation where the generals want war and the politican restrains them. But it seems to me that the generals here quake before the enemy. Do they think I am so stupid that I cannot judge correctly the strengths and weaknesses of the enemy?'

In the winter of 1940 I often found such evening conversations very stimulating. Hitler might deliver a comprehensive monologue on the problems of running the war, for example. The Balkan peninsula and the threat to the Romanian oilfields interested him intensely. The question of Great Britain and the American Presidential elections in November also featured regularly. I never perceived in Hitler any mental inflexibility or arrogance. In the main it was always possible to advance a counter-argument in an attempt to change a view he held, although it would have to be sound and convincing. It might be that he would want to reflect on it, but he always admitted the validity of an argument once he accepted that it proved him wrong. His memory was very good and his knowledge of many subjects such as music, history and the natural sciences above average. He was self-taught, but this self-education had been continuous over decades and had an unusually broad basis. Even if many of his scientific or historical assertions would not bear academic scrutiny, nevertheless he could argue in depth over a far wider range of subjects than most. He was not often contradicted, however, for few experts in any field were to be found in his intimate conversation circle, in which good listeners preponderated. In conversations generally I admired Hitler's calm manner. I never found him to be an unpleasant person. On the contrary, for me he was an aesthete, and his open-mindedness, tolerance and chivalrous manner were the reasons why all people who came into really close contact with him found him human and congenial.

CHAPTER THREE

1941

The winter of 1940/41 was a time for reflection, planning and decisions, and for this purpose Hitler spent much time at Obersalzberg, where he could work in peace. So how did he arrive at his decision to attack the Soviet Union before he defeated Britain? This is, it seems to me, the decisive question of the war. Hitler was convinced that Churchill was waiting for either the United States or the USSR to enter the war against Germany. In Hitler's judgment, the United States would not be in a position to intervene in Europe until 1943: the Soviet Union would be ready by the autumn of 1942. The Russo-German pact was useless as a guarantee of peace. Stalin would wait for the German forces to weaken sufficiently as a result of their military efforts in the West and then overwhelm Europe with little risk to himself. Hitler intended to prevent this, whatever the cost. Germany could not fight on numerous fronts at the same time, and so it became his design to knock out one enemy after the other either by negotiation or warfare. Secretly he always hoped for an understanding with Great Britain, although he had known since the autumn of 1937 of Britain's predominantly anti-German policies.

He worried about 'growing old'—that there was nobody with the capability to succeed him in his work. Of course, his enemies inside Germany called this self-aggrandizement, arrogance, megalomania and so forth. Hitler knew all this and indeed mentioned it frequently in the daily situation conferences.

The year 1941 was to be exclusively that in which the account was settled finally with the Soviet Union. Hitler made his preparations so that he could attack in about mid-May. His plan was for his forces to operate from centres in the north and south and, after the conquest of Leningrad and Rostov, to stream them out on both flanks in a great encircling movement east of Moscow which would, as he believed, so weaken the Red Army that it would capitulate. This would allow him to land the killer punch with all the military might at his command against his last enemy, Britain.

Decisions

In his New Year speeches to the Wehrmacht and the German people Hitler mentioned the military developments of 1940 and promised that 'The year 1941 will see the German Army, Luftwaffe and Kriegsmarine much stronger and better equipped', while of the air war he said, 'Herr Churchill was the man who suddenly discovered unrestricted air raids as the great secret for victory. This criminal has been bombing German cities by night—a horror which, in a military sense, has no more than nuisance value—for three and a half months . . .' This presaged a more painful type of warfare, yet it had a mesmerising effect on the people. The patience of the German masses was astonishing. Most said that the Führer knew best what was to be done. They were all harnessed up for war work and simply carried on zealously and conscientiously.

On 8 and 9 January the military leadership assembled at the Berghof for one of the most decisive meetings of 1941. Hitler told them: 'Spain has dropped out; France is against us. Russia has recently made new demands—Finland, the Balkans and Mariapol. Romania is on our side; Hungary has no obstacles to joining us. In Yugoslavia everything remains open. Bulgaria is very cautious because they don't want to risk the dynasty.' Britain wanted to dominate the continent; therefore they would need to defeat us. He intended to be so strong that this objective could never be achieved. British hopes rested on the USA and USSR; 'But we cannot deliver the final blow to Britain by invasion,' he admitted. In 1941 the situation in mainland Europe would have consolidated so that we could see our way clear to continue the war against Britain and, if necessary, the United States.

Of the new British Foreign Secretary, Eden, Hitler said that here was the man who wanted to collaborate with the Soviets. Stalin was clever and cunning. 'He will just demand more and more. A German victory would be intolerable for Soviet ideology. It must be our decision to force Russia under as soon as possible. In two years the British will have forty divisions. This could tempt Russia into a pact. To grapple with the Russian question gives Japan a free hand against Britain in the East. Japan is ready for a serious collaboration.' Russian equipment was obsolescent; the Red Army had no well-thought out organisation.

For the first time before such a large circle, Hitler mentioned the idea of fighting in North Africa. The possibility of internal political collapse in Italy could not be risked. The problem was that in North Africa the Italians lacked modern equipment. Here Germany would have to assist with a support force.

Hitler stated that he would go to war with the USSR this summer. Originally he had intended to start in the second half of May, but because of developments in the Balkans and North Africa he had now had to postpone the attack date—possibly until June. Those present listened to all this dumbfounded. Not a word of opposition was raised to any of it. Their faces had a set expression. I doubt if any of them saw the need for war against Russia. Only after leaving were the first serious questions asked.

At the beginning of 1941, therefore, I did not view the future with optimism: if matters followed the course outlined, outright victory no longer seemed to me to be possible. I concluded that Hitler wanted to take over the Soviet landmass as a Reich dependency whose purpose was to supply us with the raw materials necessary to continue the war against Britain. This seemed even more important if we were going to have to take on the Americans too at some stage. It was not yet obvious that this would be the case, but the reports from our diplomats in Washington were not promising. Roosevelt's utterances had lately become considerably more critical and negative towards Germany, and anti-German feeling had begun to gain ground amongst the American people. I guessed that Churchill had won Roosevelt to his programme. Hitler repeated constantly that we had to settle the account with the USSR before the USA came into the war, but presumably this had now gone by the board.

The Mediterranean and North Africa

On 11 January Hitler signed Directive No 22, 'Assistance by German Forces in the Mediterranean Theatre'. In paragraph 1 of this document Hitler ordered the C-in-C Army to set up a blockade zone which 'by defending Tripolitania' would render our Italian allies 'valuable service'. From Sicily Fliegerkorps X would attack British naval forces and shipping. Hitler discussed this directive in detail with Mussolini in Salzburg on 19 and 20 January. Mussolini was very anxious for German troops to arrive in North Africa soon.

In January Fliegerkorps X moved from northern Italy to Sicily in readiness to attack British seaborne targets. OKH had sent General Freiherr von Funck to Italy and North Africa to reconnoitre the operational possibilities for panzers. He returned on 1 February and gave Hitler his report, which read unfavourably, but Hitler distrusted him and in any case the transfer of a light division was imperative because the British were already at El Agheila.

Rommel had been appointed German commander in North Africa and arrived at Tripoli in early February. He was accompanied by Schmundt, who had been acquainted with all the pros and cons of desert warfare. Schmundt returned after a few days and presented Hitler with a clear and sober account of Libya. He considered the outlook for operations in this theatre as favourable and advocated the swift transfer of a substantial German force. As to the military strength of the Italians, he was very tight-lipped: he seemed to think they were almost useless. The German 5th Light Division would be put in the front line in Libya as soon as they had disembarked in order to shore up the hopeless situation the Italians had made for themselves. Rommel was predestined for the task. He enjoyed Hitler's special confidence, earned by swift and effective leadership in the French campaign. Unselfishly he saw only the job in hand and set about improvising with the few German troops he had until others arrived. The British had had to send men to reinforce Greece and Crete and this eased his initial problems.

Hitler was not so much interested in pulling Mussolini's chestnuts out of the fire as in keeping his promise to assist the Duce: he believed that a German force in North Africa would help raise the Italian fighting level. However, it forced him to advise OKH that the attack on Russia would have to be put back by a few weeks. This highly disadvantageous delay provoked little reaction from the Army leadership—a fact which surprised me, for at least five months had been estimated as essential for the Russian campaign. Thus, at the end of January 1941, it was already clear that the campaign could not be concluded before winter set in. I spoke to Hitler about this in the Chancellery one evening and discovered that he had reached the same conclusion. He explained that the German Wehrmacht would inflict such catastrophic damage on the Soviet Union during the summer of 1941 that only a short campaign would be necessary to finish them off in 1942. I was by no means comfortable with this reply and told him so. After this conversation I had the feeling that North

Africa had not previously featured in his plans but that he had had no choice because of his loyalty to Mussolini.

On 27 January we travelled by train to Munich, where Hitler visited the architects Frau Troost and Professor Giesler and had a long consultation in their studio over his plans to redevelop Munich. At midnight we returned to Berlin, arriving next morning. Next day Hitler was advised of the death of the Reich Justice Minister Dr Franz Gürtner. Although Hitler did not like jurists very much, he thought highly of Gürtner and over the next few days spoke frequently of his achievements.[7]

Planning for 'Barbarossa'

In the afternoon of 3 February Hitler had a conference lasting several hours with Brauchitsch, Halder, Heusinger, Keitel and Jodl, the idea being to solicit basic thinking about Operation 'Barbarossa'. Jeschonnek joined in later. Halder estimated the Soviet forces at 121 rifle and 25 cavalry divisions and 31 motorised mechanical brigades—about 180 groups in all. Against them the Germans would array 104 infantry and 20 panzer divisions, the Kavallerie Division, and thirteen motorised plus a few Romanian divisions. Halder estimated that the Russians had about 10,000 tanks against 3,500 German panzers, but he rated the quality of the Russian tanks as poor, although one should be prepared for unpleasant surprises. Their artillery was numerically strong but mostly obsolete. The German attack was planned with three Army Groups and four Panzer Groups strung along the whole front. Supply was to be fully motorised on account of the shortage of railways.

On the whole Hitler was satisfied with the planning but repeated his idea of how the operation should develop. After the initial battles to overcome the frontier troops, he wanted Army Groups North and South reinforced along the line Pleskau–Smolensk–Kiev so that they could advance respectively to the Baltic as far as Leningrad and in the south to the area around Rostow. Army Group Centre would if necessary delay their attack on Moscow until the 1942 campaign. Hitler emphasised that the primary aim for the year 1941 was the conquest of the entire Baltic area, plus the city of Leningrad. The Army must always keep this objective in mind and ensure that the Russians gave up the Baltic.

He then spoke about various individual problems associated with the first attacks and the problem of supply. An important point for Hitler was the flak situation. It was expected that the Soviets had an air force of note, and Hitler drove home the importance of air raid precautions and flak. He accepted the Luftwaffe operational plan for the campaign in the East. In the first three days German bombers would destroy the Russian fighter force and so enable the panzers to make swift inroads across country.

In the course of this long conversation about how to conquer an uncommonly large area of the Earth I thought it almost impossible that the set objectives could ever be achieved. Before the French campaign, Brauchitsch and Halder had expressed their doubts repeatedly and made clear their opposition to the offensive in the West. Now they accepted Hitler's instructions to invade the Soviet Union without a word of protest. It occurred to me that they knew that the operation was ultimately doomed but had decided to let Hitler dig his own grave. This idea alarmed me, but I was daunted by the very scale of the Russian land mass. To this had been added in the spring of 1941 the North African adventure to prop up an ally of dubious value. The whole thing seemed very risky.

Before the Balkan Campaign

In the evening of 6 February Hitler travelled to the Berghof, where, except for a few short breaks, he remained until mid-March. February was a very pleasant month on the Obersalzberg. The duties were few and the preparations for 'Barbarossa' and to assist Mussolini in Greece were going according to plan. The air war over Britain had slackened on account of adverse weather conditions. Amongst Hitler's guests were the Yugoslav President Zvetkovich and Foreign Minister Cincar-Markovich. Hitler was determined to persuade Yugoslavia to join the Axis, but despite frank talks the question remained unresolved.

In Munich in the afternoon of 24 February Hitler delivered his Party Foundation Day speech in the banqueting hall of the Hofbräuhaus. Speaking of Mussolini, he stated: 'Our opponents still do not understand that once I accept a man as my friend, I stand by him and refuse to bargain my attitude.' He then went on to speak about the achievements of the Wehrmacht and German people and left no room for doubt but that 'just as in the past this struggle has been blessed by Providence, so shall it be blessed in the future'.

In the evening of 28 February his train brought him to Vienna, where on 1 March he participated in the ceremony at Schloss Belvedere accepting Bulgaria into the Axis. Amongst those present were Ribbentrop, the Bulgarian Minister President Filoff, Count Ciano and Ambassador Oshima. Even while this was going on, German pioneers were at work erecting three great bridges over the Danube, by which German troops in Romania could cross into Bulgaria and march on Greece. This was Hitler's deliberate riposte to Russia. On his visit to Berlin in November 1940, Molotov had expressed the Soviet Union's strong interest in Bulgaria. At the time Hitler had not given him an answer. Now he had it.

That afternoon in Vienna Hitler had a very comprehensive conversation with Ciano. He saw it as important to give the Italians a clear idea about the coming war with Greece. He spent the evening with Gauleiter Baldur von Schirach and his wife, both of whom Hitler esteemed highly. He had known Frau von Schirach as the small daughter of his official photographer Heinrich Hoffmann. Early next morning, when our train made a 90-minute stop at Linz, Hitler wandered in the town before the morning traffic set in. Later he discussed his plans for development work along the Danube and the new Nibelungen bridge.

At Obersalzberg the daily situation conferences with Keitel and Jodl began to occupy more time. Hitler received a number of visitors important to him on account of the impending Balkans operation. On 4 March the Yugoslav regent Prince Paul called. Hitler was primarily interested in winning him over to the Axis. A polite official discussion ensued which seemed unsuccessful. Hitler said that possibly in a few weeks Yugoslavia would decide to join, although he did not seem all that confident.

Jodl was working on the Japanese angle. He interpreted General Oshima's return to Berlin as ambassador as implying the readiness of Japan for a military collaboration if not a close alliance. He suggested that Hitler sign an instruction which considered the possibilities, and accordingly Directive No 24, 'Regarding Co-operation with Japan', was issued on 5 March. The first sentence explained: 'The aim of co-operation founded on the triaxial pact must be to encourage Japan to become actively involved against Britain in the Far East as soon as possible . . . a common aim of the policy will be the swift defeat of Britain so as to keep the United States out of the war.' The Directive concluded: 'No hint is to be given to the Japanese about the "Barbarossa" campaign.'

On the evening of 12 March we returned by the train to Linz, where Hitler visited the Hermann Göring Werke the following morning. He spoke of an increase in the current steel stocks which would be necessary to step up panzer and anti-tank gun production.

Hitler made his annual *Heldengedenktag* (Remembrance Day) speech at the Berlin Arsenal on 16 March, mentioning attacks by British bombers which portended that 'in this war the homeland will have to suffer heavier casualties than previously. And it will be not just the men, but above all the women.' Thus did Hitler warn for the first time of the horror of the impending air war against German cities, as to the extent of which at that time we had had no premonition.

During the intervening quiet period up to 25 March Hitler received Rommel, and, after awarding him the Oak Leaves to his Iron Cross, Hitler discussed with him his plans to regain Cyrenaica in North Africa. Rommel was a great optimist. He foresaw no difficulties and was looking forward to the arrival of the 15th Panzer Division with its entire corps, with which he was proposing to move eastwards at once.[8] His manner and energy pleased Hitler, who later praised Rommel highly and saw the development of the situation in North Africa in a very positive light. For the first time the newspapers spoke of an 'Afrika Korps'. Subsequently Rommel made a surprise attack at Agedabia which set the tempo for his offensive. On 4 April he took Benghazi and shortly would besiege Tobruk.

Hitler arrived in Vienna on the morning of 25 March. The Yugoslavs had announced their desire to join the Axis, although they would not sign until they had obtained from Germany a guarantee of their neutrality. The signing would be celebrated with the usual due ceremony and breakfast at Schloss Belvedere. Afterwards Hitler spent a carefree evening with the Schirachs, happy in the knowledge that the last of the Balkan states had joined the tripartite pact—although he had no great confidence in the durability of the Yugoslav Government.

Operation 'Marita'

Two days later diplomat Hewel brought news that Prince Paul and his government in Belgrade had been ousted the previous night: there was unrest throughout Yugoslavia and rioting had been reported in the capital. Young King Peter had assumed the monarchy by decree. Hitler remarked that this *putsch* had at least come at a convenient point: if it had happened during 'Barbarossa' it would have caused him much more anxiety. Now he still had time. So saying, he ordered OKH and OKW to draw up the usual agenda for discussion. At 1300 that day a large number of Army and Luftwaffe senior commanders assembled in the conference room. I also saw Ribbentrop, Göring, Brauchitsch, Keitel, Jodl, Halder,

Hoffmann von Waldau, Bodenschatz and Heusinger. Hitler described the known facts and added that Serbia and Slovenia had never been pro-German. He had taken the decision to attack Yugoslavia at once with the aim of dismantling the state. He would not wait for some sort of declaration of loyalty. The operation would be linked to 'Marita', the attack on Greece. German forces would head from Sofia towards Skopje, and stronger units would go for Nis and Belgrade. A thrust from the Graz and Klagenfurt areas would have the objective of destroying the Yugoslav Army. The Luftwaffe reported that von Richthofen's Fliegerkorps VIII was at immediate readiness in Bulgaria, though units of Fliegerkorps X would not ube so until two to three days later. Hitler ordered all preparations set in train and requested that Army and Luftwaffe make known to him their intentions. That same day Jodl committed Hitler's ideas to paper in Directive No 25. Thus the Balkans campaign entered a new stage. We reckoned with its beginning in just a few days.

Matsuoka

In the afternoon of 27 March Hitler welcomed the Japanese Foreign Minister Matsuoka. During the wait Hitler had been in a state of agitation. He was very keen for Japan to take measures against Britain. He did not know how far Japan was prepared to go nor to what extent he ought to let them know of his intentions. He hinted to Matsuoka that the current relationship between the Reich and the USSR could change precipitately and said that war against Britain had been unavoidable on the grounds of Britain's attitude. As yet he did not foresee the involvement of the United States. Matsuoka remained impassive. I had the impression that it was a fact-finding mission for his part. His travels took him to Rome and back and he broke off his return journey in Moscow to sign a Non-Aggression Pact with the Soviet Union. This was a clearer statement than anything he had said during his visit to Germany.

On his departure from Moscow there was a very impressive scene on the station platform when Stalin made known how much value he placed on the assistance of our military attaché and ambassador and the importance he attached to friendly Russo-German relations.

Hitler's Attitude to the Russian Enemy

On 30 March Hitler summoned the Wehrmacht leaders to the Cabinet Office, where he delivered a 2½-hour long speech. 'Britain is placing all her hopes on the United States and the USSR,' he began. The maximum armaments output of the United States would not be reached for three to four years. 'Russia is the last enemy factor in Europe. She must be destroyed during this year and the next. Then we will be in a position as regards *matériel* and men to control the air and seas. What has to be achieved in Russia is the destruction of the Red Army and Soviet state. It is a war of two world viewpoints. Bolshevism is comparable to an asocial criminal system and offers enormous danger for the future. We much dissociate ourselves from any idea of soldierly comradeship with the enemy. A communist can never be a comrade-in-arms. It is a war of extermination. If we fail to see it in that light, then even though we will defeat him, in several years the communist enemy will rise once more against us. In the war against the Soviet Union what will be important is the extermination of the Bolshevist commissars and intellectuals. The battle is against the poison of degeneration. Our troops must defend themselves by the same means as those with which they are attacked. Political commissars and GPU people are criminals and must be treated as such. In the East, hardness now means mildness for the future.'

Hitler mentioned next the large numbers of Soviet tanks and aircraft, only a few of which met modern criteria. The great Russian continent and the endless expanses of terrain made concentrations at decisive points essential. It was important to amass our panzers and Luftwaffe at decisive spots. After the first battles for air superiority, the Luftwaffe must work closely in support of the land operation. The Russian would fail once he came up against the panzers and Luftwaffe *en masse*.

After a late breakfast Hitler resumed that afternoon, emphasising the necessity for haste in the Balkans. Even so, the beginning of the Russian campaign had to be postponed by about a month. The Balkans offensive would start, at the latest, in about a week.

It was at about this time that I noted down something of especial significance. Between 1 and 3 March Oberst (Ing) Dietrich Schwenke of the Reich Air Ministry had paid a visit to Russia to inspect Luftwaffe facilities there under the Russo-German agreement. I heard about this trip from various service centres of the Ministry. Unfortunately I did not get to speak to Schwenke personally, but the head of the Foreign Air Forces Section at Luftwaffe General Staff let me have some important points from his report. From these there could be no doubt that Russia was arming on a grand scale. Newly built aircraft factories of an enormous size were nearing completion. A huge number of airfields had been laid down. Everyone seemed to be very busy indeed. When I mentioned this to Hitler, he said that Göring had already told him. One should take this military build-up very seriously. He was firmly convinced that the justification for the war with Russia would be realised at the last moment.

On 5 April Hitler was advised that the Soviet Union had terminated her Friendship and Non-Aggression Treaty with Yugoslavia. Hitler accepted this report with a certain satisfaction, for it proved that the Russians wanted to go their own way. A few days later the ambassadors of Yugoslavia, Norway, Belgium and Greece were expelled from the Soviet Union since Stalin no longer considered these to be sovereign states.

The Balkan Campaign

Our attacks on Greece and Yugoslavia began on Sunday 6 April. Hitler had ordered a very heavy air raid on Belgrade, which came as a complete surprise to the civilian population and caused many casualties. At the same time the invasions were reported in the Reich by a proclamation in which Hitler described his efforts 'to spare the German people this altercation'. He placed the blame for the situation in the Balkans squarely on the British, who had had a foot in Greece for some time. 'May people who are blind to the fact recognise that they have to thank for this the worst of "friends", who for the last 300 years have been occupying parts of the continent', and in an Order of the Day to 'Soldiers of the South-East Front' he reproached the British for 'making others do their fighting for them'.

Just before Hitler transferred his HQ to the south-east of the Reich, he was surprised in Berlin by a very heavy British air raid. On the night of 10 April the State Opera House, the University, the State Library and the Palace of the Crown Prince were hit. Heavy damage was caused. The Opera House was completely gutted. Hitler was outraged and as a result he had a furious argument with Göring. I heard Hitler's reproaches about the useless Ju 88 with which the bomber squadrons had been saddled. They would rather have the He 111 back. Göring did not dispute the allegation about the Ju 88 but explained to Hitler that the competent director at Junkers, Koppenberg, had reported to him that the fault had been ironed out in the newest machines and that the models coming off the line in 1942 would have more powerful motors.[9] Göring usually had the knack of mollifying Hitler. The Führer gave Professor Speer the job of rebuilding the Opera House.

That night Hitler left Berlin for his FHQ at Mönichkirchen, where we arrived 24 hours later. This small village lay at the end of a tunnel on the main railway line between Vienna and Graz. Makeshift platforms had been erected and a military signals station set up. The train remained in sidings here for the next fourteen days. The campaign was under the control of OKH and went off without any real problems. The only difficulty lay in the inadequate highways.

In a letter I informed my uncle: 'This time we have our HQ in the train which has been marshalled in the south-east corner of the Reich. From here the Führer directs the operation. Since midday it is quiet on the Yugoslav Front. It is a good thing that we have got it over with so quickly for there is nothing down here worth winning. Let's hope that it will tail off soon in Greece too. The British are clearing out from there, so it looks like the other side thinks it's not worth the candle. The battle in Yugoslavia was easier and we had fewer casualties than expected. The only difficulty was the terrain which held up the panzer divisions. The Greeks put up a fierce resistance on their side of the Bulgarian passes (Rupal Pass) and the individual bunkers fought bravely. At the moment our troops are in action on both sides of Mount Olympus. According to the latest reports, however, the British and Greeks seem to be beaten. They are pulling back everywhere. It is good that the Balkans question is being resolved. It was always an uncertain factor. I fear that the arrival of the Italians in Dalmatia will not contribute to peace. The Croats are already saying that they want the Italians out of the Balkans altogether. If they have the weapons they can do it. The Turk seems to be maintaining an honest neutrality. But the British are doing all they can to buy influence. They pay better than we do. We have now only one objective—to reorganise our divisions in readiness for fresh missions. The big question remains to be settled this year, then we can fight the war against the Anglo-Saxon democrats to its bitter end.'

The Greeks fought a brave and tough battle and held up our troops along the frontier; but, ultimately, inexperienced Greeks and Yugoslavs were no match for battle-hardened Germans. Fliegerkorps VIII contributed to a substantial acceleration of operations. The Yugoslavs capitulated on 17 April, the Greeks on the 21st. Their capitulation to the Twelfth

Army gave rise to an incident. Hitler had instructed C-in-Cs to ignore the Italians in all questions of armistice negotiations and accept any offer without hesitation. The Italians were still in Albania, where they were making very heavy going of it. The C-in-C of the Greek Epirus Army stated that he would only surrender to the German High Command and not to the Italians. After the armistice had been signed there was a lot of ill-feeling which culminated in the Italians' declaring that they would only recognise the treaty if they were present at a re-signing. Feldmarschall List refused to go through it all again and so Jodl had to do it instead.

After the surrender of Belgrade I flew there in a Fieseler Storch on 14 April. The city was still in disorder. The air raid two days earlier had caused serious damage. Bridges were down. I obtained a motor-car at the airfield for sightseeing. Most striking was the state of the so-called Government Hill, where the villas of Prince Paul and King Peter were to be found. Both houses were undamaged. The doors were open but nothing had been touched. Personal effects lay around in the king's villa: it looked as if the occupants were likely to return at any moment. This impressed me very much, for it gave me a clear picture of how war and peace were bedfellows.

The days of the South-East campaign passed calmly at FHQ Mönich-kirchen. I concluded from conversations with Hitler that his thoughts were more on 'Barbarossa' than in the Balkans. He posed many questions about equipment of the bomber squadrons but weapons and munition stocks of the Flak Korps interested him more. He was expecting heavy air attacks against the invading groups and said that we would not be able to rely on empty skies as in previous campaigns.

The increase in British air raids against the Reich was causing him concern. Göring had apparently promised him that the weaknesses in the German Luftwaffe would be overcome in the winter, although he evidently did not believe these assurances entirely. I had to tell him in all honesty that I had seen no Luftwaffe figures which supported this assertion. The interruption to Ju 88 production seemed too fundamental to be overcome as quickly as claimed. Airmen were saying quite openly that the Ju 88 was an absolute disaster. This conversation pained me, but I could only report the facts as I knew them. I put Bodenschatz into the picture about what I had told Hitler and asked him to advise Göring. Bodenschatz was well aware of the Ju 88 problem and said that he would do the necessary. I found out later that he probably did tell Göring something, although I think he was not as forthright with the Reichs-marschall about the difficulties as he might have been.

During the stay at Mönichkirchen Hitler received several visitors. On 20 April the OKW chiefs called by to offer birthday congratulations. Ambassador von Papen came to FHQ to enquire about the course of German-Turkish relationships at a time of radical change in the Balkans. Hitler told him very clearly that it was not his intention to perturb the Turks. King Boris of Bulgaria and the Hungarian Regent Admiral Horthy came on 19 and 24 April, respectively, both intimating an interest in annexing certain parts of Yugoslavia. In these talks Hitler remained re-served but polite and said he would consider their wishes once the occu-pation of the territories had been completed.

Another caller was Oberleutnant Franz von Werra, a Luftwaffe fighter pilot shot down during the Battle of Britain. He had been transferred to a prisoner-of-war camp in Canada, from where he escaped to the United States and then to Mexico. Finally he had returned to Germany—un-doubtedly an unique achievement. Hitler was delighted to meet him, asking for his experiences and any information he had picked up which might be useful for the war. Amongst other things, von Werra reported a new British anti-submarine search system which seemed to be successful.

Jodl presented Hitler with fresh directives, numbered 27 and 28. The first was dated 13 April and concerned the conclusion of operations in the Balkans, recording that 'the mass of the groups deployed are being withdrawn for a new purpose'. The other, dated 25 April, referred to Operation 'Merkur', the invasion of Crete. Jeschonnek considered this operation essential with reference to the Greek theatre and to make se-cure Rommel's position in North Africa.

The train arrived back in Berlin on the morning of 28 April. Once again Hitler was returning from a victorious campaign and in the Chan-cellery he was feted by a mêlée of curious callers, congratulating him and attempting to obtain more details from Hitler himself about the cam-paign. But Hitler allowed little time—except at table—to relate events. He had nothing but praise for the Greek Army, which in his own words had 'gone down fighting'. Accordingly, he had allowed the officers to retain their weapons. As to the fighting quality of the Italians, he re-mained silent but spoke up for Mussolini on account of his loyal comrade-ship in the war against Britain. In the same breath, however, he criticised the Italian Army leadership and the royal house, which were pro-British.

All Hitler's free time was now claimed by the final preparations for 'Barbarossa'. One evening the opportunity arose to speak to him about the campaign. I told him that earlier in my military service I had arrived in Russia on 5 May 1929. From that time on, as I recalled, I had experienced only dry and fine weather. Therefore I could not imagine why the Wehrmacht should waste two good months on account of the handful of divisions that we were waiting to withdraw from Greece. Hitler listened in silence and announced after some reflection that Halder, with his 'old-fashioned' ideas about modern warfare, had learned very little. He would speak to him again. As I later discovered, Halder referred to transportation difficulties and the need to rest the men—reasons which I found unconvincing. However, in practice Hitler would not interfere in Halder's measures once he had failed to convince the latter of the correctness and logic of his own appreciation of the situation. Apparently Halder had not been impressed, and so Hitler accepted Halder's programme to bring up the divisions from the Balkans first.

On 29 April Hitler addressed 9,000 Wehrmacht senior cadets awaiting commissions. He described the war successes to date, lauded the bravery of the German soldier and demanded of his listeners 'never to capitulate . . . one word I do not know and will never know as Führer of the German people and your Supreme Commander is capitulation, submission to the will of another. Never! Never! And you have to think in the same way.'

On 30 April Hitler discussed with Jodl details of the commencement of 'Barbarossa', which Jodl later communicated to the Wehrmacht in his bulletin of 1 May. This set the date at 22 June and meant that the general movement order would take effect from 23 May. Revising the respective ratio of strengths, Jodl reported a substantial increase in Soviet forces along the southern sector of the front. Although the Russians were lately drafting increased numbers of troops to the central area, the German Army still had a strong superiority there. On the basis of OKH estimates, Jodl reckoned that there would be up to four weeks' fierce fighting along the border. The Russian soldier could be expected to stand and fight to the last. Hitler co-operated in the draft of this communiqué, which amounted to its seal of approval.

On the evening of Sunday 4 May Hitler made the usual speech to the Reichstag at the conclusion of a successful campaign, emphasising the strength and achievments of the Wehrmacht. 'The year 1941 will go down in history as the greatest year of our revival,' he said. He was not thinking of the Balkans but of 'Barbarossa'. Throughout the Reich the impending invasion of Russia was an open secret. The soldiers at battle readiness in Poland; the congregation of supply formations; the conglomeration of signals groups—all this left little room for doubt of Hitler's intentions. The build-up for the campaign was on such a scale that its purpose could scarcely be disguised.

After the Reichstag session Hitler travelled to Danzig and Gotenhafen, where the new battleship *Bismarck* and heavy cruiser *Prinz Eugen* were working up for Operation 'Rheinübung', an Atlantic raiding cruise. Hitler spoke to the Fleet Commander, Admiral Lütjens, saw over the flagship and obtained an impression of the ship's company. On his return he was full of praise for the battleship and her crew. He had complete confidence in the ship and said that the commander would set out on the voyage without anxieties. The only danger which might threaten them in certain circumstances was an attack by aircraft flown off a carrier—his own greatest fear. He told Jodl that in his opinion heavy ships were now superfluous in warfare: they were always at risk from aircraft bombs and torpedoes and there was nothing to protect them against the danger. Thus whilst he had pride in German naval might which *Bismarck* represented, he kept himself fully informed as to the progress of the voyage and remained very thoughtful. We left Berlin for Obersalzberg, where we arrived late on 9 May. Hitler made the observation that he wanted a few days' peace and quiet so as to return to Berlin in June fresh and rested for the fray. He wished Keitel and Jodl 'restful days' in the lead-up to the attack on Russia.

The Flight of Rudolf Hess
In the morning of 11 May, Pintsch, one the two adjutants of Rudolf Hess, reported to the Berghof with a letter. Hitler, who was in bed, rose quickly and went into the hall to read it. Then he asked Pintsch if he knew what the letter contained, and he received an affirmative reply. Pintsch and the other adjutant, Leitgen, were arrested at once and taken off to a concentration camp. They had disobeyed Hitler's orders to maintain a special watch on Hess. Göring, Ribbentrop and Bormann were summoned at once. Göring came accompanied by Udet. There was a long discussion in which Hitler repeatedly expressed the hope that Hess would be shot down. He was furious that Hess must have had the freedom to

make the preparations for his flight in minute detail despite the flying ban Hitler had imposed on him personally. He attributed the behaviour of Hess to certain 'delusions' under which he was labouring and on 12 May explained the defection of Hess in an announcement, stating that 'A letter he left unfortunately shows in its confusion the evidence of a mental derangement which leads us to fear that Party Member Hess has fallen victim to a delusion.' Following this broadcast, the British confirmed the safe landing of Hess in Scotland with the assurance that he was in a good state of health. Hitler reacted by having inserted in the *Nationalsozialistische Parteikorrespondenz* a footnote to his original statement in which he further explained that Hess 'was suffering from bodily ills and was motivated to flight on the basis of astrology and magnetism'. The statement ended: 'Respecting the continuation of the war enforced upon the German people by Britain, it changes nothing.' And that was the last which the German public heard about the defection and its cause.

On 13 May Hitler gathered all Reichs- and Gauleiters to the Obersalzberg and provided them with a full explanation. Bormann had to read Hess's letter aloud. Hitler spoke briefly about the case and saw in Hess's behaviour an abnormal interpretation of the political events of the time. Hitler nominated Reichsleiter Bormann to be Chief of the Party Chancellery under his personal command.

I had known Rudolf Hess for four years through his various visits to Hitler, when I listened to various conversations he had had, and on many other occasions. Had Hess fallen prey to mental delusions? I think that a night flight in a twin-engined Me 110, alone and without a navigator, could only be undertaken by a person in a sound mental state. In my opinion, Hess was sane and in full control of his faculties. His wish to engage in a dialogue with the British about the future of the war between Britain and Germany seemed to me unexceptional. Hess knew Hitler and his ideas about the war, especially the intention to invade Russia. I considered the flight to be a manifestation of his fear respecting the outcome of the war and of his helplessness to do anything about it. I shared these fears, and in subsequent months found out that I was by no means alone in that.

Crete
On 20 May paratroops and an air-landed force under General Student began the invasion of Crete. This risky operation lasted until 2 June,

when the whole island finally came under German control. We had suffered heavy losses and had to fight for every inch against entrenched British Empire defenders. In the initial few days, when the operation threatened to collapse, Jeschonnek flew to the Peleponnese and took command, ordering the transfer of the entire 22nd Infantry Division to begin at once. This operation cost the Luftwaffe a large number of Ju 52 transports, but our forces on Crete were substantially reinforced within a few days and the enemy evacuated the island shortly afterwards. The success was of significance for the war in the eastern Mediterranean.

I wrote to my uncle on 23 May: 'Since the 20th the battle for the last piece of Greek soil, Crete, has been raging. Almost two whole divisions were flown in, which should be enough to take the island. The British Fleet turned up but was driven off by our bombers. Crete has shown again that a fleet is at risk if one does not control the air . . . it is not easy for Rommel at Tobruk. But there is no worry. The conquest of Crete will make it simpler for him . . . the Führer selected General Rommel for the role personally. The Army had suggested another general.'

Battleship *Bismarck*

On 18 May *Bismarck* and *Prinz Eugen* sailed from Gotenhafen and, after having refuelled near Bergen, headed north-about for the Atlantic. They were maintaining radio silence, and we had to wait for reports from enemy sources. On 24 May *Bismarck* sank the most powerful British warship afloat, the battlecruiser *Hood*, in the Denmark Strait. Raeder telephoned the Führer to report the success personally. Hitler congratulated him, but after that his mood changed and he became very edgy. Nothing further could be done to influence events, and unfortunately *Bismarck*'s voyage developed in the manner Hitler had feared. The Home Fleet shadowed the battleship, continually increasing the number of units in the area, which included the aircraft carriers *Victorious* and *Ark Royal*. A hit in the forepeak during the battle with *Hood* had caused some flooding: *Bismarck* was a little down by the head and had lost a few knots in speed. For this reason Admiral Lütjens decided to abandon the mission and make for St Nazaire. For a while the ship managed to shake off her pursuers, but in the morning of 26 May the British re-established contact and that evening *Ark Royal*'s torpedo aircraft attacked and obtained a hit astern which jammed her rudder. *Bismarck* was now only able to proceed in a broad circle and British heavy units closed in for the kill.

Shortly before midnight *Bismarck* signalled: 'Ship unmanoeuvrable. We fight to the last shell. Long live the Führer.'

Hitler and I sat alone in the small living room at the Berghof and waited for fresh reports. At 0036 a signal was transmitted addressed to the Führer personally: 'We fight to the last in belief in you, *mein Führer*, and with rock-solid confidence in Germany's victory.' I took down Hitler's reply: 'All Germany is with you. What can be done is being done. The fulfilment of your duty will fortify our people in the struggle for their existence. Adolf Hitler.' I telephoned the text to SKL at once. Then it fell quiet between us for some time until Hitler broke the silence and asked for the strength of *Bismarck*'s complement. I told him there were 2,300 men. As the night progressed Hitler grew ever more irritable. He said that he would never allow a battleship or cruiser out into the Atlantic again.[10] Between two and three that morning he retired to bed. I joined my wife and in a drained mental state discussed with her at length our first major naval defeat of the war. Late next morning SKL reported officially that *Bismarck* had been sunk.

On 2 June Hitler had a long conversation at the Brenner with Mussolini concerning Hess, the sinking of *Bismarck* and general military matters. No mention was made of Russia. On the 4th the report was received of the death of the former Kaiser, Wilhelm II. Hitler sent telegrams of condolence to the widow and Crown Prince and assigned the Reich Commissioner for the Netherlands, Seyss-Inquart, and Luftwaffe General Christiansen, Wehrmacht senior commander in Holland, to attend the funeral at Doorn.

On 12 June, in Munich, talks were held with the Romanian head of state. Antonescu said he was very interested in regaining Bessarabia and promised to send Romanian troops to fight alongside the German armies in Russia. Hitler was very reserved when it came to promises like this made by persons of Balkan origin, and made no comment.

Final Preparations for 22 June

The Commanders-in-Chief of the Army Groups, Armies and Air Fleets destined for the Eastern Front were summoned to the Chancellery on 14 June. To avoid the influx of General Staff officers becoming too obvious, a strict agenda of arrival routes, times and car parking was enforced. After a few words of welcome, Hitler invited each commander to report on his intentions for his personal sphere of operations during the opening days of the campaign. This provided an overview of the strengths of the groups, the numbers of panzers and so on. Hitler interrupted rarely and listened attentively. The reports gave an optimistic opinion about the quality and equipment of the Red Army.

After lunch Hitler spoke to the gathering for about an hour. He said that this was a war against Communism. He reckoned that the Russian soldier would fight hard and offer tough resistance: 'We must expect heavy air raids and take steps to protect ourselves through skilful air defences. The Luftwaffe will win quick successes and thus lighten the load for the Army Groups. We will have the worst of the fighting behind us after about six weeks. But every soldier must know what it is we are fighting for. It is not the teritory that we want, but rather that Bolshevism is destroyed.' He spoke in bitter tones against Britain, which preferred an understanding with the Soviet Union to one with Germany: these were the politics of the nineteenth, and not the twentieth century. Hitler proved with these words that his alliance with Stalin had been a purely political device to regain Danzig and the Polish Corridor without becoming embroiled in a European war. He continued: 'If we lose this war with Russia, then all Europe will become Communist. If the British cannot see that, they will lose their leading role in world affairs and with it their Empire. To what extent they will trust themselves to the hands of the Americans remains to be seen. But the Americans are interested in this war only for what they can get out of it.'

In the afternoon Hitler had further talks with the commanders of Army Group South, which would be driving into a vast and expanding area. He said that the mass of Russian troops was expected on the Central Front: once these were defeated, Army Group South would be reinforced from Army Group Centre. Brauchitsch and Halder made no comment.

On 21 June Hitler dictated a proclamation to the German people describing his policies since the outbreak of war. 'The reawakening of our people from despair, misery and an abusive disregard is the sign of a pure inner rebirth. This was no threat to Britain. Nevertheless they resurrected their hate-filled policy of encircling Germany. Within that nation and externally there has been a conspiracy between Jew and Democrat, Communist and reactionary, with the single objective of preventing the reconstruction of the new state of the German people, to uproot the new Reich and return it to impotence and misery.' Despite all friendly conversations Moscow had been preparing systematically for war. The

German build-up on the Eastern Front was now concluded. 'The task of this front is . . . no longer the protection of individual nations, but the defence of Europe and the salvation of all . . . May God help us in this struggle.'

In 1941 I was asked repeatedly if the Russians knew of or suspected our intention to invade. At that time I could only answer that I supposed their long-range reconnaissance aircraft must have seen the build-up of our land forces along the border. What they could not know was when and how we would operate these units. Not until long after the war did I discover from an official on the staff of Carl Goerdeler, Oberbürgermeister of Leipzig, that he had been present at private talks in the Hotel Kaiserhof with Molotov in 1940. Apparently they had told Molotov of Hitler's plan to attack Russia in 1941 but Molotov had not wanted to believe this and would not take them seriously. After his visit to Berlin, however, Russia began large-scale preparations for war. When they invaded in 1941, German troops came across vast new fortifications, new airfields and so forth. The Soviets had been expecting our invasion, but not in 1941. They had decided it would be later.

In the last few days before the commencement of the Russian campaign Hitler was increasingly nervous and troubled. He was garrulous, walked up and down continuously and seemed to be waiting anxiously for news of something. Not until the early hours of 22 June did I hear his first observation about the opening campaign when he said, 'It will be the most difficult battle which our soldiers will have to undergo in this war.'

I tried to picture the general situation and deduce what confronted us over the next few months. The war with Britain would go on as before. Hitler planned to attack Britain in the summer of 1942. This seemed to me to be wishful thinking. I considered a direct invasion of Britain possible in the autumn of 1942 at the earliest—if by then we had managed to see off the Russians. But I doubted Hitler's optimistic judgement of the Russian situation. The prognosis looked very complicated to me. Even more threatening was the United States. I feared that their entry into the war could not be too far off. Then we would really have a struggle on our hands. If Hitler failed to obtain a clear victory against Russia before the Americans came in, we would be faced—in the most favourable way of looking at it—with a long, hard war of attrition, the outcome of which was highly doubtful. Accordingly I judged the general situation at the outbreak of war between Germany and the USSR as not in our favour. The only chink of light seemed to be that our enemies, seeing our strength along the Russian border, had decided to wait for the time when they could match us in armaments. That might be years, and in that time, I believed, it might be possible for us to defeat one of our two main enemies and so be free to take on the other.

The Army High Command was expecting a conventional war, but most generals were not in favour of fighting it for the reason that we would now have a war on two fronts which in the long run Germany could neither win nor see through to a satisfactory conclusion. Hitler's concept was quite different from that of the Army. He saw a confrontation with a hard and ruthless enemy, indicative of this being his 'Commissar Order', by which he required German troops to shoot out of hand all political commissars they happened to come across. This order had caused much disquiet and I knew that not all commanders had passed it on. It was the first major opposition to a Führerbefehl I had heard of and probably it was not the first. I had observed, for example, Halder's oppositional stance to many of Hitler's instructions and noticed how he had now ceased to argue. I had the impression that Halder had decided to swallow his pride and keep silent, but perhaps he had his revenge by sabotaging Hitler's orders subsequently. Thus as we embarked upon this truly massive offensive we had not only a disjointed leadership, but some were pulling in different directions, and in this I saw a great danger for the success of the operation.

For his part, Hitler stood in the highest favour with the German people and had the unconditional support of the Party functionaries and membership. He had never lost a campaign and he felt sure he was going to win this one. He even spoke of the United States reconsidering involving itself in the European war. The struggle would be very hard—of that he had no doubt. He expected the enemy to be ruthless and wanted to encourage German troops to be the same. The Commissar Order was a means to this end. Lenin and Stalin had grabbed power and maintained their stranglehold on the Russian people by eliminating their political enemies. Hitler proposed that the political commissars, who were instrumental in this policy, should be eliminated summarily in their turn.

Wolfschanze

Hitler launched his campaign against the Soviet Union in the early hours of 22 June 1941. At midday on the 23rd he boarded his private train for the new FHQ in East Prussia, where he arrived late that evening. The site, known as Wolfschanze, lay in a small wooded area east of Rastenburg. It had been built the previous winter and was well camouflaged against aircraft. At the heart of the complex were ten bunkers with a two-metre thick concrete roof over the rear section where the sleeping quarters were located. The forward part housed the military planning rooms and offered splinter protection only. The daily situation conferences were held in a large room in Keitel's bunker. The corresponding room in Hitler's bunker was set aside for small-scale conferences. In the middle of the camp were the dining barracks with two tables seating twenty and six respectively. We moved into Wolfschanze for an indefinite period and settled down to await the first reports of this great war. Warlimont's planning staff and the FHQ Kommandant and staff were accommodated in normal barracks with a number of bunkers set a little apart from the camp. The OKH quarters were located a few kilometres to the northeast, close by the Rastenburg-Angermund railway line, while Göring and the OKL were accommodated in trains in sidings near Goldap and in the Johannesburger Heide.

Among the first reports which the Press Chief brought was a statement by Churchill. He had been a lifelong opponent of Communism, he said, but he now allied himself totally to Russia and against Germany. 'We will never parley with Hitler and his gang,' he promised. Hitler had expected nothing else from him.

The daily routine in FHQ Sperrkreis I, as the core area was known, differed little from the usual pattern in Berlin. Each day at twelve Hitler would make his way to Keitel's bunker for the main situation conference, which would normally last about ninety minutes. Once or twice a week Brauchitsch, Halder and Heusinger would attend these briefings. In the afternoons Hitler would have conversations and dealings with non-military callers, but the subject was always to do with the war. The evening situation conference, chaired by Jodl, followed at six. Hitler usually ate punctually at two in the afternoon and at seven-thirty. If no special visitors were expected, he would take his time at table—often up to two hours. In 1941 and 1942 Bormann's companions Heinrich Heim and Dr Henry Picker took down the text of many of these conversations in shorthand and they were subsequently published after the war in numerous reprints under the title *Hitlers Tischgespräche* (Hitler's Table Talks). In these two years at mealtimes Hitler spoke freely on many subjects. It might happen that now and again he would seize on a subject, be it about the passion for hunting or horsemanship or whatever, in order to 'deal a blow' to somebody.

Meals were Wehrmacht catering and consisted of soup, meat and a dessert. Hitler had his own vegetarian menu which he drew up at breakfast time. The seating arrangement never varied. Hitler sat in the middle with his back to the windows. To his right sat Press Chief Dr Dietrich, to his left Jodl. Directly opposite him was Keitel, to his right Bormann and to his left Bodenschatz. If there were guests they would sit between Hitler and Dietrich or between Keitel and Bodenschatz. The atmosphere at table was free and unforced. Conversation was spontaneous and there was no kind of compulsion about what could be discussed. On subjects of general interest, when Hitler contributed his opinion silence would be maintained. It occurred occasionally that he would hold the floor, so to speak, for up to an hour, but this was the exception rather than the rule. The extended mealtimes often forced many younger diners to excuse themselves from table for duty. Hitler never took this the wrong way.

First Successes
In the first week of our stay at Wolfschanze Hitler forbade the broadcasting of Wehrmacht bulletins. The operations on the Eastern Front were going to plan. There was patchy stiff resistance which would have to be smashed by panzers and artillery. It soon became clear that this delaying resistance was directed by specially able officers, NCOs or political commissars who dominated the men under them and made it violently clear that they were there to fight. If these leaders were captured they were summarily executed. However, the overall picture in the first few days was, as expected, variable. A comprehensive letter which I wrote to my uncle on 28 June conveys my impressions at that time:

'. . . Reports about the advance and operations have been withheld so as not to provide the Russians with a picture of the situation. The first bulletins will probably start tomorrow. The initial evidence is that Russia has made far greater preparations for this war than we assumed, but probably they did not expect a date before 1943, by when the build-up and arming of their forces would have been completed.

'The Russian Army made a stand with assault groups and motorised units first around Lemberg, then at Bialystok and finally Kovno. Their defensive installations were still under construction. North-west of

Lemberg, near Rawa-Ruska and north-west of Grodno bunker installations were discovered which were laid out on the Westwall pattern. The front line was completed but the two rear sections were still under construction.

'The ease of our early victories along the whole front came as a surprise to both Army and Luftwaffe. Enemy aircraft were parked in neat rows on their airfields and could be destroyed without difficulty. Four Panzer groups carried the weight of our attack: Kleist from Lublin towards Rowno-Shitomir, Guderian via Brest to Minsk, Hoth from Gumbinnen via Wilna to Minsk and Höpner north of Gumbinnen via Kowno to Dunaburg. A part of Guderian's group is heading for the Beresina near Bobruysk . . . the Russian is putting up a good fight everywhere, sometimes so tough and determined that our troops have a fierce battle. The main reason behind it is undoubtedly the Communist commissars who, pistol in hand, force their men to fight until shot dead. The Russian Communist propaganda has succeeded in convincing their men that they are fighting a war against barbaric savages and that no prisoners are being taken. This explains why many soldiers, but especially officers and commissars, commit suicide when faced with surrender. Often they place a primed hand grenade against the chest.

'Our advance has gone off surprisingly swiftly. On the northern flank in Lithuania and in the centre around Bialystok the enemy is falling apart. Their command structure has failed completely. Individual groups are trying to break out of the cauldron. From Dunaburg our forces are heading to the Peipus Sea to block their escape. The stiffest resistance is in the south. Here the leadership is good. Rundstedt, who is commander there, says that he has not come up against such a good opponent at any time in this war. Since yesterday evening, however, the enemy seems to be weakening. Therefore we are hurrying to form a bag. From northern Romania a German army will meet up with the Romanians and connect up with Kleist.

'Those are broadly the opening operations. The next major targets will be the Donetz basin, Moscow and Leningrad. The men are saying that the Russian gives a repulsive impression. They are a confused racial mix with Asiatic appearance and manners.

'Russian tanks and aircraft are poor, much inferior to ours, and tend to be deployed in small numbers. This enables our forces to score highly. They seem to have a good supply of tanks, but our troops are so superior that we can look to the future with confidence.'

These were the first impressions our troops had gained of the enemy. I flew in a Storch to the front to obtain an idea of affairs for myself. In the Lithuanian area, for example, a German unit came across a giant field of corn. There was a lot of shooting coming from within. Gradually we established that the cornfield concealed hundreds of young Russian Asiatics who had been thrown into the fray and left to it. There was fear in their faces since they were expecting to be shot out of hand. It took an age to round them all up.

The month of July found most in an optimistic frame of mind at FHQ. Hitler saw himself confirmed in his judgement. Neither Brauchitsch nor Halder, Keitel nor Jodl had a word to say to the contrary. Whether they all shared Hitler's outlook I was unable to determine. However, as we know from his published diary notes, on 3 July Halder considered that the campaign against Russia would be won within the next fourteen days if it was not already won.

Personally I did not share this opinion. There was certainly an astonishingly high bag of prisoners—Army Group Centre reported over a quarter of a million on 9 July—but it was a permanent flow, constantly increasing. On 16 July Hitler went so far as to create the Ostministerium covering Russia and the Baltic, and awarded the competent office to Reichsleiter Alfred Rosenberg. This decision caused a mild sensation and many difficulties were predicted with it—as, indeed, duly came to pass.

Mölders and Galland

That month Hitler awarded to Oberst Mölders as the first Wehrmacht recipient the Swords and Diamonds to the Oak Leaves of the Knight's Cross; in January 1942 Galland was similarly honoured. The two airman maintained a friendly chase. Hitler took the opportunity to discuss with them in detail problems of the air war in the West. From both I gained the impression that they were anxious to give voice to certain doubts and worries. They spoke frankly and without reserve. Hitler listened attentively. Galland complained of false Press and radio reports and of the condescending and arrogant tone adopted when referring to the RAF. At the conclusion of this conversation Hitler gave Galland to understand—in the winter crisis of early 1942!—that Germany had already broken the back of the Red Army. I can still hear Galland's question to me afterwards—'Is that right?' I did not reply.

Discussions Concerning the Attack

In those July days of 1941 it seemed to me that Hitler was overestimating the operational success of the campaign. The number of prisoners taken by Army Group Centre was no doubt impressive, but Russia had an immeasurable reserve of people. Furthermore, as our divisions rolled ever onwards into the vastness of the Russian hinterland, we would encounter greater problems. Above all we would need time. Hitler's intentions, ever since the initial plans had been first drafted, was to seize all Baltic ports, including Leningrad, and in the south the entire Black Sea coast as far as Rostow. In order to hammer home this point afresh with the military commanders on the spot we flew to Malnava, Army Group North, on 21 July. Generalfeldmarschall Ritter von Leeb had been firmly opposed to the campaign from the start but exuded optimism and saw no obstacles blocking his advance, provided that he received reinforcements from Panzer Group 3. Hitler reminded him of how much importance was being attached to the taking of the Baltic ports and the setting up of a link with the Finns through the port of Leningrad.

OKH and, so it appeared, Army Group Centre had certain reservations about the operation which Hitler did not share. The arguments were still going on at the end of July when Hitler fell ill for a few days. He failed to appear for meals and the daily situation conferences: it was quite obvious from his appearance how miserable he felt. Dr Morell said it was probably a slight apoplexy. Hitler's heart and circulation were not in good order, but within a short while he would return the Führer to his former self. After a few days there was a noticeable improvement. We were ordered to observe the strictest silence about Hitler's condition. This was a health crisis with potentially serious consequences, however, and it worried me sufficiently to confide it to my brother on 30 July.

On 3 August we flew to Borissov to see Bock, C-in-C Army Group Centre. Brauchitsch and Halder were also there. Hitler had long talks with them. In the forefront of these conversations was the ratio of strength, opposing troop numbers and the size of the territory to be conquered— twelve per cent of the world's land surface. All three generals stressed the idea that Army Group Centre should have the single objective of taking Moscow. They were in an optimistic frame of mind, and said that, after a few days to re-equip and re-group, they could go on to take Moscow before the bad weather set in. Hitler did not approve this proposition, referring to the view he had asserted prior to the campaign that Army

Group Centre was to halt beyond Smolensk while Army Group North took Leningrad and Army Group South took Rostov. Subsequently the two Groups would stream out from these two centres and drive in the direction of Moscow, the two spearheads meeting up east of the city. Both sides were stubborn and no decision came despite the length of the talks.

I remember Borissov for another reason. Two royal princes whom I knew through my service spoke to me about Hitler's order that all descendants of the former German ruling houses were not to fight at the front but be placed in positions to the rear. All they wanted was the chance to do their duty as any other front officer. Basically Hitler held the princes in high esteem and recognised their bravery in the field. I have described the political reason for this order and Hitler's uncompromising stand on it. I was unable to help the princes in any way. They understood this and went off considering themselves second class officers.

On 14 August we received the report that Churchill and Roosevelt had held talks aboard the battleship *Prince of Wales* and had issued a declaration known as the Atlantic Charter. In paragraph 1 this document states that the United States and Britain renounced any enlargement of state territory. The remaining seven paragraphs contained general but very reasonable sounding concepts about 'rights of peoples', 'world trade' and the 'elimination of force'. Hitler flew into a passion of rage and was particularly upset by point six which promised 'the final elimination of the National Socialist tyranny'. He said that was something they would never achieve.

Hitler advocated single-mindedly his military plan for the East. OKH opposed him with all means at their command. On 18 August Brauchitsch argued, in his memorandum 'The Further Operations of Army Group Centre', for the immediate resumption of the drive on Moscow. Panzer Groups Guderian and Hoth needed rest: after they were ready he estimated two more months to achieve the goal. Hitler's answer of 21 August expressed the opposite opinion: 'The Army's suggestion as to the continuation of operations in the East does not coincide with my intentions . . . the most important goal to be achieved before the onset of winter is not Moscow but the Crimea, the coal and industrial regions of the Donetz, cutting off oil supplies from the Caucasus and in the north the capture of Leningrad and the establishment of a corridor to the Finns.'

Four further points explained what was required of the three Army Groups. Halder described this directive in his diary as 'decisive for the outcome of the campaign'.

The long argument between Hitler and OKH got on one's nerves. I remember exactly what Hitler had said before the campaign. Over and over he emphasised his conviction that Leningrad and Rostow were the key cities. He said several times that Moscow need not be taken until the second operation—perhaps not until 1942. Therefore the current controversy went back to the planning stages. Even Guderian was drawn into it. Bock thought it was a good idea to send Guderian, commander of Panzer Group 2, to FHQ to put forward the case for moving on Moscow. He arrived on 23 August, presented the argument and was seduced by Hitler's counter-argument. Hitler was incensed by the time that was being wasted on the matter.

Mussolini and Horthy at the Front

On 25 August Mussolini arrived at Wolfschanze to inspect Italian units fighting alongside Army Group South. Next day Hitler accompanied him to Brest-Litovsk and then onwards to FHQ South, from where, on the 28th, they dropped in on an Italian division moving up to the front. It was not pleasant. Mussolini had no concept of the Eastern Front and the problems confronting Hitler. After his guest had departed, Hitler expressed his disappointment to his circle of officers. The Italians could offer very little on the Eastern Front. They had no fighting strength worth speaking of. He said wryly that they were here for the purposes of good morale. He spoke often about his long discussion with Mussolini, emphasising that it was still necessary to flirt with the Italians since the fighting in the Mediterranean theatre was not yet over.

The Hungarian Regent Admiral Horthy stayed at Wolfschanze from 6 to 8 September at Hitler's invitation. Hitler gave him a broad picture of the situation at the front and discussed with him the different problems which the war in general was causing. Horthy also visited Göring and Brauchitsch, and at Marienburg Hitler invested him with the Knight's Cross—as he explained later, a purely political gesture. At Wolfschanze later I as usual listened with interest to Hitler's comments about one of his state guests. As far as the war was concerned, Germany was expecting nothing from Hungary, he said, but for peace in the Balkans; good neighbours were important, and, after all, Germany was still dependent on the Romanian oilfields. Thus he was satisfied that the object of the visit had been achieved.

Despatches submitted during August by Army Group South contained reports of the first atrocities committed by Soviet troops. They were so appalling that even Hitler was doubtful ,and he sent me to Nikolayev to check with the 16th Panzer Division. I spoke there with General Hube and a very good friend of mine, Udo von Alvensleben. They described to me the discovery of the corpses of more than 100 murdered soldiers of 6/Rifle Regiment 79 (i.e. the 6th Company of the 79th Regiment) at Grigovo station. At another place German prisoners had been drawn and quartered alive. Our troops had responded accordingly. When I explained the facts to Hitler at Wolfschanze he thought about it for some time and said finally that General Staff ought to know: then they might take a different view of the sort of enemy we were fighting against.

Private Arguments

When Admiral Canaris called into FHQ at about this time, he made an allegation against me to Schmundt. Canaris had told him that on a certain date before the beginning of the Russian campaign my wife had telephoned one of her sisters at Halberstadt and told her that Hitler would attack Russia on 22 June. Schmundt had been obliged to inform Hitler, who dismissed the whole thing at once with a wave of the hand. Schmundt was very impressed by Hitler's reaction. I told Schmundt that, if he had discussed it with me beforehand, I could have shown him that when the telephone conversation was supposed to have been made, the date for the attack had not been set and that Canaris's report was false. I heard nothing more about the incident either from Hitler or from elsewhere.

The 'Final Solution'

Also in August Goebbels appeared for the first time—at Hitler's wish—in FHQ. In the two days of his stay he had private talks with Hitler on several occasions. It seeped out eventually that the Jewish question had been discussed. Goebbels and Heydrich were pressing for a solution. Goebbels wanted Hitler's permission to expel Berlin's remaining 70,000 Jews. Hitler was not yet ready for this but agreed that Jews should be distinguished by a special badge. On 1 September a Police Decree published in the *Reichsgesetzblatt* ordered that henceforth all Jews were required to wear prominently a yellow Star of David on their clothing. It appeared that the problem would not be finally resolved until after the conclusion of the Russian campaign and then *in grosszügiger Weise*—on the grand scale. I did not understand the cynicism of this remark until after the war, when, in the summer months of 1945 and later at the Nuremberg Trials, the extent of the Jewish Holocaust became known. The Berlin Police Decree was the intial stage of preparation for the Final Solution in which Göring, in his police function, had a significant involvement. Personally I had no knowledge of the activities of the SS and Police Einsatzgruppen responsible for the murder of large numbers of Jews in the occupied territories, nor did I know of the transportations of Jews to death camps in the East after 1941 from a catchment area comprised of all conquered European countries. I also knew nothing of the Wannsee Conference of 20 January 1942.

After the war, particularly from many conversations when in custody, I was able to put together certain circumstantial pointers which really ought to have given me cause to reflect towards the war's end on the significance of Hitler's increasing anti-Jewish sentiments or on some incidental remarks made by senior SS officers. Along with many others, I believed the explanation for the rumoured Jewish deportations to the East that they were required there as a labour force for important war factories. In view of the increasing use of domestic and foreign forced labour at the time, this was not implausible. I know now of course that I was the victim of a wicked deception.

I find it extraordinary that it was possible to conceal this genocide behind a veil of secrecy. My family and my wife's family had no Jewish friends or acquaintances and during the war we lived in a certain isolation. Neither my family, nor any of our relations, friends or service comrades, received knowledge by direct means. Führerbefehl Nr 1 had been effective here. In a system such as that of National Socialism, with an efficient secret police which spied on civilians and military alike, certain themes were taboo—even in our circle. In any case I am absolutely convinced, even in the absence of documentary evidence, that the extermination of the Jews resulted from Hitler's express order, since it is inconceivable that Himmler and Göring could have operated an independent policy without his knowledge. Certainly Himmler would not have informed him as to the individual details, but in this matter Himmler acted with Hitler's full agreement and approbation.

Autumn 1941: Russia, Bohemia and Moravia, and North Africa
Despite the bickering with OKH, Hitler still took a positive view of the
war situation in the summer of 1941. He was of the opinion that during
September Stalin would be forced to bolster the front with his last reserves. If these could be bled white, resistance would cease and our units
could roll onwards. This outlook lasted for some time until the receipt of
fresh reports which spoke of tough resistance and heavy fighting. Thus it
seemed that the Red Army retreat was either organised or ragged depending on location.

The question as to whether the attack on Moscow should be carried
out this year or next was finally settled when Hitler gave in to the
Army's entreaties, and on 6 September Jodl issued Directive No 35 that
'the operation by Army Group Centre against Timoshenko is to be
prepared in such a manner that the attack can be mounted early [at
the end of September]', and not until the expected victory over the
mass of Timoshenko's Army Group had been achieved 'can Army Group
Centre set out in pursuit towards Moscow'. Jodl was convinced that this
battle would deprive the Russians of any real potential to defend their
capital, and he repeated this opinion in subsequent situation conferences.

On 2 October Hitler travelled to Berlin for the opening of the Winter
Relief Programme and in his speech harangued Great Britain as usual.
Of the Russian campaign he observed that we had come as close as a
hair's breadth not only to the destruction of Germany 'but of all Europe'. He continued: 'I can say today that this enemy has been broken
and will never rise again. He had been building his strength against Europe, something of which most had unfortunately no suspicion and many
today still have no suspicion. It would have been a second Mongol invasion by a new Genghis Khan.'

On the conclusion of this speech Hitler returned to Wolfschanze at
once. The events on the Eastern Front preoccupied him. The twin battle
of Briansk-Wiasma between 2 and 12 October was expected to create a
favourable centre for the advance: in the event, over 660,000 prisoners
were taken and many tanks and field guns captured, and it seemed that
an open road to Moscow lay before us. But then came the rains, earlier
than normal, and with them the mud. Many units stuck fast in the mo-
rass. Our troops tired. The enemy used the time to regroup, block the
gaps and structure new resistance, and with that the advance came to a

halt. Pessimism began to gain ground, fed by false rumours and gossip; some of it percolated through to FHQ and Hitler himself.

A much-discussed change at the end of September was the replacement of Baron von Neurath by SS-Obergruppenführer Reinhard Heydrich as Reich Protector for Bohemia and Moravia. Heydrich, a capable and determined SS functionary, presented himself in advance of the official call and set out at once to cut down the Czech resistance movement. Although he was a radical and uncompromising National Socialist, he carried out his mission in Prague with great skill and not solely by the use of police brutality. He succeeded in subduing the region, kept the armaments factories working and paved the way for a positive development of the relationship between Germans and Czechs.

In North Africa, meanwhile, Rommel had been beaten back. The British had been strengthened and the relationship with the Italian ally was not good. There had been serious problems of supply. Thus not much had gone right for Rommel in the summer of 1941, and he had been forced to let the British drive him back. Hitler was not too concerned: he knew Rommel well enough to realise that eventually he would return to the offensive, even without much in the way of reinforcements.

Equipping the Luftwaffe
Since the beginning of the Russian campaign I had actually been without special duties. The Luftwaffe had transferred its rested units to the East, where, in the opening days of the offensive, they had destroyed huge numbers of Soviet warplanes on the ground. Afterwards, their activities were reduced to a support role for the Army. Here von Richthofen's Fliegerkorps VIII distinguished itself. The general spent all day aloft, mostly in a Storch, flying from one hot spot to another, and was correspondingly often better informed about the ground situation than most senior Army commanders. His advice led to considerable debate on occasion, but generally he got his way. In the summer weeks I spent a good deal of time with Luftwaffe units and gained the impression that the Army did not make the best of its opportunities. This was due in part to the great distances involved and the tendency of many Army commanders to rush things. In general, however, the Luftwaffe showed little understanding either.

Jeschonnek's door was always open to me and he kept me informed of affairs. He was in despair at the renewed postponement of the Luftwaffe

115

aircraft production programme. He said we could not afford to lose any more time because in recent weeks aircraft losses at the front were not being made good. He wanted a substantial increase in production immediately, since the deployment of the Luftwaffe along the Channel coast remained crucial. He said that if Hitler would not allow the programme to go through, this alone could prevent us ever winning the war against Britain.

I broached the subject with Hitler. He knew about the problem but said the Army had priority. This state of affairs would change in the spring of 1942: then he would switch all production capacity to the Luftwaffe. I also mentioned to him that although for the present the British appeared content to mount relatively minor air raids on our cities, we had to reckon with an escalation in due course. He agreed, but believed that the Luftwaffe could bridge the gap. I could not accept this opinion and contradicted him. He nodded and said he would discuss the question with Göring.

My duties as Luftwaffe adjutant began to have a larger dimension. There was no set schedule for me to follow and I arranged my tasks to suit myself. Until now Hitler had interested himself almost exclusively in the numbers of operational aircraft. Questions were now being put about when such-and-such squadrons were going to be equipped, when aircraft requirements would be met and the like. Therefore I had to keep myself permanently supplied with statistics and update my own records accordingly.

Obtaining details about flak was not a job which I did with much relish, but it was essential because Hitler laid value on it for a special reason. On the Eastern Front large numbers of Russian tanks were appearing which were better armoured that anything we had come up against previously, and these could only be knocked out with the 8.8cm flak gun. Hitler hammered the point hard that the Flak Korps on the Eastern Front was to be equipped exclusively with the 8.8cm in order to be able to engage these tanks and take part in the land fighting.

On 1 November, at OKH, an exhibition of Army winter uniforms was put on display. The Quartermaster-General, Wagner, assured Hitler that work on winter clothing was in hand and that sufficient quantities would be made available to men in the field. Hitler took note of the report and appeared satisfied. On the 7th he went to Munich to make his annual speech to the 1923 veterans. On the 9th he addressed the Reichs- and Gauleiters before returning immediately to Wolfschanze.

116

Cure at Constance

I parted from Hitler at Munich to take the cure at Constance. My wife accompanied me. A special diet was prescribed for my nervous stomach condition. The four weeks preceding 8 December passed without special incident. From what I could make out, all movement on the front had stopped. There were few fresh reports in the Press. I was shaken to read of the deaths of Udet and Mölders. Udet's death on 17 November was supposed to have occurred in a flying accident, but I thought this unlikely and established from telephone enquiries to Berlin that he had committed suicide. I felt the loss keenly. I knew him well from my flying days. He was a person of rare likeability. Göring had appointed him Generalluftzeugmeister. The post handled aircraft production and supply, and Udet considered it a step down. He was a bachelor who enjoyed life, always surrounded by a circle of good friends. They offered him support but he saw things differently and could not be influenced. His death affected the whole Luftwaffe. Mölders was killed on 22 November on the way to Udet's funeral when the aircraft in which he was a passenger crashed while making an intermediate stop at Breslau. His death was a serious blow, especially for the fighter arm.

At War With the United States

My wife and I arrived at Berlin Anhalter station early on 9 December. Loudspeakers urged all passengers to hurry since the platform was needed urgently. I knew that this was the particular platform alongside which Hitler's special train usually drew and assumed that he was returning to Berlin. From my apartment I telephoned the Chancellery and found that Hitler was expected. I dressed in my uniform and was driven there. I had no presentiment of how the political situation had changed nor of what lay ahead in the next few weeks.

I reported to Hitler. He was very friendly and asked me how the cure had gone. I had myself informed as to recent events, the most important of which was the Japanese attack against the US naval base at Pearl Harbor without a declaration of war on 7 December. Hitler had interpreted this event as the signal for Germany to declare war on the United States.

I was appalled at his unworldliness and innocence as to an industrial potential which just over twenty years previously had been decisive in the Great War. It exposed the amateurism of his foreign policy and his deficient knowledge of the world beyond Europe. He was relying for the foreseeable future on the hope that the conflict between the USA and Japan would keep the Americans out of the European theatre. He was convinced that his *'Weltblitzkrieg'*, as the historian Andreas Hillgruber calls it, in which all enemies are vanquished swiftly one after the other, would be successful. Presumably this also meant that he would hasten to the aid of Japan, since he spoke repeatedly of the need for closer German-Japanese military cooperation. If so, I thought this would not be a good move. At the time his preferred foreign policy conversational partner was Hewel, but ultimately Hitler's extra-European political ideas were based more on his wishes than on reality.

Winter Crisis

The day of my return was one of turmoil. Many visitors gathered in the Chancellery in the hope of obtaining from the horse's mouth the latest about the war situation, but the matter was not for discussion. After lunch Hitler spoke with Ribbentrop, Himmler, Todt and Göring. The rooms emptied. Schmundt supplied me with the business of the day. Then I was left alone with Hitler and we talked. In the evening we strolled the winter garden. He was wrestling with the question of the Army High Command. He had had no confidence in Brauchitsch for some time and was looking for a replacement. Schmundt had recommended that he assume supreme command of the Army himself, at least temporarily. Hitler had bristled at the very suggestion, but after the declaration of war on the United States he saw a new situation developing and began to incline more and more towards Schmundt's suggestion. Hitler was of the opinion that many generals needed to be rested. He had sent Rundstedt on leave on 1 December and was worried about Guderian, who was totally 'drained'. He had given Army Group South to Reichenau, whom he trusted implicitly.

Hitler was very concerned at the situation with Army Group Centre. He assumed that the Russians were planning a major counter-attack. Kluge spoke of nothing but drawing back. 'How far back does he want to come?' Hitler asked. 'We have no prepared positions to the rear. The Army must stop where it is.' Then he reproached the Army supply organisation. The Army had no winter clothing, no protection against the bitter cold and no efficient means of catering. Hitler was outraged. How could the Army not have prepared for it? The Luftwaffe had managed to provide its units with all their winter requirements.

Hitler said that the Russians were now attacking everywhere in large numbers with the T-34. The Army had no effective anti-tank gun against it: even the short-barrelled Panzer Mk IV found it a handful. 'If we didn't have the Luftwaffe 8.8cm flak, these Russian tanks would go where they liked,' he said. In the T-34 the Russians had a weapon of note, and he did not yet know in what numbers it was being supplied. It would soon be confirmed in 1942 that it was arriving at the front in constantly growing numbers. Our own panzer production was satisfactory, but we needed to accelerate the pace. Hitler also mentioned American supplies to the Russians. He knew for certain that they had been supplying lorries and provisions to the Soviets for some time because German units had identified them. He was mentally at the front and always trying to imagine ways to help the men in the field. But he kept repeating, 'They must stand where they are—not a step backwards!'

Hitler convened the Reichstag for three o'clock on the afternoon of 11 December. He made a long and comprehensive speech about the whole political situation without working up to any special high point. Upon our return to Wolfschanze on the morning of 16 December the situation at the front was confused and worrying. That night Hitler decided at last to assume command of the Army; he had been thinking about it for several days. Schmundt welcomed his announcement, if only because it brought to an end the daily struggle with Brauchitsch. Hitler had considered entrusting the High Command to Manstein or Kesselring, but Manstein was unsuited by temperament and Hitler needed Kesselring as Luftwaffe C-in-C in the Mediterranean because he did not want to unsettle the Italians with a surprise change.[11] On 18 December he replaced Bock with Kluge as C-in-C Army Group Centre. The day had begun with a number of urgent telephone conversations, all of which requested permission to pull back Army Group Centre under the weight of the Soviet counter-offensive. Hitler would not concede a step and insisted that they stay where they were. At Kluge's request Guderian was sent on leave for Christmas and New Year. The two generals could not stand each other.

Hitler and Halder were spending hours each day in conference. It was always the same theme: to stay put or draw back. Meanwhile the front was being shored up by reinforcing the sections under the heaviest threat and throwing in the last reserves. Just before midnight on 30 December Hitler began a two-hour long telephone conversation with Kluge, who wanted to retreat 35 kilometres. Hitler refused and told him to stand his ground. This undoubtedly saved the situation, although serious crises still lay ahead over the next few weeks.

After the declaration of war on the United States, we knew that now we faced virtually the whole world—knowledge which made it difficult for me to continue to believe in victory. In Germany opinions began to shift. The vast majority of the people remembered Hitler's successes and either did not or could not believe that the man who had restored German prestige in the world could be taking a false path. Amongst them were many who no longer expected outright victory but who said that such a great man would find the way to maintain the welfare of the Reich. Other people of this group—and there were many—had no opinion at all and were happy to let events take their course. There remained a small, even a very small circle who perceived clearly Germany's great misfortune, who discussed it and who were even prepared to risk everything to destroy it—individuals from the churches, landed gentry, diplomats, government officials and military officers. The Gestapo knew all about them. They had most of the names in their card indexes. They took no action for the number was small and there was no evidence to go on. Himmler kept Hitler advised, and the latter knew the names of most of the active opposition. Since even in early 1941 Hitler had spoken out vehemently against critical trends, it was not surprising that opposition should increase at a time of winter setbacks.

A Separate Peace with Russia?
At the time I believed that the Soviet Union, which since June had been taking very heavy punishment, would find it impossible to recover quickly. I thought there was still a chance to strike at Russia before America, with all her enormous potential, entered the fighting proper. As far as I could judge, this was also Hitler's view. He was certain he would defeat Russia in 1942.

Ribbentrop was advising Hitler to seek a peace treaty with the USSR. He believed he had got to know Stalin very well in 1939 and considered that not all possibilities had yet been exhausted. He argued his case in depth but Hitler said that a peaceful solution was impossible.

Stresses and Strains
In his New Year statement to the German people and an Order of the Day to the Wehrmacht, Hitler admitted the difficult situation in which

Germany found herself in these winter months, but he left no doubt that he would regain the initiative and continue the struggle for *Lebensraum*: 'Whoever fights for the life of his people, for their daily bread and for their future, will be victorious. But whoever by this war, with its Jewish hate, seeks to annihilate the people, will fall,' he exclaimed. His Order of the Day concluded with the words: 'The blood spilled in this war will be—this is our hope—the last in Europe for generations. May the Lord God help us therein in the coming year.'

In the autumn and winter months of 1941 Hitler experienced for the first time how a retreat fanned enemy resistance into flame. His assumption of supreme command of the Army was a successful move since it prevented the catastrophe into which a withdrawal would have degenerated. Instead, the German soldier found new reserves of strength and confidence from the knowledge of his superhuman achievement in holding off a superior enemy sometimes twenty times his own strength.

Hitler would not countenance withdrawals to gain freedom of manoeuvre or to spare his forces. His burgeoning mistrust of the generals—a sentiment of which he was never to rid himself entirely—cramped him, since he insisted now on reserving to himself even the most minor tactical decisions. The lack of fresh, rested divisions (Hitler had thrown all 41 available divisions into the front) was the reason for the reckless deployment of men. He had no reserves worth speaking of. The Russian landmass was too big for the German Wehrmacht. It was almost 2,000 miles from Leningrad to Mt Elbrus in the Caucasus. At the outset of the campaign Hitler assumed that he would quickly break the enemy's back as he had in former invasions. But Russia was different. The enemy had inexhaustible reserves. Over the winter of 1941/42 it became apparent to Hitler that his Army was too small. As we know today, Stalin was able to leave his far Eastern Frontier unprotected because the Communist spy Richard Sorge in Tokyo had shown him that the Japanese did not want war with Russia. This knowledge, together with American assistance, gave Stalin strength to withstand the German attack, to put Hitler's armies on the defensive and, in the winter of 1941/42, to push them to the edge of the abyss.

This was the great turning point of the war. Hitler's optimism in his war against the world remained unimpaired, for he still believed that Britain, if faced with losing her Empire, would rather abandon the war against Germany. This was a slim hope, but Hitler saw Britain relying increasingly on the United States and from this he inferred the central importance of the USA.

Hitler still considered that he could strengthen and consolidate the German position in the spring of 1942. In the event the Red Army attacked repeatedly all along the German front. They achieved limited success, but even though they broke through the German lines in some places a really significant penetration eluded them. The encirclements at Demyansk and Cholm proved how it was possible to make a heroic stand when adequately supplied from the air.

Hitler and the Army Generals

Despite Schmundt's efforts, an improvement in Hitler's relationship with the generals was scarcely to be hoped for. When speaking with Bormann, Göring or Himmler about them, Hitler was often dismissive or harsh in his condemnation. Few of the generals who came into contact with Hitler knew him sufficiently well. They behaved correctly, and were inhibited about informing Hitler of problems or difficulties. As adjutants we used to speak to these visitors beforehand, suggesting that the best approach was to be unselfconscious. A few succeeded. Most natural were the young officers who came to receive the Knight's Cross or other decorations from Hitler's hand. In my experience these were always Luftwaffe officers, and there was scarcely one who lost his tongue in Hitler's presence. He could be told unpleasant truths and in fact he valued receiving bad reports as early as possible. The manner in which they were presented was naturally important.

Udet and Milch

In the Luftwaffe a basic change resulted from the death of Udet: Hitler and Göring transferred to Milch responsibility for all Luftwaffe production and supply. Göring did this reluctantly, but Hitler willed it and probably Göring saw no other solution. Milch was robust, inconsiderate, demanding, radical and hard with himself. He was appalled at the disorder in which he found the office of Generalluftzeugmeister and determined to put things straight. His priority was to increase the monthly production of aircraft. For 1942 he wanted to double the December 1941 figures from 250 to almost 500 machines monthly. He would not go so far as to authorise the changeover to four-engined bombers at this stage. He saw as his principal task an increase in fighter aircraft. He knew about current British aircraft production and their huge bomber programme. Against these Milch would need primarily fighters and flak. At the end of January 1942 he presented his ideas at FHQ. Hitler made his stock reply that for the time being the Army took absolute precedence. This was understandable, but nevertheless I took the opportunity to bring up again the subject of Luftwaffe difficulties. I foresaw, as did Milch, British air raids escalating without there being sufficient air defences to combat them. Hitler pointed to the end of 1942 when Russia would be broken. I did not believe that, but said nothing. The fact was, Hitler had always turned out to be right in the end.

CHAPTER FOUR

1942

Hitler's great concern at New Year was to keep the Eastern Front intact. Having been implored by Kluge to do so, he gave his reluctant authority to bring back the front to an agreed line, allowing it to be straightened out at the same time. The worst of the difficulties were overcome by rushing in replacements. The railway situation was chaotic. German locomotives were not designed to operate in temperatures of −30°C and were to be found on railway tracks almost everywhere, frozen and immobile. Transport Minister Dorpmüller presented to Hitler evidence that the problems had been identified and that energetic action had been taken. Hitler later praised the efforts that had been made.

Malta

At the end of 1941 Hitler had transferred the bulk of Kesselring's Air Fleet 2 to Sicily and North Africa for a proposed attack on Malta. Kesselring's feasibility study showed that an invasion was possible, although the Italians wanted to wait for the spring. From the beginning of January, Italian and German aircraft kept up an unceasing aerial bombardment of Malta, but when Kesselring asked for a decision at the end of March the Italians were still unready. Kesselring's other tasks were to support the Afrika Korps and escort seaborne supplies across the Mediterranean. These duties made great demands of the Air Fleet, so that his interest in the important bastion of Malta tended to diminish.

Kesselring was the right commander for the Mediterranean. He was a likeable man, a warm-hearted and cheerful optimist with an open manner, and for this reason found all doors open to him—an inestimable benefit in the onerous liaison he had to maintain with the Italians. Kesselring understood the needs of the Afrika Korps and did what he could to equip Rommel for his planned thrust into Egypt. For his part,

Rommel often made impossible demands—which did not help. Hitler had great confidence in Kesselring, which was not misplaced.

The 'Channel Dash'

The battleships *Scharnhorst* and *Gneisenau*, and the heavy cruiser *Prinz Eugen*, were bottled up at Brest, where they had been for the better part of 1941. There was no possibility of future Atlantic operations, and they were in constant danger from the RAF. Hitler thought they would be more useful for coast defence duties in Norway, where he feared that the British would eventually attempt landings. At the beginning of January the Kriegsmarine informed him that they proposed to extricate the three units through the English Channel. Hitler expressed surprise that they wanted to do it in daylight, but gave his approval nevertheless. The group would sail beneath an extensive air umbrella composed of Galland's fighter force based in northern France. In the evening of 12 February the ships slipped their moorings at Brest and headed undetected into the Channel. At about midday on the 13th they passed through the Dover Strait. The British were taken completely by surprise, and not until they were almost in the North Sea did the German ships come under attack. *Scharnhorst* and *Gneisenau* both received slight damage when mined, but neither was seriously delayed. All three heavy units reached their intended ports of destination. The RAF lost about sixty aircraft. The 'Channel Dash' was a complete success: Hitler was overjoyed at its manner of execution and often referred to it later as an example of how complete secrecy contributed to the success of an operation.

As January progressed, activity on the Eastern Front began to diminish. Russian attacks seemed easier to beat off, and the German line began to consolidate. Hitler was concentrating on his new operational plan for the summer. He told Jodl that he had in mind an offensive at the southern end of the front, where his objective would be to cut off the supply from the Caucasian oilfields. In the north, Leningrad would be captured and the territorial link with Finland established. All preparations were to be completed by 1 May.

Höpner Relieved of Duty

The dismissal of Generaloberst Höpner gave rise to considerable disquiet. On 8 January, at the high point of the crisis in Army Group Centre, Höpner had reincorporated Materna's XX Army Korps into the 4th

Panzer Army without having first obtained authority from Kluge's Army Group and, worse, Hitler. The latter was extremely irate when he found out and Höpner received no sympathy whatever. On 9 January Kluge was obliged to read Höpner the following text of a Führerbefehl: 'Generaloberst Höpner has endangered my authority as Commander-in-Chief of the Wehrmacht and as Head of State of the Greater German Reich. Generaloberst Höpner is dismissed from the Wehrmacht with all the consequences that that implies.' Fortunately Schmundt intervened to prevent the worst. Contrary to what is often stated, there was no court-martial and Höpner took his retirement at the end of June, drawing the usual pension for his grade and continuing to live in Army quarters. In this way Schmundt interpreted in the widest sense Hitler's orders that Höpner's family should be cared for.

As the anniversary of the seizure of power approached, Hitler contemplated whether he should fulfil the annual engagement of addressing the German people from the Berlin Sportpalast on 30 January. Goebbels pressured him to do so, but Hitler was so involved in his plans for the summer offensive in Russia that not until the last moment, at midday on the 29th, did he board his train for Berlin. He spoke at five on the evening of 30 January. Goebbels made the introduction. It was a skilfully arranged event with an extraordinarily responsive audience, mostly Berlin armaments workers, military nursing sisters and wounded servicemen. Hitler touched on many old themes. The British and the Jews, the arch-enemies, came under immediate fire. The he mentioned the three great 'have-nots', Germany, Italy and Japan, who were in this struggle to win. He drew much enthusiastic applause, which buoyed him up in his planning for the summer.

Speer Succeeds Todt

On 31 January he was back at Wolfschanze, and it was there on 7 February that he discussed with Dr Todt the armaments production programme. Todt had arrived at Rastenburg in a Heinkel 111 bomber which he had obtained for his own use at the end of December 1941. It was his intention to fly out in it early next morning. There was a Führerbefehl in effect that all high functionaries were forbidden to fly in any aircraft having less than three engines. I explained the order to Todt and banned his flight. He was beside himself with rage and informed me that Hitler's order did not apply to him. That evening, after he had left Hitler's bunker,

I was sent for and Hitler asked me how my encounter with Todt had come about. I explained that I had merely been following his own strict instruction. Subsequently Hitler gave in to Todt and told me to have the Heinkel serviced for next morning. I also arranged for a check flight. Next morning, shortly before dawn, the flight captain of the Führer-Kurierstaffel got me out of bed to inform me that Dr Todt's aircraft had crashed on take-off. I dressed and went at once to the airfield, where I saw a great smouldering heap of wreckage. There were no survivors. When Hitler rose I informed him of the tragedy. He was visibly upset and made no comment for some time. Then he asked if I knew the cause. I did not, but the weather was not good. Sky and snow-covered ground would have merged into a greyish shade in the darkness, leaving no visible horizon, and I hazarded a guess at crew error: the pilot did not have sufficient experience for the conditions. An investigation into the accident was undertaken by the RLM and SS but the cause was never established.

Hitler decided at once to appoint Speer as successor to Todt. Speer came to FHQ directly to receive Hitler's instruction in his new duties. It was obvious to all that a radical change of direction was in the wind, and within a few weeks the first positive signs were evident. Hitler paid Dr Todt special honour by delivering personally the obituary in the state ceremony at the Chancellery. He described Todt as 'a National Socialist from the bottom of his heart' and mentioned as his greatest achievment the construction of the autobahns. He said that Dr Todt had never had an enemy, and I believe that in Todt the Third Reich never had a better servant.

On 13 February Speer called a meeting of the heads of the armaments industry and the responsible government offices in Berlin. Amongst these men were some with ideas for hiving off large sections for their own ambitions. Speer had agreed with Hitler beforehand that those 'interested' should be invited to attend at the Chancellery forthwith to hear Hitler's views, and at this second reunion Hitler spoke of the importance of armaments and of gathering everything into a single hand. With these words all personal schemes were swept from the table and Speer was confirmed as the new supremo of Dr Todt's empire.

On 15 February Hitler addressed senior cadets in the Sportpalast. The great successes of 1941 were the centrepoint of his speech. Of the difficulties in the East he left his young listeners in ignorance. In any case, all they wanted was a chance for glory at the front. Of himself he said, 'I am proud beyond description that Providence granted me the opportunity to lead you in this inevitable struggle.' Göring then referred to the achievements of the first year of war. As Hitler left the platform there burst forth such applause and jubilation as had seldom been experienced before. On the return journey to East Prussia, Hitler received the report that Singapore had fallen to the Japanese. Whilst praising the Japanese Army, he added that, from the Russian side, it would be seen as irresponsible to rejoice too much at Japanese victories.

Stabilisation in Spring

On the whole March and April were relatively quiet months, and it was assumed that the Soviets either were so depleted that they lacked the strength for a major attack or were planning an onslaught requiring substantial pre-planning. Hitler was calm and level and devoted most of his energies to discussing armaments with Speer or scheming his summer offensive. He stressed here that the most important aim was to cut off supplies from the Caucasus oilfields. If this could be achieved, the Russians would be reduced to indolence. The purpose of his attack in late spring would be to straighten the front at Kharkov and occupy the Crimea and the fortress of Sevastopol; after this he would press on at once for Stalingrad and the Caucasus. Schmundt was given the job of setting up a new FHQ in the Ukraine near Winniza so that Hitler could be nearer the front in the summer.

Hitler returned to Berlin for *Heldengedenktag* on 15 March. It was becoming vitally important for him again to influence opinion with his speeches. In this discourse he described the fierceness of the Russian winter and the enormous difficulties which our soldiers had had to overcome. But he praised the German fighting men, who, despite the violence of the enemy and the severe weather, had helped to keep the front solid. Full of reverence—and this seemed to me to be no empty pathos—he spoke of the fallen, who had not sacrificed their lives for Germany in vain.

On 21 March Hitler gave to Gauleiter Sauckel of Thuringia—ignoring Speer's preference for Karl Hanke, Gauleiter of Lower Silesia—the job of organising the armaments workforce. As General Plenipotentiary for Industrial Employment responsible to the General Plenipotentiary for the Four-Year Plan, he had extensive powers to seek out, pool and distribute the workforce throughout the armaments industry. Sauckel's

Right: Von Below watches over Hitler's shoulder as he corrects the draft manuscript for his 'An das Deutsche Volk' speech following the declarations of war on 3 September 1939.

Left: Von Below accompanies Hitler at a flak battery during Wehrmacht manoeuvres in Mecklenburg, September 1937.

Above: In the Führer's personal aircraft: left, von Below
with Hitler; right, an exhausted adjutant.

Below: Von Below with his wife Maria during a visit to
the Berghof, summer 1938.

Above: Hitler with Ambassador Bernardo Attolico, Rome, May 1938. *Courtesy of Dirk von Below*

Below: Hitler with Frau von Below at the Berghof. *Courtesy of Dirk von Below*

Left: Hitler with his personal pilot, Captain Hans Baur, at Saarbrücken, July 1939. *Courtesy of Dirk von Below*

Right: During leave on the Bühlerhöhe: von Below with his wife and Wilhelm Brückner, Hitler's personal ADC.

Left: Frau von Below (right) at table with Generalleutnant Stumpff, Luftwaffe Chief of the General Staff, and his wife.

Left: At the Berghof with Speer (far left), Frick, Ribbentrop, Goebbels, Bormann (obscured by Hitler) and Bouhler.

Above: Hitler with (on his left, in the bowler hat) Gustav Krupp; Albert Krupp is to the left of the photograph, in a soft hat. 1939. *Courtesy of Dirk von Below*

Left: The French Ambassador Coulondre is received in the forecourt of the Berghof. From the left: Meissner, Coulondre, von Below, and Brückner.

Left: The entrance to the Old Reich Chancellery, Wilhelmstrasse, Berlin.

Right: The Marble Gallery, New Reich Chancellery.

Left: At the situation table in the Great Hall of the Old Reich Chancellery, from 26 September 1939 the Führer Headquarters in Berlin. From the left: von Puttkamer, Schmundt, Hitler, Jodl and Keitel.

Right: Hitler admires his 50th birthday present from the Luftwaffe—a collection of models of all the German warplanes. Von Below stands next to him.

Left: At a private birthday party: from the left, Frau Anni Brandt with her son; Frau von Below; and Hitler.

Above: The Berghof in Obersalzberg.

Left: A view of the hallway on the ground floor.

Right: Hitler's study on the first floor.

Left: Frau von Below with Albert Speer on the terrace at the Berghof. *Courtesy of Dirk von Below*

Right: Hitler with (far right) von Below, Poland, September 1939. *Courtesy of Dirk von Below*

Left: Von Below celebrates his promotion to the rank of Major, surrounded by Luftwaffe colleagues.

Left: A conversation with Jodl during the Balkans campaign. Von Below is in the background.

Right: Situation conference for 'Barbarossa', June 1941.

Left: Hitler's dining room in FHQ Wolfschanze.

Left: Mussolini during a visit to the Eastern Front, August 1941. The location is Brest-Litovsk airfield.

Right: Christmas 1941 at FHQ with Schmundt, von Puttkamer, Gabriel and others.

Left: Von Below with Rommel at FHQ, summer 1941.

Above left: Oberst Lützow receives a decoration from Hitler at FHQ.

Above right: Summer 1942: von Below with Generalfeldmarschall Milch at Romintern.

Above: Von Below with his brother at Wolfschanze.

Left: A pause for rest at FHQ Winniza, summer 1942.

Above left: Von Below with Bodenschatz at Romintern, summer 1942.

Above right: Von Below with Oberst Rudel at FHQ on the occasion of Rudel's receipt of the Golden Oak Leaves with Swords for his Iron Cross.

Above: Hitler's birthday, April 1943: the Führer and his staff at Obersalzberg. Von Below stands at the back, second from the right.

Left: Three adjutants at Wolfschanze, September 1943: on the left, von Szymonski; centre, von Below; and right, John von Freyend.

Above: Conference at Wolfschanze: from the left, Student, Hewel, Wagner, Göring and Dönitz.

Below: Fifteen Luftwaffe Oak Leaves recipients proceed to Hitler's bunker to receive their decorations.

Above: Hitler with Bormann and Jodl after the attempted assassination of 20 July 1944.

Below: The wrecked situation conference room after the bomb explosion.

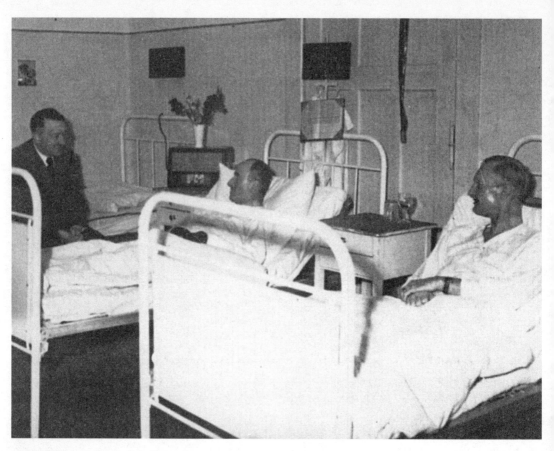

Above: Hitler paid visits to those injured during the Bomb Plot explosion. He is seen here with Admiral von Puttkamer and Kapitän Assmann.

Below: A copy of Hitler's private testament, with the signatures of the witnesses.

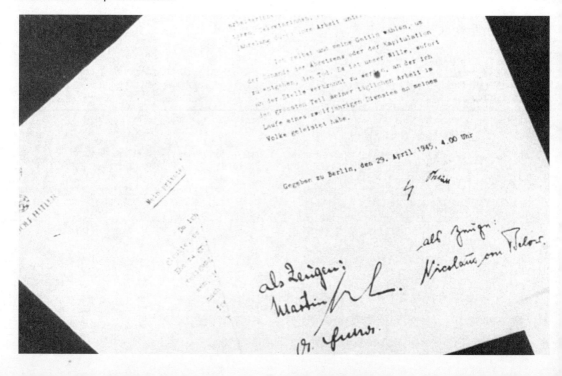

principal source was foreign forced labour, mainly workers from the East. What had been originally designed as a co-operative effort for Speer's benefit developed increasingly into a rivalry since Sauckel, one of the oldest Gauleiters, knew that Hitler smiled kindly upon him.

On 25 March Fritz Wendel, Messerschmitt's chief test pilot, made the first jet-powered flight in an Me 262. The second flight took place on 18 July. Despite the many modifications which were necessary, the manufacturer could speak justifiably of the enormous significance of this aircraft, but it was not until 1943, after Galland and Steinhoff had flown it and recognised its fantastic superiority, that Messerschmitt was given the go-ahead for mass production. By then it was too late.

The Air War Intensifies

March 1942 brought the opening of the British bomber offensive. On the night of the 3rd the RAF bombed a Paris factory, leaving 800 dead. The next raid occurred on the night of 28 March when 234 bombers dropped about 300 tons of incendiaries and high explosive on Lübeck. The old city centre was devastated, the aftermath chaotic; 320 civilians were killed. Lübeck was the first German town subjected to carpet bombing.[12] Hitler said that terror must be answered with terror but would not go so far as to accede to Jeschonnek's request to transfer aircraft from East to West, since that was precisely what the British bombing had set out to achieve. He could not and would not give in to it. As a reprisal, Luftwaffe bombers based in northern France embarked on a series of attacks on English towns such as Exeter—the so-called Baedeker raids—but, lacking numbers, they failed to achieve an appropriate impact.

Planning the Summer Offensive

On 5 April Jodl issued Directive No 41. This was the culmination of Hitler's concentrated thinking as discussed in detail with Halder and OKW. While he waited with great impatience for the mud roads of southern Russia to dry out, he used the time to rest, re-equip and re-arm his divisions. The directive stated that Army Group Centre would remain where it was, and Army Group North would capture Leningrad and establish the land link with the Finns. All available units in the southern sector were to be grouped up, with the objective of taking the oilfields at Maikop and Grozny and the passes over the Caucasus mountains. Jodl pinpointed the attack on Voronezh as the principal primary target, after which the operation would be geared 'to reach Stalingrad itself and at least subject it to the effects of our heavy artillery so that it ceases to function as an armaments and communications centre'.

Reichstag Session, 26 April

On 24 April we travelled to Berlin for a Reichstag speech on the 26th. The reason for it was the pending action involving Höpner. A trial of strength was in the offing between Hitler and the Wehrmacht judiciary, who did not want to proceed, with the harshness demanded by Hitler, against either Höpner or any other general who had been deemed out of step during the winter crisis. In a long speech, his last to this forum, Hitler depicted the struggles of the past and outlined his plans for 1942 before delivering to great acclaim a declaration subsequently published in the law journal *Reichsgesetzblatt* on 27 April under the heading *Übermächtigungsgesetz*—Law of Supreme Empowerment: 'There can be no doubt that in the present time of war, when the German people are engaged in a struggle to be or not to be, the Führer must have the right claimed by him to do anything which serves to secure, or contributes to, victory: therefore, in his capacity as Führer of the nation, Supreme Commander of the Wehrmacht, head of state and supreme holder of executive power, as senior law lord and leader of the Party, he must always be in the position, if necessary, and without being bound by existing law, to impose upon every German—be he ordinary soldier or officer, lower or higher official or judge, leading or serving Party functionary, worker or employee—by all appropriate means the duties he has to fulfil, and in default thereof after investigation, but without recourse to so-called well-established rights, to require of him due expiation without the need to first institute those prescriptive procedures befitting his office, rank or position.'

This decree formally bestowed on Hitler unlimited power. He was no longer bound by the rule of law, and it made many people sit up and take notice for the first time. The masses, however, were content to accept the measure and its consequences without much reflection, seeing such powers vested in the Führer as justified by present circumstances. Those alarmed by the introduction of previous illegalities condemned this new law as an excess without precedent.

The increasing British bombing of German cities was a warning of the gradual deterioration in the overall situation. The entire population now formed a front line. Personally I was amazed at how calmly the people accepted these fearsome air raids. For their part the British no doubt imagined that civilian morale could be broken in this manner, but the air offensive against civilians and residential districts did not bring them the desired success.

Conquest of the Crimea

Hitler went from Berlin to Obersalzberg and met the Duce at Schloss Klesheim on 29 and 30 April. Mussolini was fed a very optimistic picture of affairs. On 1 May Hitler returned to Wolfschanze to resume plotting the summer offensive. In southern Russia, when the weather had warmed up sufficiently to dry the mud roads, Manstein's Eleventh Army was the first to roll eastwards for the Crimea. Across the approaches to the Kerch peninsula the Russians had excavated an extensive system of trenches. These were broken down by heavy artillery, Stukas and landing craft to enable the whole Crimea to fall into our hands by 16 June. A second operation by Army Group South to clear a pocket south of Kharkov was scheduled to commence on 17 May, but the Russians broke out on the 12th and headed north. Bock was sufficiently alarmed to solicit permission from Hitler to pull back, but Hitler refused and ordered up Kleist's Army Group from the south. The encirclement succeeded on 22 May at Isyum. Plunder and innumerable prisoners were netted. While this was going on, Manstein had set off to capture Sevastopol. An artillery barrage on 3 June was followed by the first attack on the 7th, but Sevastopol held out until the beginning of July. Hitler considered the conquest of the whole Crimea as a great victory for the German forces and the basis for future successes this year.

Flying to See Kesselring and Rommel

In the last week of May I flew to Sicily and North Africa to see Kesselring and Rommel, respectively. On the outward flight I went to Derna, where Kesselring had an outpost of his HQ. He received me very warmly and I remained his guest for two days. We discussed Rommel's intention to take Tobruk and then push on for Egypt. Kesselring and Rommel did not get on. Crüwell had been earmarked as Rommel's successor by Panzer Army Afrika Command Staff and Kesselring was looking forward eagerly to the change. Kesselring was an optimist and was positive about Rommel's plan, although he did not believe that our forces would stretch all the way to Egypt. Even to take Tobruk, Rommel would need a surprise attack. He was dependent on the Italians for his supplies and his losses were likely to be high.

In the morning of 1 June we were horrified to learn that the British had taken Crüwell prisoner. Kesselring's hopes for an early change in command had evaporated. I was surprised at how philosophically he took it. We set out in two Fieseler Storchs to meet Rommel about 30 kilometres south-west of Tobruk. His camp looked like a disorganised mess in the middle of the desert. Kesselring discussed with him what he needed in the way of air support. Rommel said that everything depended on successful operations in the next few days if Tobruk were to be taken. That afternoon we flew back to Derna.

Göring's Star Wanes

On my return to Wolfschanze I found a very unpleasant atmosphere. On 27 May an attempt had been made on the life of Heydrich in Prague; he died of his injuries a week later. On the night of 30 May the RAF had attacked Cologne with 1,000 bombers. When I reported to Hitler about my North African impressions, he replied by deploring bitterly the attack on Cologne. He complained about the poor flak and said that from the beginning the Luftwaffe had not given flak the attention it merited. This was the first time I had heard him criticise Göring. Hitler never regained absolute confidence in the Reichsmarschall and complained that he, Hitler, now had to involve himself personally in organising air raid precautions within the Reich. From now on he frequently mentioned to me that the Luftwaffe command—he meant Milch and Jeschonnek—must pay more attention to defence of the home territory. I inferred from these conversations that Hitler expected no end to the British air raids and saw in them a great danger for the Reich. I discussed this very closely with Jeschonnek.

How seriously Hitler viewed the murder of Heydrich, which had been arranged by the Czech government-in-exile in London, was demonstrated by his presence at the state funeral in Berlin on 9 June. Himmler delivered the obituary; Hitler added a few words. When he greeted the Czech President Hacha he warned him forcefully against any further terrorist activities against German rule in the protectorate. If this happened, severe reprisals would have to be taken.

During a stay at the Berghof after the burial of Heydrich on 20 June, Hitler visited the Reichswerke at Linz. As usual he urged them to step up heavy panzer production. In general I observed that Hitler could judge at a glance a factory's possibilities and know if his demands were capable of being met.

From Linz he went to Munich to attend the funeral of NSKK leader Adolf Hühnlein, a 1923 veteran, whom he considered exceptionally able and proven. On the evening of the 26th we returned to Berlin. On the way Rommel's report announcing the capture of Tobruk reached Hitler. He was delighted at this success and promoted Rommel to General-feldmarschall at once. He endorsed Rommel's plan to continue the operation to the banks of the Nile—which was contrary to the wishes of the Italians, who wanted to occupy Malta.

Summer Offensive

On 28 June an attack code-named 'Blau' (Blue) began along the front between Taganrog on the Black Sea and Kursk. Two Army Groups involving five armies took part. Once the Russian front had been parted, the advance proceeded according to plan in the direction of Voronezh, which was surrendered by the Soviets on 6 July. Following the River Don, units of the Sixth Army continued the advance towards the southeast. A sharp controversy now arose involving Hitler, Halder and Bock. At the beginning of the operation, Hitler had made it perfectly clear that the advance of the panzer divisions was to be pursued without pause in order that retreating Russian units should be overrun and crushed and the Volga reached as soon as possible. There had been a 48-hour rest at Voronezh. Hitler had censured this severely and was so infuriated that he relieved Bock and replaced him with von Weichs. He added to this directive the observation that he would not allow the generals to jeopardise his plans as they had done in the autumn of 1941.

German troops advanced very smartly along the whole front but found that the Russians had vanished. The tally of prisoners was relatively light and led to the conclusion being drawn that the Russians either had withdrawn knowing details of the attack in advance or were too short on the ground to resist effectively. This was debated endlessly at FHQ. Hitler emphasised that the Russians were at their end and urged his units to hasten. Unfortunately, after initial successes a shortage of fuel obliged the motorised units to wait several days for supplies to arrive.

On 16 July FHQ was transferred forward to Werwolf, near Winniza. Hitler did not feel well here. He found the heat oppressive and the place was plagued by flies and mosquitoes. During these weeks I spent as much time as I could in the air, keeping in touch with the HQs of Göring and Jeschonnek to the rear.

At mealtimes Hitler was very open to conversation and talked at length with Admiral Theodor Krancke, Raeder's representative. The usual wide range of subjects was discussed. A particular talking point was the mysterious British landings at Dieppe on 19 August. I have never been clear what the purpose of this operation was. Enemy commandos came ashore on heavily fortified beaches, and after suffering heavy casualties left twelve hours later. Hitler and Krancke examined the affair from all angles but neither could come up with a satisfactory explanation.

Hitler was extremely indignant for several days following an unofficial Gebirgsjäger operation on 21 August when the highest peak of the Caucasus, the 5,600-metre high Elbrus, was scaled in order to place the German war flag on the summit. Although undoubtedly a great mountaineering feat, it served no military purpose, and such 'events' were expressly forbidden. Hitler's permission had not been sought beforehand and he learned of the feat in a cinema newsreel preview. Every effort was made to track down the culprits, but they were never identified.

Hitler was soon forced to address more serious problems. On 23 August advance units of General Paulus's Sixth Army reached the Volga. This good report was overshadowed by news confirming that—as expected—the Russians had recovered some lost territory from Army Group North. The Eleventh Army had been moved up from South Russia to lend weight to the effort to capture Leningrad in Operation 'Nordlicht', but now Manstein had to be diverted to help beat off the Soviets in the energy-sapping Battle of the Ladoga Sea. It succeeded, but the last chance to take Leningrad had gone.

When List, C-in-C Army Group A (Caucasus), reported to Hitler on 31 August, it was clear that he was close to the end of his strength. Everywhere in that vast expanse he was running up against stiff resistance. Hitler was influenced by the calm manner in which List presented his report and showed understanding for the situation of the Army Group, but insisted that the set objectives had to be kept. Hitler was still thinking of a thrust to Astrakhan and the shores of the Caspian Sea.

Around this time I made a longish visit to the front at Stalingrad. I went first to the 71st Infantry Division south of the city and advancing towards the Volga. My brother was Chief of Staff of this division. He was confident and gave me a comprehensive impression of the situation. It appeared that recently the Russians seemed stronger, but he had no concerns about it. What worried him was the question of supply. Ammunition and fuel were needed urgently.

My next call was to the Sixth Army General Staff. I knew several staff officers well and was announced to Generalleutnant Schmidt. I gained a positive impression of matters despite the shortages and other worries, which included the long supply line behind the Axis armies on the Don. Covering the rear were Romanian, Italian and Hungarian armies, one of each, which in his opinion did not amount to satisfactory protection. Schmidt said that the Russians' presence was growing in size daily and that they were occupying an area which was difficult to observe. I found this very unsettling. I could speak openly with Schmidt and he was frank with me. After a brief call on General Paulus I flew to meet General Hube, commander of XIV Panzer Korps as successor to Wietersheim, whom Hitler had just relieved of command.

Halder Dismissed

On my return I found Winniza plunged in gloom. Hitler had withdrawn into seclusion. The situation conferences were no longer being held in the Wehrmacht Command Staff house but in the large study at Hitler's quarters. When one entered he would not offer his hand but acknowledged the caller's presence by merely extending his arm. He dined alone in his bunker. Two female Reichstag stenographers took down all his conferences, including the situation conferences, verbatim. We military adjutants had then to check the resultant typed scripts for accuracy—a considerable undertaking. And what was responsible for all this? After List's visit, Jodl had flown to Army Group A to size up the situation and talk over the next move. When he delivered his report to Hitler subsequently, a violent argument had erupted. Hitler had told Jodl that he had not sent him to the Caucasus to obtain an account of their misgivings. Equally vehemently Jodl had shouted back that nothing else could be expected from the bringer of impossible orders. At that Hitler had left the conference room and had not returned since. The only person he had spoken to was Schmundt, in order to discuss with him the coming reshuffle. Hitler had got rid of List and announced his intention to dismiss Halder. Schmundt advised him strongly to appoint General Zeitzler as Halder's successor. Hitler decided to think about the changes for a few days.

I waited until the waters had calmed before reporting on my trip to Stalingrad. Hitler was much calmer and gave me his usual welcome. To my surprise I found that he shared Schmidt's reservations about the Don area. He said that he had put the 22nd Panzer Division in reserve behind the front as a precaution but had the impression that Halder did not see any danger there. That did not coincide with his own appreciation. He would speak to him about it. Then, angering swiftly, he complained of the little understanding which Halder had for the difficulties. Halder could see a situation developing on a map, but had no ideas for solving it: he was dispassionate and dry and held quite false notions of how the campaign should proceed. Therefore Hitler was determined to make the change. He added that the mass of older generals were past their best and must be replaced by younger officers. Schmundt would take over the Army Personnel Bureau, where he would arrange matters. Personally I thought that these were enormous changes which were bound to transform the Army substantially, but I said nothing. Basically I was happy that Halder was going. In my opinion his departure was long overdue. Whereas he may well have been a good General Staff officer, he was never the right partner for Hitler as Army leader. I always had the impression that the Army General Staff, with Halder as its head, were not well disposed towards Hitler's plans and intentions and pursued instead quite different objectives.

My 35th Birthday

Despite the general air of upset at FHQ I had a very pleasant 35th birthday celebration on 20th September. Hitler presented me with a kilo tin of caviar which Antonescu had given him. I took this generous gift as the incentive to invite both Adjutantur to a small party. This was in fact the only occasion when we all got together—the stenographers Fräulein Wolf and Fräulein Schröder, Schaub, Albert Bormann, Puttkamer, Engel, Schulze-Kossens, Brandt and Hewel. Unfortunately Schmundt was absent from FHQ that day. After the evening situation conference we finished off the caviar and conversed openly about our concerns. A confidence existed amongst us that we could speak freely without the fear of unpleasant consequences. I noticed that we were all capable of making independent judgements.

On 24 September Hitler dismissed Halder. Zeitzler was made Chief of the General Staff in the rank of General der Infanterie. He set about his new task with verve and commitment. He had got himself a difficult C-in-C, but Hitler had great confidence in him and more or less left him to his own devices. This would show through more clearly in a few weeks as the situation worsened at Stalingrad.

As promised, Hitler gave Schmundt the Army Personnel Bureau. His predecessor, Keitel's brother, had not been equal to the task for some time. Schmundt had not been particularly anxious to take on the office since he had quite enough to do as it was. Nevertheless Hitler eventually talked him round. I thought the decision was correct. Schmundt knew better than anybody Hitler's ideas about the Army High Command and was also in a position to reflect their thinking. In the year and a half that he ran the office, he often contradicted Hitler and got his own way. Schmundt was a good advocate for the Army officer corps.

Towns Bombed and Industry Destroyed

In September it became obvious that the purpose of the British air raids was to build a second front. The RAF attacked Munich, Bremen, Düsseldorf and Duisburg. As the aircraft crossed into Reich territory, air raid alarms were given for vast areas, sending people down into the shelters for hours at a time. This brought a damaging loss of production, particularly serious for the armaments industry, in its train. Quite apart from the damage and casualties inflicted by the bombing itself, these alarms imposed a great strain on people. Hitler spent much time contemplating how he could combat the problem. It had always been his principle to retaliate like for like or worse, but that was not now possible.

The Ju 88 was still not being turned out in satisfactory numbers. The He 177 was a complete disaster.[13] Hitler had had grave doubts about the design from the start and was now confirmed in his opinion. Hopes were focused on the Ju 88, but Milch, who was responsible for aircraft supply, was concentrating on producing fighters to improve air defence. I was amazed that Hitler expressed satisfaction with all this and did not attempt to interfere. He told me that he trusted Göring, who had promised an early improvement in the state of the Luftwaffe.

At the end of September Hitler flew to Berlin to make three speeches and keep a number of important appointments. On 28 September he addressed 1,200 newly commissioned officers fresh from training school and made emphatically clear to them their duty. They had to understand that the war with the Soviet Union had increased in bitterness, but he was certain the German soldier would win. On the 29th he had a long meeting with Rundstedt, recently appointed C-in-C West. Hitler feared British landings and wanted to discuss defensive strategy. Rundstedt was not pessimistic on this point: what concerned him was the unoccupied part of France. He considered the area to be a reservoir of saboteurs and spies safe from our attentions. Hitler said he would deal with this problem soon.

Next day he spoke at the Sportpalast at the opening of the War Winter Relief Work. I was surprised here at his openness. He said that capitulation was unthinkable; the British had declared that the second front had arrived, for which they proposed to step up extensively the bombing war. Hitler described this as 'insane utopia'. His critical listeners could decide on the truth of this for themselves.

On 1 October, in a visibly heartfelt reunion, Hitler received Rommel and awarded him his Feldmarschall's baton. During a long conversation Hitler spoke of his doubts and worries. The inadequate supply of weapons and equipment was an especial headache. He feared that one day the British would arrive with a large, superior force and then he would have 'difficulties'. Rommel's army was at El Alamein, which he had well fortified. He was still very confident. Hitler asked him about the reported British air superiority. Rommel replied that the situation was not critical. Afterwards both went into the Chancellery gardens, where an impressive display of new weapons, including assault guns and a Tiger tank, was on show. Rommel requested them for the front as soon as possible, which Hitler promised to see to. I had the impression that he was beginning to deceive himself. He was underestimating the fighting strength of the Russians and also had the wrong idea about the British. That same day he addressed the Gauleiters. I did not hear this speech but feared that it would be cast in too optimistic a vein. Over the next few days he had various talks about armaments before we returned to Winniza on 4 October.

Threatening Developments in the East

Generaloberst von Richthofen always managed to hit the right note in conversations with Hitler. He spoke frankly and critically and avoided naming guilty parties. He was very worried about the Eastern Front and described situations which the Russians might seize for their own advantage. Hitler's concern coincided with that of Richthofen: they both thought it very possible that the Red Army on the Don would break out from the woodlands on the north bank of the river. Hitler said he would talk this over with Zeitzler. Richthofen referred to the latter disparagingly as 'fat and merry'.

Hitler often put himself in the shoes of the Russians. He felt he should draft in additional reinforcements to bolster the sector where the non-German Axis armies were concentrated, but his warnings met with little success. The department for 'Foreign Friendly Armies East' at OKH was not expecting a Russian attack against the Sixth Army on the Don, but against Army Group Centre.

Hitler was becoming very uneasy at the increasing reports of saboteur commandos behind the German lines in both Russia and France: their aim was to disrupt the supply organisation. As far he could see this was a new form of warfare. For this reason he authorised the 'Commando Order', instructing German troops to execute summarily all captured commandos. Jodl added a rider to the order that in essence it was to be regarded as a companion to the 1941 'Commissar Order'. Hitler's fears were justified, for in the northern sector a huge partisan area had come into being. It was commanded by my Russian namesake, General von Below. Hitler often told me wryly that I ought to bring my 'relations' to heel.

During the stay at Winniza a young lieutenant of the FHQ signals train told me that he had witnessed a terrible massacre nearby. While working on communications equipment he had come to a gorge, where he discovered an SS-troop shooting a large number of men and women. He was very distressed by what he had seen and thought he ought to report it. I spoke to the SS liaison officer, Gruppenführer Wolff, and asked him to investigate and report back. After a few days he supplied me with a very ambiguous answer and hinted at sabotage in the rearward areas. I was requested to take no further steps in the matter. I was satisfied with the explanation and forgot the incident. I was not aware of similar reports subsequently.

British Offensive in North Africa
On 23 October the British attack in North Africa expected by Rommel began. Montgomery was the British C-in-C. His force was about twice as strong as Rommel's and was equipped with a large number of Sherman

tanks. Hitler did not consider the situation to be critical because Rommel had so fortified his positions that even a much superior enemy could be held off. Rommel made a hasty return from leave and was horrified by what he found. The Italian units had melted away into the desert. The German line had held except for some minor penetrations which they had failed to stem. On 2 October Montgomery drove forward again and his tanks broke through the front. Rommel lacked the fuel and ammunition necessary for a mobile engagement of this nature and on the 3rd he appealed to Hitler for help, reporting that he had taken heavy losses and the British had won ground in a successful advance. Hitler replied in a signal that he must remain where he was and not concede a single step; new units would be supplied swiftly. Rommel had already decided to draw back without OKH approval and Hitler saw from his report of 3 November that he had made an unuathorised retreat. Hitler became irate but attributed negligence to FHQ Command Staff. Fortunately Schmundt was able to placate him sufficiently so that no dire consequences ensued: for a short while Warlimont fell into disfavour and a reserve major, the duty officer, suffered a temporary demotion. But Rommel had lost much of the glamour he had attracted in the outward campaign. From now on he was the commander of an army driven ever westwards across the desert towards Tunisia for a last stand in May 1943. But by then, events elsewhere had reduced this theatre to little more than a sideshow.

Stalingrad

The fighting at Stalingrad became very fierce in the autumn of 1942. Frequently reports would come in describing bitter fighting for a block of flats. Hitler insisted that at Stalingrad every house had to be fought for. Only in this way could the Russians be forced out of the city. I believed that we had arrived at the crossroads of events. Hitler often seemed unduly pensive and far away—almost as if he no longer had confidence in the strategy. The extent of the fronts had become enormous, the supply of weapons and munitions problematical. But Hitler made increased demands. Did he truly believe even now that the war could end in a German victory? The question was surfacing for the first time. The answer could not be fathomed.

On 1 November we had had a very pleasant surprise on our return to Wolfschanze. All concrete bunkers had been fitted with a large wooden barracks annexe which made the place much more habitable. Hitler's barracks had a large study added for the daily situation conferences. On the 6th, whilst we were proceeding by the train to Munich via Berlin, a very disturbing signal was received from the Mediterranean. For days our agents had been reporting the assembly at Gibraltar of a large troop convoy, and this had now sailed eastwards. Towards Munich our train was stopped at a station in the Thuringian Forest to receive a Foreign Office communiqué that a US expeditionary corps was disembarking in Algiers and Oran. Ribbentrop was waiting for our train at Bamberg. He had summoned Ciano to Munich, but wanted to speak to Hitler beforehand. He suggested contacting the Russian Embassy in Stockholm to arrange an approach to Stalin proposing far-reaching concessions in the East. Hitler brushed the idea aside. A moment of weakness was not the proper time to negotiate with an enemy. Instead he issued orders for the American landings in Algeria to be repelled. Jodl was instructed to organise the Wehrmacht for the defence of Tunis. As it happened, Oran lay just beyond the range of our bombers and so no attacks were possible.[14]

On 8 November Hitler spoke to the Party veterans. I had the impression that the Algerian affair had winded him. He spoke only of driving the Americans out, but as he stepped up to the platform to address the auditorium he appeared to be bursting with confidence. They applauded him and followed his arguments in a state of rapture. Actually he had nothing new to say. He spoke of the bitter fighting in which our soldiers were embroiled and said that it was about 'the right of our people to be or not to be'.

In the evening of the 10th he had talks with Ciano and Laval. Neither could influence his decision to occupy Vichy France, and next day German troops began the invasion, which proceeded swiftly and without especial incident. It took a few days to capture Toulon and in this time the French scuttled the remnants of their Fleet there.

Hitler retired to Obersalzberg for a few days' rest on 12 November. After the unsettling stop in Munich I had the opportunity to speak to him privately for the first time. He was depressed. The Western Powers—the USA and Britain—had begun to take an active role. He judged this to be a very serious development. Moreover, there was the difficulty of shipping supplies across the Mediterranean. The British had increased the number of their submarines there. He had no confidence in the

Italians: they were pro-British, and he had no doubt that they were reporting the movement of German transports to the British.

Another theme that weighed down on him was the Luftwaffe. Göring had also been in Munich, and it struck me then that Hitler and Göring no longer talked together as they had done previously. Hitler said that Göring did not keep himself properly informed, and Hitler preferred to discuss current problems with Jeschonnek for that reason. He spoke to me in forceful tones about the air defence of the Reich. More flak had to be produced, for our fighters were seldom available in sufficient numbers, or they went to the wrong area, or they were hampered by bad weather. We also needed more flak towers, for example in Munich and Nuremberg. In Berlin and Hamburg these structures had proved themselves in practice.

He hoped that there were no new surprises in store on the Eastern Front, although he suspected that there would be a new Russian offensive at the start of winter. He had drawn this conclusion on the basis of the British and American operations in North Africa.

On 19 November Zeitzler called Hitler to inform him that the Red Army had begun a great winter offensive along the Don. After heavy artillery preparation, Russian tanks and motorised infantry had moved south in large numbers and broken through the Romanian lines. The Romanians had broken and run and the Russians were advancing almost unopposed. Hitler ordered General Heim's XXXXVIII Panzer Korps, in reserve, to move to intercept. Hitler had been misled as to the quality of this Panzer Korps. Its German division was still in formation and the other unit was a Romanian tank division which proved no match for the Russians and was finished off in a few days. Hitler was outraged by Heim's conduct, although really he had been put into a hopeless position through contradictory orders and the enemy's strength. Heim was relieved of command and condemned to death, although Schmundt obtained a reprieve in due course.

On 20 November Hitler ordered Manstein's Army Oberkommando 11, which had been transferred from Army Group North to Army Group Centre at Vitebsk, to be renamed 'Army Group Don' as a new Command Staff to support the threatened front of Army Group South. Hitler was aware of the critical turn of events but did not believe that the Russian penetration would have serious consequences. He accepted that the Sixth Army might be encircled for a few days but considered that he could put that right by a counter-offensive with a few extra reserves. As the developing situation swiftly showed, he was underestimating the Russian forces considerably.

The miserable weather of the first two days was disastrous. Frost, fog, snow and appalling visibility prevented any aircraft from taking off. A second Russian movement, also south of Stalingrad, which began on 20 November confirmed the intention to encircle the city. This they achieved on 23 November.

Zeitzler's reports were becoming so alarming that during the late evening of the 22nd Hitler decided to leave for East Prussia in his train. The journey took twenty hours. Every three to four hours we made a long stop for a telephone conversation with Zeitzler. He was making urgent demands for permission to extricate the Sixth Army before the net closed. Hitler would not allow a single step back. If in the first few days he was thinking that he only needed to mop up the spearhead, now he realised that he was going to need a newly formed Army to contain the Russian divisions at Stalingrad. This would require considerable preparation, and for the time being General Paulus would have to hold his trenches.

After we arrived at Wolfschanze, Hitler's initial worry was to supply Sixth Army from the air. He had long conversations with Göring and Jeschonnek about this. Göring assured him that the Luftwaffe could supply the Sixth Army for a certain time. Jeschonnek did not contradict him. Therefore Hitler decided that Paulus could be supplied by air and that he would eventually be in the position to fight his way out of the pocket.

As soon as it was reported, Göring's statement was disputed vociferously. Even Zeitzler did not believe Göring and told Hitler so forcefully. In the Luftwaffe, Richthofen was very dubious. He considered an air lift out of the question and based this opinion on the weather situation, which was already bad enough and would deteriorate as the winter set in. Moreover, there was a shortage of transport aircraft. Hitler received Richthofen's opinion but rejected it. The distance between Stalingrad and the German lines was growing daily. The Russians had demolished Italian and Hungarian sectors of the front and there was a 300-kilometre long gap along the Don.

Soon after the first Russian breakthrough Hitler had ordered up Hoth's 4th Panzer Army from Kotelnikov south-east of Stalingrad for a counter-attack scheduled for 3 December but eventually postponed until the 8th and then the 12th.[15] At the outset Hoth was quite successful, but when he got to within about 60 kilometres of the ring around Stalingrad he found himself heavily outnumbered and had to give up.

Between 23 and 28 December we lost the airfield at Tazinskaya, which was of special importance for supplying our troops within the cauldron. Flights to and from the airfields inside Stalingrad were increased by 100 kilometres, and this reduced dramatically the already inadequate supply situation. In these circumstances, on 27 December Zeitzler demanded that the Caucasus Front be drawn back. Hitler gave his permission but retracted it shortly afterwards. However, Zeitzler had wasted no time in communicating Hitler's first decision by telephone and he reported to the Führer that the withdrawal could no longer be stopped.

I followed the developments at Stalingrad from 19 November to the end of December with a certain dread. My first impression while at Obersalzberg was of a catastrophe. I had paid a short visit to the Don front at the beginning of November and had obtained reports about the condition of the troops which held out little prospect of a lasting success there. The basically positive attitude of the officers was tempered by depressing admissions about unit and company numbers. On average, they were having to make do with less than 50 per cent of permitted strengths. Commanders had had to come to terms with this. In the six months since June 1942 the German Army had fought without replacements and was now exhausted. Even though reinforcements were being pushed forward in December, it seemed unlikely that a strong defence of the Don front would be possible in the face of a determined assault. Thus the Sixth Army at Stalingrad had to stay where it was, for there was no prospect of its achieving a successful break-out to the German lines. From the end of December I saw its task to be that of tying down the encircling Russian forces for as long as possible to give the Don front time to re-form. But the men in Stalingrad were of course doomed. For all his efforts to help the Sixth Army, I firmly believe that Manstein thought the same. He knew that, primarily, he had to close the gap along the Don and erect a new, sturdier front.

From 1 December I received regular correspondence from the Stalingrad cauldron. That day Generalleutnant Schmidt wrote: 'Now we have our ardent all-round defence. I have enough weapons but little ammunition, little bread and spirit, no wood for burning or building materials to

160

go below ground and keep warm, and the men, who remain astonishingly confident of victory, are daily losing their strength.' On the 8th his No 1 orderly officer, Hauptmann Behr, wrote: 'Condition of the men is unfortunately shit, living on 200 grams bread ration and for the most part sleeping in the open. Not short of pasteboard though so morale excellent.' And on 26 December he said, 'Here on the edge of the other event we think ourselves at the moment a bit betrayed and sold down the river . . . I would like to tell you quite honestly that there is simply nothing more to eat here . . . the black bread stocks have run right down . . . in my experience of the German soldier it is quite reasonable to expect now that his physical will to resist will become weaker in the cold and the moment will come when the individual says "It's all the shit-same to me whether I live or die" and he simply allows himself to freeze to death or lets the Russians overrun us.'

In his letter of 11 January 1943 Behr wrote: 'It has become so bad that German soldiers are going over to the other side.' Two days later he had the unbelievable good luck to be ordered to fly out with the Sixth Army War Diary. My brother, who was 1st General Staff Officer of the 71st Division, and then of the Sixth Army, and who had flown back to Stalingrad in early January after recovering from an illness, wrote me on 13th: 'It does not look good here. There is no doubt whatever that things are coming to their close.'

I showed Hitler these letters and read him the pertinent extracts. He made no comment except to remark on conclusion that the fate of the Sixth Army was for us all a profound duty in the struggle for the freedom of our people. In January 1943 I had the impression that Hitler knew that a war against both the Russians and the Americans—a war on two fronts—could no longer be won.

Together with Ribbentrop, he considered the idea of driving a wedge between his two major enemies. Ribbentrop's plan was for a peace treaty with the Soviets, but Hitler said that that solution was not yet to be pursued. It remained his intention to mobilise the entire German people, involving every German in the war process. Milch would have to do more to frustrate the British air raids while he would devote himself day and night to the task of building up his defensive front. With Speer he discussed armaments projects: Gauleiter Sauckel should pool all labour within reach. The result of all this activity was an astonishing upswing in the whole field of armaments production in 1943.

CHAPTER FIVE

1943

In January Paulus sent two emissaries, General Hube and Hauptmann Behr, from the Stalingrad cauldron to report to Manstein and Hitler. At a situation conference Behr delivered a clear and simple picture of the condition of the Sixth Army. According to him there was no hope. A man fought and fell where he stood. There was no talk of negotiating with the enemy. Supply to the units was no longer possible as there was no means of transportation. It was the absolutely unequivocal picture of a lost battle. I knew Behr, my future brother-in-law, very well and could judge how his report was to be interpreted. Hitler admitted afterwards that only very seldom had he received such a clear and sober view of a situation. Hube presented a broader account, but from his words too it was obvious that events in the Stalingrad cauldron were approaching an inevitable conclusion. Nothing could be done. Nevertheless, on 15 January Hitler asked Milch to make a last attempt to deliver to the Sixth Army a significant quantity of supplies. Despite being severely shaken in a collision between his panzer and a locomotive, Milch set to the task energetically. The bitter winter weather hindered the work on the airfields, and whilst attempts were being made to prepare the aircraft and runways the airfield inside the cauldron was lost and then the supplies could only be parachuted down. Many of these drifted to the enemy. There was no doubt that Milch had been given the job far too late, and Hitler told him as much when Milch made his report to FHQ in early February.[16]

Whilst the fighting for Stalingrad was still going on, I had the impression that Hitler was considering alternative ways to remedy the catastrophic situation. He was convinced that the Anglo-American and Russian forces were harmonising their measures. Hitler knew that there were at OKW officers who had abandoned hope for a positive end to hostilities. He never betrayed a sign of weakness nor indicated that he saw any situation as hopeless. He considered it necessary to spread confidence in victory, and henceforth he ensured by his attitude, mood and appearance that none of his visitors nor his trusted companions should infer from his demeanour how he really judged the war situation. This led to his adopting an outward expectancy that one day the tide would turn in Germany's favour. It fascinated me to see how he contrived to put a positive value on setbacks and even succeeded in convincing those who worked most closely with him. Nevertheless, I could no longer share the confidence in victory which he expressed in his New Year speech. On the other hand, I did not believe that we would actually lose the war. I envisaged a sort of compromise European peace solution which, despite everything, seemed to be still attainable with a little goodwill. Everything achieved so far need not have been in vain. From opinions garnered at FHQ it was clear that this point of view was as widespread there as in the Wehrmacht generally.

Raeder Steps Down

On 6 January Raeder reported to Hitler; the conversation was held partly *in camera*. Raeder requested to be allowed to resign his post on 30 January. At first Hitler would not hear of it, but Raeder made a plausible case as to why there should be a change at the top. He said that he was no longer competent to fulfil the high demands of his office and feared that one day his shortcomings would be discovered. He suggested that he be given the title of Admiral-Inspekteur, so that the Press, and particularly people abroad, would not read too much into the change. Hitler consented, not least because the era of the surface fleet which Raeder had championed seemed to be at its close. To succeed him Hitler nominated Dönitz, head of the U-boat arm, with immediate promotion to Grossadmiral. I did not know the background to the change then, although the previously good relationship between Hitler and Raeder had been sour for some time. I assumed that the 'Regenbogen' fiasco—the unsuccessful action by the heavy cruisers *Admiral Hipper* and *Lützow* and six destroyers in the Arctic against Allied convoy JW.51B at the end of 1942—had something to do with it. Konteradmiral Voss replaced Admiral Krancke as personal representative of the C-in-C Kriegsmarine at FHQ.

Casablanca, North Africa

In January Roosevelt and Churchill conferred at Casablanca; De Gaulle and Giraud also took part. It was here that the joint decision was made to continue the war until Germany surrendered unconditionally. The conference was surrounded by a great deal of publicity and was not without its effect on Hitler. He mentioned the agreement repeatedly and stressed that any idea of 'coming round' would now be completely senseless.

Further bad reports were received from North Africa. Montgomery's pressure on Rommel had increased, and on 23 January, when Tripoli fell, almost all of Libya was in British hands. To the west, the Americans were camped on the Tunisian border facing the German rear line. North Africa could obviously not be held much longer, but the melting away of the Italians was very disappointing.

Manstein and Hitler

On 6 February Manstein visited Hitler at Wolfschanze to discuss the division of command since Hitler had made himself C-in-C, and, in the autumn of 1942, had also taken personal command of Army Group A. Manstein wanted to propose the appointment of a general as C-in-C Army, or at least of the Eastern Front. If Hitler did not think that would be possible, then he might at least consider ending the dual command structure by combining the Army General Staff and Wehrmacht Command Staff under a General Chief of Staff. Calmly and objectively Hitler answered each point of Manstein's argument. He would not give way. He knew no general in whom he had sufficient confidence to place those powers demanded by Manstein. Thus the situation remained unchanged. Manstein also discussed his future intentions at the front, for which in the main Hitler gave him a free hand.

On 7 February all Gau- and Reichsleiters assembled at FHQ to hear a wide-ranging speech covering the events of the winter. Hitler had designed it in such a way that none of his listeners would have the slightest hint of the catastrophic situation. It contained neither uncertainties nor expressions of disappointment. Without beating round the bush, he admitted the Russian successes and set out his programme for clearing up the mess. I was astonished at how this approach convinced them. He also mentioned the Casablanca Conference and the enemy's joint declaration for 'unconditional surrender'. This decision had freed him completely from any ideas of peace negotiations anywhere in the world. His audience left visibly happier and returned home full of enthusiasm for the fray.

Winrich Behr married my sister-in-law on the family estate in Saxony on 13 February. It was all the more happy an affair for the salvation of the bridegroom from his fate at Stalingrad. During the month Hitler spoke frequently with Göring, Jeschonnek, Ribbentrop, Goebbels, Himmler and Speer and with his military advisers at OKH and OKW. On the 16th he promoted von Richthofen to Feldmarschall: I telephoned Richthofen at his HQ with the news.

Manstein's Offensive

Manstein was planning to embark on his push to the Donets and Kharkov on 19 February and suggested that Hitler should observe the campaign from his Ukraine FHQ at Winniza. Thus with Zeitzler's support he flew with a small retinue to Manstein's Army Group HQ at Saporoshye for two days. The mood was even but tense, as Manstein recorded in his memoirs. Hitler was interested almost exclusively in the operations of Army Group South, as Army Group Don had been renamed at the beginning of the month. The Russians had not so far managed to stem its advance to the south-west: it was breaking a vast area of virgin territory. This advance influenced Hitler's return to Winniza on 19 February. Both Manstein and Richthofen recommended that he leave Saporoshye because they feared that a Russian battle group might make a surprise raid against the airfield, leaving Hitler stranded. As we left that afternoon, we heard MG and shell fire not far from the airfield. I remember Saporoshye if only because Hitler promoted Engel and myself to the rank of Oberstleutnant there. We also noticed the coldness and reserve of the officers of this command; it was obvious from their demeanour that they were unable to muster much belief in Hitler's plans.

We resumed residence at the pleasant Winniza HQ for almost four weeks to 13 March while Manstein's panzers forged ahead. Hitler followed the movements of the attacking divisions very closely. In mid-March they reached the Donets, the goal of the operation. On the 10th Hitler flew out to Manstein and in recognition of his success awarded him the Oak Leaves. It was extraordinary to observe the change of mood within the officer corps of that Army Group since the previous visit. Now they had quite a positive outlook on matters.

Accusations Against the Luftwaffe

On 1 March the RAF bombed Berlin: 250 heavy bombers dropped 600 tons of bombs on the capital, destroying 20,000 houses and making 35,000 homeless. 700 were killed. This prompted Hitler to make a severe outburst against the Luftwaffe. When Goebbels visited a week later on 7 and 8 March, Hitler had long talks with him about the escalation in the British air raids. He struck out in all directions and included the generals for good measure. Even though he attributed the main responsibility for the defeat at Stalingrad to the three foreign Axis armies, he did not exempt the German generals: they did not believe unshakeably in the righteousness of this war; they had no understanding of weapons and equipment; they watched developments at the front full of misgivings. Hitler often became so worked up that he could not be interrupted. Returning to the original theme, he ordered the Luftwaffe to nominate a young, experienced officer as *Angriffsführer England,* to whom would be assigned a number of bomber crews whose duty would be to make continual concentrated bombing raids on British cities. Twenty-nine-year old Oberst Dietrich Peltz was selected, but as he lacked sufficient aircraft his operations were never really effective.

Planning for 'Zitadelle'
On 13 March Hitler returned by air to Rastenburg, making an intermediate stop at Army Group Centre HQ Smolensk, where he had a long and optimistic talk with Kluge. He said that one never knew if the Russians might not be near the end of their strength, and in fact he was now planning an offensive in the East. The first objective was to retake an prominent bulge around Kursk. The operation was code-named 'Zitadelle' (Citadel).

The second leg of his flight from Smolensk to Rastenburg passed without incident, and not until after the war did I learn that a General Staff Officer of the Army Group, Oberst von Tresckow, an opponent of Hitler, had placed a bomb in the aircraft. During my own return flight over a vast area of woodland—I was piloting an He 111—I remember wondering what would happen if Hitler's FW 200 crashed into a dense forest without making a distress signal.

The interlude at Wolfschanze passed relatively quietly except for renewed outbursts against the Luftwaffe following heavy air raids on Nuremberg and Munich. As soon as he arrived at the Chancellery on 20 March Hitler tackled Göring about the raids and the uselessness of the Luftwaffe generals. He also accused Göring of incompetence, although this did not affect their personal relationship at all.

On the 21st Hitler made his annual speech at the Berlin Arsenal to commemorate *Heldengedenktag*. He spoke with reverence of the 542,000 men who at that date had fallen for Germany in this war and said that they 'lived on eternally in our ranks, the heroes and pioneers of a better age'. Oberst Baron von Gersdorff, a General Staff officer of Army Group Centre, claimed after the war that during this ceremony he was carrying explosive charges in the pockets of his uniform greatcoat for the purpose of making an attempt on Hitler's life. Hitler's hasty tour of inspection of the Arsenal had prevented the time fuses being set. I remember Gersdorff. The sartorial elegance of his uniform made him stand out from the crowd. He accompanied Hitler's retinue like a creeper and held long conversations with Keitel's ADC von Freyend. However, I do not really think he had explosives on him.

On the Eastern Front it was the muddy season. Neither side could mount a major attack, and a tense inactivity prevailed which gave no clue as to where or in what direction the opening moves would be made. On 22 March Hitler decided to retire to Obersalzberg for a few weeks. This was a taxing and depressing period, but Hitler invited my wife to the Berghof, which helped.

Tunis

At the end of March I flew to Taormina in Tunisia to see Kesselring. His reports were hard to fathom, for he spoke in a very optimistic vein about holding Tunis but was pessimistic about everywhere else. He told me clearly that Tunisia could not be held much longer. Next morning I flew with him to the Southern Front to meet von Arnim, C-in-C Armee Afrika. He held the same opinion as Kesselring. I spent the hours of darkness with the Hermann Göring Division, where I knew several officers, including the commander, Generalleutnant 'Beppo' Schmidt. Schmidt took me to the front line that evening. It was very thinly spread; he doubted it could withstand an American attack. That evening he told me his men's worries. I replied that compared to the Army units I had seen recently his division was in a fantastic condition. He did not deny this but stressed that, even so, he could not hold off the Americans alone. Next morning I met Kesselring in Bizerta and we flew back to Taormina, where I took the opportunity to ask several of his staff officers if they thought an American invasion of Sicily launched from Tunisia could be countered. Opinions were divided, although they believed there was no possibility of holding it off in the long run.

I gave Hitler a detailed report. He received the bad news calmly and said very little. It seemed to me that he had already written off North Africa. As for Sicily, he thought that Italian forces would fight better when actually defending Italy. I expressed my negative opinion of Italian troops. I did not imagine there was even one Italian division capable of making a stout resistance for any length of time. Above all, the Italian officer corps was not up to it. Hitler was angry when he thought of the uselessness of the Italians. Basically the Italian forces did not want to fight. They would rather throw away their arms and go over to the enemy *en masse*—and today was better than tomorrow to do it.

Visits by Allies

King Boris of Bulgaria led the queue of foreign government heads. As far as I was concerned, his visit on 3 April was merely to glean Hitler's views about the catastrophic situation in Russia. He spoke very frankly with Hitler and held nothing back. But Hitler said he was sceptical that the Russians had anything more up their sleeve. The talks took place in a very tactful and moderate tone, but Hitler told us afterwards that he had been blunt with the king about the Russians and said he did not share the widespread opinion of Russian might.

Next evening we travelled by the train to Linz to visit the Reichswerke Hermann Göring and the Nibelungenwerke at St Florian. Pleiger, the Minister for Coal and managing director of the Reichswerke, met Speer in Linz and accompanied Hitler on his tour of both factories. In the Reichswerke Pleiger had achieved a substantial increase in production and in the Nibelungenwerke the new Panzer Mk III and IV models were beginning to roll off the line.[17] Hitler had been waiting a long time for this news and looked pleased. He decided at once to postpone 'Zitadelle' to enable his panzer force to be strengthened. The Chiefs of the General Staff were very reluctant to accept this postponement; even Richthofen pressed for the attack to be made. But Guderian, who since the end of February had been General Inspector of Panzer Troops, supported Hitler's view and the attack was put off until June. I could not understand Hitler's decision because this delay of almost six weeks was of greater benefit to the Russians than ourselves. If they were not planning an attack, then they would reinforce their defences so strongly that an attack from the German side would be rendered much less likely to succeed. But Hitler could not be dissuaded.

April brought more visits by pro-Axis politicans—Mussolini, Antonescu, Horthy, Quisling, Tiso, Pavelic, Laval and Oshima. Mussolini stayed three days at Schloss Klesheim and attempted to influence Hitler to end hostilities with Russia. This was an old bone which Hitler had already rejected. Mussolini was not interested in anything else and was very quiet. It was obvious that he considered the war to be lost and in his opinion Italy had no further role to play. When I gave Hitler my impression he replied that Mussolini could no longer influence operations. He feared that political change in Italy might soon be to our disadvantage.

To Admiral Horthy's enquiries about the general situation Hitler gave a synopsis with a very favourable slant. I thought that Horthy heard it out in his usual amiable way and did not believe a word of it. Ribbentrop then accused him of dragging his feet about the Jews. There were 800,000 Hungarian Jews who had to be transported to the East. But Horthy would not be drawn. On the whole all visitors this month were not disabused of the misgivings which had been fostered in other countries. They had been shown evidence of the ever-increasing American and Russian build-up and were in no doubt that the major push would begin in 1943. Yet Hitler was still hopeful that the Russians were weak and put his faith in 'Zitadelle'.

Hitler Demands Stronger AA Defences

My conversations in April with Hitler about the bombing were extremely worrying. The British were keeping up their horrific attacks on German cities and Hitler was at a loss as to how they could be countered. Almost every evening after dinner he would call me into the large hall, where we would stroll up and down for up to two hours deep in conversation. Hitler recognised the aerial superiority of the British and spoke forcefully about the need to strengthen our flak defences. I gave him my frank opinion that I would not expect too much even from a gigantic flak network. Flak might divert bombers from a straight approach and bomb run, but there was no effective defensive weapon in Germany against night bombing. He did not contradict me and so I assumed he agreed. It was depressing to have to hear his opinions about Göring; he had not forgotten my criticism of Göring in 1940. The bombing gave him renewed cause to criticise Göring's contribution as Luftwaffe C-in-C. In April 1943, at the Berghof, I gained the impression that Hitler had had enough of him, speaking of him in terms harsh and dismissive. In mitigation I pointed to the way in which the war in the East had developed and the Luftwaffe shortages of aircraft. He acknowledged this, but I had to accept as justified his criticism of the failure to produce new aircraft designs, especially bombers.

He drew comparisons with the U-boat arm. Heavy losses had been suffered in 1942 because of new British locating devices. Dönitz had decided to curtail U-boat activity until he had an effective answer to British radar. The stage would soon be reached when that would be achieved. Kriegsmarine efficiency was worthy of recognition and was a great help for him since he no longer needed to worry himself about naval problems. Earlier he had had no reason to watch over the build-up of the Luftwaffe and had not understood much of it in any case, but here he was having to concern himself with all the details and take a much closer interest in what went on. In the daily round with Göring, however, Hitler allowed no sign of his aggravation with Göring or the Luftwaffe in general to make itself known.

In the last days of April Army Group Centre at Smolensk reported extensively on the discovery of mass graves in the Katyn Forest. The Foreign Office despatched an international medical commission there. It was composed of important judicial forensic experts from the Universities of Ghent, Sofia, Copenhagen, Helsinki, Naples, Agram, Prague, Pressburg and Budapest. By 30 March the corpses of 982 Polish officers had been disinterred. The officers had been murdered by a shot to the back of the head. When Hitler read the report of the commission he gave voice to all his hatred for the Soviet regime and its assassins. He said he would not have expected anything else of the Russians and this discovery merely confirmed his impression of them.

May 1943 brought no great events on land. Hitler's efforts to increase armaments production and reduce the bombing stood in the foreground. Speer was the active type of minister who knew how to mobilise industry and step up its output month by month. Every fourteen days he reported to Hitler, usually in the company of a couple of industrialists who could answer Hitler's questions. I recall sessions in which Hitler conversed solely with financiers. He kept the main armaments figures, including the current monthly outputs, in his head. Many industrialists found it hard to answer all Hitler's questions. From what they said, it was amazing how little real effect the bombing had had on industry. The

RAF attacked mainly residential districts because they thought that that was the way to break the will of the people. In 1943 it was noticeable how little success they had doing this: certainly a huge number of families were bombed out of their homes and many killed, but the impression remained that these air raids did not have a demoralising effect.

In the morning of 2 May Hitler left for Munich, where a conference had been arranged for the 4th about 'Zitadelle'. Kluge, Manstein, Guderian, Jeschonnek and others had been summoned. Hitler discussed it beforehand at the Berghof with Model, who advised him to postpone the offensive for another month to July to allow himself the maximum number of panzers in hand for the operation. Hitler was very much inclined to take this advice and eventually decided to ignore the opinion of his generals in Munich.

We returned to Berlin on 7 May to attend the state funeral of SA Chief of Staff Viktor Lutze, who had been killed in a road accident on the Berlin autobahn. Goebbels led the orations and Hitler added a few words, from which it was apparent how deeply he mourned the loss. After the ceremony he invited the Party, SA and SS leaders to lunch and subjected them to an impassioned discourse about 'motorway madness'. Then he ordered that the cars of the Party leaders should be adjusted mechanically so that they could not exceed 80kph.

On 12 May we flew to Wolfschanze, where Hitler received next day von Arnim's report from Tunis that all German forces in North Africa had capitulated. Hitler had seen it coming but had been unable to do anything to help. He criticised the Italian supply organisation which in the final months had got out of control. Between the 13th and 15th Hitler had detailed discussions with Speer and several arms experts and saw a display of new panzers and anti-tank guns. His decision was invited. He conferred upon Speer an honour.

Holiday in Prague and Vienna

At the end of May I took extended leave with my wife. We had decided to see Prague and Vienna before they were reduced to rubble. We went by train from Berlin to the Czech capital, stayed a week in an hotel on the Wenzelsplatz and quickly forgot the war, although in the first few days we were shocked to read of the British 'Dambusters' raid. In Prague we visited the opera and theatre, but most of all we loved the fine old buildings which gave the city its special appeal.

From Prague we travelled by rail to Vienna. The train was packed and in conversations the dominant theme was the war. Our fellow passengers held very critical opinions of events, but all were convinced that Hitler was the custodian of affairs and that the war would end in our favour. In Vienna we were surprised to be met on the platform by Reichsleiter Baldur von Schirach's ADC, who escorted us to our hotel. I had phoned Schirach previously and asked him if he could assist us as tourists in the city. He treated us with great hospitality.

After sightseeing we saw a presentation of *The Merchant of Venice* at the Burg Theatre and then in a restaurant discussed the military situation. Schirach shared my opinion that the war could not be won with our present forces. He was very annoyed that Ribbentrop, Keitel and others were not honest about matters with the Führer. I was compelled to contradict him on this point. I mentioned the Casablanca Conference and unconditional surrender. Schirach said one should not take this declaration too seriously since there was always room for a compromise.

Hitler Criticises the Luftwaffe
On 14 June I returned to Obersalzberg. When I reported my presence to Hitler at the Berghof, after a few words of greeting he went directly to the main theme, the constant bombing. They had ruined the Ruhr and there was no way of telling when it would end. The Luftwaffe had next to nothing to fight them with. Then he switched subjects to Sicily. He was extremely concerned here because he had no faith in the Italians and was short of German troops to defend the island; he was relying primarily on the Luftwaffe to help out.

A few days earlier, on the 11th, Richthofen had come to the Berghof to receive command of Air Fleet 2 in Italy. This would relieve Kesselring, who until then had commanded it as C-in-C South, for a more comprehensive task, even though at first he would be to some extent a general without men.

The overstretching of resources in Italy at this time is demonstrated by a telegram sent on 11 June to the Command Staff, Air Fleet 2, and of which I have the original: 'All fighter pilots stationed in Italy are to be informed that they are the most pitiful bunch of fliers I have ever commanded. If by chance they happen to encounter the enemy they allow themselves to be shot down without obtaining any successes in return. Until further notice I forbid any leave in order that I do not have to be ashamed of these miserable personalities in the homeland. Göring.'

That first evening of my return to Obersalzberg I spent hours in conversation strolling up and down with Hitler. He spoke primarily of his fears about Italy. He judged the American moves as very weighty and said that our forces were insufficient. If the Luftwaffe did not succeed in driving off the American landings in Sicily then he had no hope for the entire Italian peninsula. He had great faith in Richthofen and hoped he could pull it off. I took the liberty of reminding him clearly of my opinion of our Luftwaffe, which would never again be the equal of the British, Americans or Russians. He mentioned Göring, who, like himself, could make the impossible possible. I suggested that that might no longer be the case. The 1941 and 1942 aircraft designs were missing and we were still flying more or less the same aircraft types with which we had begun the war in 1939. He did not reply to this, but I noticed that his belief in Göring had returned.

On Corpus Christi, 24 June, Baldur von Schirach came to the Berghof with his wife. He had a long talk with Hitler, the content of which I did not hear until a few evenings later. Schirach had stated his opinion quite unambiguously that, one way or another, the war had to be brought to an end. Hitler said, 'How can he think like that? He knows as well as I do that there is no way out. I might as well shoot myself in the head as think of negotiating peace.' He was highly indignant about Schirach and made it quite clear that he wanted nothing more to do with him. That was their last meeting.

'Zitadelle'

On 29 June Hitler returned to Wolfschanze for a conference on 1 July with all senior commanders. He delivered a long statement about the general situation and 'Zitadelle', which was scheduled to roll finally on the 5th. He was confident and expected victory. He did not believe that the Russians had the strength to strike a telling blow against our Eastern Front. He feared only for Sicily because he was doubtful about the Italians. On the 5th the Army Groups of Kluge and Manstein attacked from the north and south, respectively, towards Kursk. Before the attack the Russians pounded the German front with a heavy artillery barrage. The date had been discovered.

Sperrle's Forty Years

The same day Hitler gave me an errand in France. I flew to Paris and saw General Koller, Chief of Staff to Feldmarschall Sperrle. We discussed the air war against England. Koller thought that the Luftwaffe should not be used as the Army's artillery elsewhere. The continuation of bombing against England was very urgent and Oberst Peltz should be given the squadrons he needed. Sperrle was not in Paris but in his summer HQ at St Jean de Luz on the Biscay coast south of Biarritz. It was very remote and Sperrle was attended only by a physician, an ADC and an orderly officer. I arrived that afternoon. The HQ did not look a very military set-up. I fulfilled my task by offering him Hitler's congratulations on the fortieth anniversary of his military service together with a cheque for 50,000 Reichsmarks. We discussed the situation. Sperrle seemed impressed by some of Hitler's ideas. I stayed twenty-four hours in this small circle to soak up the restful atmosphere.

From the south of France I returned directly to FHQ to find a witches' brew of toil and trouble. On 12 July the Russians had attacked our advancing front at Orel. Next day Hitler discussed with Kluge and Manstein the continuation of 'Zitadelle'. Manstein was unconditionally in favour, but Kluge, whose units had taken the full brunt of the Soviet attack and who doubted if he could hold it, wanted the operation called off. After long conversations Hitler decided to abandon 'Zitadelle' and thus the last German offensive of the war on the Eastern Front miscarried.

Break with the Italians

From Italy came reports that indicated a political revolution; the American landings in Sicily on 9 and 10 July had brought it about. Our 'strong man' there was Hube, but he had too few troops to defend the whole coastline. The enemy's air superiority made itself felt. As for the Italians, they abandoned their weapons and made off. One American and one British army took the island during the next four weeks. In this turbulent period Hitler considered it indispensable to speak to Mussolini, and the two leaders met on 19 July at Feltre near Belluno in Upper Italy. Mussolini brought a number of companions with him but they were unable to follow the conversation. Hitler spoke reproachfully to Mussolini but had the impression that the Duce was resigned to his fate. He was in a very ungracious mood on the return flight to Rastenburg as he ruminated with anger and suspicion on the events unfolding in Italy.

At six in the evening of 24 July the Grand Fascist Council convened at the Palazzo Venezia for the first time since December 1939. Reports of what was being discussed were scanty, leaving Hitler in an impatient frame of mind. Ribbentrop, Göring, Goebbels and Himmler all took part in excited conversations. At FHQ on the 26th we learned that the Council had voted by a large majority to request the king to take personal command of the armed forces. A leading figure of this Council was the fomer Italian ambassador to London, Grandi. On the afternoon of the 25th Mussolini had been asked to present himself at the royal palace, where he was informed that Marshal Badoglio had been appointed as his successor. On leaving the palace Mussolini was arrested and taken by ambulance to a *carabinieri* barracks. For a week we had no news of his whereabouts. Hitler was horrified at the swift and bloodless end to fascist domination in Italy. Nobody had interceded for Mussolini. The Badoglio government announced that it would continue in the Axis alliance with Germany, but Hitler looked on sceptically. He had no faith in Badoglio. His main interest was to find out where Mussolini was being held, and he gave Himmler orders to set the necessary wheels in motion.

The Suffering of Hamburg

At the same time as Hitler was learning of the Italian upheaval on 26 July, Gauleiter Kaufmann reported from Hamburg the first of three fearful air raids on the city. A thousand RAF bombers had covered their approach from radar detection equipment by dropping countless tinfoil strips. Kaufmann spoke of a gigantic conflagration with thousands dead. At next morning's situation conference Hitler made a violently critical outburst against the Luftwaffe and demanded an immediate build-up in flak defences. He was expecting fresh attacks on Hamburg and in this he was not wrong. In a few days two further such raids followed, leaving Hamburg almost completely destroyed.

The Russian attack against Orel and Byelgorod was successful and we lost both cities. The Soviets remained on the offensive without respite from now until October and forced back sections of our front by 200 kilometres. Our lines at the beginning of the October muddy season stretched from the Sea of Azov through Saporoshye, along the Dnieper through Dnyepropetrovsk, Kiev and Gemel to Vitebsk. Hitler was more preoccupied by events in Italy than in the East, and by transferring several divisions to Italy he completely drained the Eastern Front of reserves.

The Russians had now gained the initiative along the whole front and were unlikely to let go. I saw our main worry in the number of fronts we were having to maintain: a growing number of divisions in Italy; a defensive front against invasion along the French coast; and occupation troops tied down in Greece and Norway.

Jeschonnek's Suicide

In August 1943 I drew Hitler's attention to a problem within the Luftwaffe leadership. Since the beginning of January the differences between Göring and Jeschonnek had multiplied and could no longer be bridged. Göring had added a number of younger officers to his personal staff and was practically conducting affairs without reference to the General Staff—an obviously intolerable situation. In early August Jeschonnek's ADC invited me one morning to breakfast. I found Jeschonnek in a state of anxiety and despair. Göring had blamed him for the continually increasing British air raids: he had been intolerable, immoderate, biased and unjust. I spoke quietly with Jeschonnek and asked him to attend that day's situation conference to discuss his problem with Hitler. The Führer agreed to hear Jeschonnek's complaint after I had outlined the facts. However, he would not allow him to resign under any circumstances since he knew of no other person who could replace Göring if need be. Jeschonnek was closeted with Hitler for nearly two hours over lunch. On leaving he thanked me for my mediation but added that he had to continue to co-operate with Göring. The differences seemed unresolved, but I could do no more.

In the morning of 19 August the ADC rang me to say that Jeschonnek had shot himself. I was taken completely by surprise. Göring arrived at Rastenburg from Berchtesgaden before the morning conference. I fetched him from the airfield. He gave me two letters which Jeschonnek had left for me and asked if he had given me any hint of his intention. I could deny this with a clear conscience. Göring also wanted to know the contents of the letters. I declined and put them in my pocket. I read them later when I was alone. Jeschonnek had set down his complaints about Göring—his continual abusive telephone calls about the British air raids and other things for which Göring had unjustifiably made him the scapegoat. He described his own abortive attempts to build an effective Luftwaffe. I was very moved by these letters and informed Hitler of the contents that evening. He said that Jeschonnek's suicide had solved nothing but only brought about personal consequences. I had the impression that Jeschonnek's intention to expose Göring's weaknesses by his suicide had been turned by Göring to his own advantage. The funeral took place a few days later near Luftwaffe HQ and Göring nominated Korten as Chief of the Luftwaffe General Staff.

Jeschonnek's death just about summed up the state of the Luftwaffe and the constant overtaxing of its resources. After the Battle of Britain it had had no operational role to play and neither did it have the capacity for major operations. The high standard of its pilots stood in stark contrast to its material failure to progress. As a ground-attack force supporting the Army it was still achieving a great deal, but in the West—as became abundantly clear in the summer of 1944—and over the Reich, it was hopelessly inferior. Pitted against the rising number of Russian frontline aircraft, the better quality of our pilots proved significant for some time but in the long run they were bound to be claimed by wear and tear. Later, when sufficient aircraft were rolling off the production lines, a different situation arose, in which the lack of fuel led to pilots with insufficient flying hours being thrown into combat to fall an easy prey to British and American fighters. Jeschonnek had had scarcely any capital to play with: Korten, Kreipe and Koller applied their different temperaments to administering the bankrupt estate. Korten took the broad view of his office and did not burden himself with too many details.

For a while Kreipe and Koller were both Chief of the Luftwaffe General Staff. Kreipe got on well with Göring and realised that nothing could be done, while Koller suffered visibly at the uselessness of what he was supposed to be attempting with hardly any battleworthy units at his disposal. To make matters worse, Koller did not see eye to eye with Göring and this weighed on him heavily once middleman Kreipe had stepped down. In the course of the next few months it was galling to observe how the Luftwaffe, in which at the outset such great expectations had been placed, burned itself out through a wide variety of errors and omissions.

In August 1943 the British carried out many more terrible air raids. Seven hundred persons were killed in an attack on the rocket development establishment at Peenemünde. The Americans were now flying from Sicily against factories in Austria and southern Germany—the aircraft works at Wiener Neustadt, then the ball bearing factories at Schweinfurt and the Messerschmitt Werke at Regensburg.

From 17 to 24 August Roosevelt and Churchill met at Quebec in order to agree their common objectives. Hitler recognised from Ribbentrop's note that Roosevelt was the big noise. Roosevelt was of the opinion that, after the defeat of the Axis, Russia would control Europe. Therefore it would be important to establish and maintain friendly relations with the Soviets. Churchill agreed and thus the traditional politics of the 'balance of power' on the European continent tilted in favour of Stalin. Hitler took the results of this conference very seriously and expected a further hardening of their attitude. Taking the lesson of developments in Italy, Hitler decided that he ought to tighten internal control at home just in case. In a reshuffle, Reich Interior Minister Dr Frick became Reich Protector in Prague while Himmler was given the Interior Ministry.

At the end of August Hitler was saddened by the death of King Boris of Bulgaria. His instincts told him that the Italian royal house was behind it. King Boris's queen was a daughter of the Italian king. Her sister Mafalda, the wife of the Prince of Hesse, had lived a long time in Sofia. Hitler had no proof, but German physicians attending the king stated that they would not rule out poison.

Pressure on the Eastern Front

Towards the end of August the Soviet Army stepped up its pressure. Kluge and Manstein fought desperately to hold the front together. Hitler concluded from this situation that Stalin was deriving comfort from the situation in Italy, guessing that Hitler would have to transfer substantial forces there from the Eastern Front. The German movement was exposing the Donets Basin, which Hitler wanted to retain at all costs.

On 8 September we returned to Winniza for a conference with Manstein. The Russians had attacked at the seam where the two Army Groups met and had made a deep penetration. The front could only be held by a retreat. Hitler saw that he had no choice but to agree.

Code-word 'Achse'

Upon our return to Wolfschanze we found a tense atmosphere. Indirect reports from Italy that their armed forces had capitulated were confirmed on 6 September. This was the signal to mobilise all German forces in Italy for the occupation of the country under the code-word 'Achse'. This succeeded and the disarming of Italian troops began. When units of

the Italian Fleet broke out, the battleship *Roma* was sunk by a glider
bomb and her sister ship *Italia* damaged. Patchy resistance was encountered, and in some places troops of the former ally were given a ruthless
response. Rome capitulated on 10 September, Luftwaffe General Stahel
being given command of the city, and a few days later the mainland
peninsula was in German hands. Himmler appointed SS-Ober-
gruppenführer Karl Wolff as 'Special Adviser for Police Affairs in Italy';
Gruppenführer Fegelein took over his role as SS liaison officer to Hitler
at FHQ.

Meanwhile Hitler had found out that Mussolini was being held in a
ski hotel at Gran Sasso in the Appenines and set up a major operation to
kidnap him. Luftwaffe General Student was asked to plan a landing on
Gran Sasso from the air. This was done in cooperation with SS-
Hauptsturmführer Skorzeny, who eventually stole the show. The operation started and finished on 12 September. Glider troops landed on Gran
Sasso near the hotel, paratroops freed Mussolini and Skorzeny made off
with the Duce in a Fieseler Storch to the nearest airfield, where a larger
machine was waiting to fly him to Vienna. From there Skorzeny rang
FHQ and reported the success. Hitler awarded him the Knight's Cross.
Two days later Mussolini arrived at Rastenburg, a broken man. I had the
impression that he was finished with politics. Hitler sent him off to Munich with a new role. He left without a spring in his step: his time had
run out. But Hitler remained his loyal friend.

A Separate Peace?

In these weeks of permanent crises the idea was circulated for a compromise with one enemy. Ribbentrop and Goebbels were behind it and attempted to win Hitler over. What they had in mind was an agreement
with Stalin. Hitler said that basically he was so inclined but it would only
be possible from a position of strength. He thought a breakdown in the
enemy alliance would be better. Any agreement with the Western powers
was out of the question, however. Churchill was his enemy from innermost conviction and would not rest until Germany was destroyed, even
if he lost the British Empire in doing so. He could not go for a compromise with the Soviets, for the Communists were the enemy of the Reich.
Thus his attitude towards separate peace negotiations in the autumn of
1943 seemed disjointed. I do not think that he dismissed them entirely
but rather held to the view that victory only came to those who fought

for it. Eventually he alone thought this. German troops were retreating on all fronts. Confidence in victory had evaporated: only the belief that Hitler would find the way out remained unbroken. This certainty increased his concept of mission. He could not believe that all the efforts, the enormous casualties in the air raids and the sacrifices at the front were in vain. In the autumn of 1943 I observed how Hitler was filled with a profound sense of mission, and even seemed to expect a miracle. The longer the fighting in Russia went on, the more unrestrained became his hatred of the Jews. He had no sympathy whatever for them. In his conversations with Goebbels and Himmler he left no room for doubt that he was not in the least concerned about what happened to the Jews. Incidentally, Goebbels seemed to me the most radical of the National Socialist leaders, whilst Himmler had an eye increasingly to the future in all that he did.

About this time people began to ask me how we could still win the war—a very difficult question for me to answer. I did not let anybody think that I believed personally in total victory. The catastrophic situation in which the Luftwaffe found itself made defeat certain unless a miracle happened. In such conversations I left no doubt however that I considered a change of fortune in our favour possible by the introduction of the new technical weapons. Here I was thinking of the new jet fighters and the development of the V-1 and V-2 at Peenemünde. Actually I did not believe in this myself. I was sure that these weapons had no significance in the final analysis. I accepted that the war would end in 1944.

I was also asked if there was no way in which a stop could be put to Hitler—in other words to assassinate him. I had to deny this for myself outright. I had now served as his adjutant for six years and had seen his trust in me grow steadily. It would have been impossible for me to have turned against him. I was determined to fulfil my obligations irrespective of what might happen. To bring about the change, others would have to do that if they considered it to be the answer.

Exit Engel

At the end of September 1943 Hitler dispensed with the services of Army adjutant Engel. He had dropped a hint about this a year or so earlier but I had thought nothing more of it. I was therefore very surprised when Engel told me one day that Hitler had released him for ordinary Army service. From Engel's reaction I saw that he had been taken completely by surprise. To leave our Adjutantur came as a severe blow to him. I suspected that General Zeitzler had had a hand in it. Engel's successor had already been found. Contrary to the previous terms of reference for the position, a 33-year-old General Staff officer, Major Heinrich Borgmann, had been appointed, and he took up his duties in early October. Borgmann was not at ease in the job and seemed to be constantly on the lookout for something else. He was seriously wounded on 20 July 1944 and was incapacitated for some time afterwards.

In the autumn of 1943 the war entered a ferocious stage. The morale of the German front soldier was admirable. Of the millions who wore Army uniform, only a relatively small number were involved in the immediate fighting at the front. Supply and catering formed a considerable part of the Army's function. Hitler regularly issued instructions to comb through the support services and reserves for young men to put at the front. I do not know why these efforts to find large numbers of young replacements only ever had moderate success. All Army front-line units were under strength. Battalion commanders were happy if they commanded 200 to 300 men. If there was an action, the numbers were quickly cut. But the morale of the men, their readiness and their will to fight, were constant, and Hitler's role as Führer was undisputed. Many men were absolutely convinced that Hitler had weapons in preparation which would pave the way to victory. Those such as myself who had an overview of the situation knew to the contrary—that defeat was just a question of time.

Landings in Italy

In September 1943 the Allies landed in southern Italy. They moved up northwards relatively quickly as far as Naples and Foggia. The latter seemed very important to them: there were airfields there and favourable terrain to lay down more. This they accomplished in a few weeks. In October the Americans flew their first major air raid from Foggia against the Messerschmitt factories at Wiener Neustadt which turned out the Me 109. Hitler sent me there at once in order to obtain clarification of the conflicting reports submitted by the flak units and Homeland Air Defence organisation about the strength and success of the attack. I had already experienced the impenetrability of the secret world of air defences. The responsible commanders here had not seen very much of what went on since there was no protected observation point where an air raid could be watched from beginning to end.

By the beginning of October almost 300,000 Italian soldiers had been transported to Germany as prisoners-of-war and put to work. The Allied land forces took their time coming up from southern Italy and Kesselring, C-in-C South-West Army Group, was not only able to marshal his few forces for a spirited defence but became so firmly established that he allayed Hitler's fears about the Italian Front. Eventually the theatre was left in his hands and Hitler hardly ever interfered there.

Further Intensification of the Air War

The Reich was becoming more and more the hapless target for British air raids. On 7 September Hitler asked Professor Messerschmitt how things stood with the Me 262, and, to everybody's surprise, if it could also be used as a bomber. Messerschmitt said that it could, and added that Milch was always making difficulties and not putting a sufficient workforce at his disposal. This struggle between Messerschmitt and Milch had been smouldering for years. Explaining the problem to Hitler, I told him that Messerschmitt had already exceeded his entitlement having regard to the stage his developments were justifying. He had a knack of presenting individual achievements in such a way that it seemed he was ready to mass-produce. I requested Hitler to discuss the question again with Milch.

Hitler's main preoccupation at this time was anti-aircraft defence. He racked his brain day and night for new ways to reduce the effects of the bombing. Earlier he had left this job to Göring, but even the latter was now dissatisfied with results. Therefore Hitler consulted only the Chief of the Luftwaffe General Staff on Luftwaffe questions and ignored Göring, who began to appear more infrequently at daily situation conferences. The air raids increased. On 2 October the fighter factory at Emden was seriously damaged, on the 4th the industrial area of Frankfurt and on the 10th Münster and Anklam in Pomerania. On 14 October the Americans carried out a heavy raid on Schweinfurt which virtually paralysed ball-bearing production. On this occasion the bombers suffered heavy losses. After this latter German success, which was due primarily to Hitler's persistent criticisms, the daylight attacks stopped. The British night attacks against cities continued, however, and Hanover, Leipzig and Kassel also received attention.

On 5 October Hitler discussed with Göring and Korten how the day attacks could be ended permanently. Hitler said that the major part of the fighter force ought to be concentrated to oppose the enemy bomber fleets. It was important to prevent the destruction of our production centres. After every air raid Hitler received reports from the appropriate Gauleiter. He was therefore in the picture about the completely inadequate Air Raid Defence organisation. Often during the day attacks it was next to useless. When fighters could not get up because of bad weather or were occupied elsewhere, this made Hitler especially irate. What made it worse was when bombers protected by enemy fighters were not engaged by our fighters because of poor direction techniques. At situation conferences Hitler was able to present detailed reports about individual air raids and was swift to jump to conclusions based partly on his misunderstanding of air defence and partly on the conflicting reports submitted.

Hitler had been made aware of the Japanese kamikaze phenomenon, which had been advocated repeatedly in Luftwaffe circles on the premise that the sacrifice was justified if victory resulted as a consequence. He was not of this view. He thought that inspired, selfless commitment for the Fatherland was right, but this price was too high. The names of volunteers were noted, however, in case the need for German kamikazes should ever arise in the future.

On 7 October the Gau- and Reichsleiters were summoned to Wolfschanze to be instructed as to the unfavourable situation and the future difficulties to be overcome. Hitler emphasised that the will of the people and 'unremitting perseverance in pursuit of the goal' must remain constant, continuing: 'Your warrior spirit, your energy, your firm resolve and utter readiness give the people backbone and steadiness to withstand above all the violence of the bomber war.' He closed with words expressing his unshakeable confidence in victory and succeeded in convincing his devoted listeners, who then returned to their Gaue in the firm belief that he had in preparation certain weapons which would yet win this war for Germany; his 'Decree Respecting Preparations to Reconstruct Bomb-Damaged Cities' reinforced their hopes.

Hitler's Intransigence
Hitler foresaw threatening developments on the Eastern Front earlier and with greater clarity than his military advisers, but he was determined

with great obstinacy not to accede to the requests of his Army commanders to pull back fronts, or would do so exceptionally only at the last
minute. The Crimea was to be held at whatever cost, and he refused to
entertain Manstein's arguments in the matter.

In October Saporoshye and Dnyepropetrovsk were lost. On 6 November Kiev fell and fierce fighting continued in the bend of the Dnieper,
yet Hitler informed Zeitzler and Jodl that our first priority was the Italian Front and the bomber war. He viewed the Russian victories on the
Eastern Front with a certain equanimity and was resting his hopes on a
new offensive in the New Year and on the new weapons which would
then be at his disposal. Zeitzler did not believe a word of it but Jodl still
cherished certain hopes for the success of the new weapons.

Getting Ready for the Invasion
On 3 November Directive No 51 was issued. It said: 'The danger in the
East remains but a greater threatens to the West—the Anglo-Saxon landings. In the East, in the worst scenario, the vast size of the territory allows a loss of ground even on the large scale without delivering us a
mortal blow. But it is different in the West! If the enemy breaks through
our defences here on a broad front, the short-term consequences are
unforeseeable. Signs indicate that the enemy will launch an invasion of
the European Western Front at the latest by the spring, but perhaps even
earlier. I can therefore no longer allow the West to be further weakened
in favour of other theatres. I have decided to strengthen its defences at
the place where we will commence the long- range battle against England. For it is there that the enemy has to attack, there—if we are not
deceived—that the decisive landing battles will be fought.' Although
drafted by Jodl, it was completely Hitler's style. He was only wrong about
when. He expected the Normandy invasion at the beginning of 1944.

On 5 November Hitler appointed Rommel as C-in-C Special Purposes and the responsibility for fortifying the invasion front devolved on
him. He had full responsibility for the security of the French coastline.
At the time Rommel was still an unconditional follower of Hitler and
obeyed his orders without protest. Accordingly he threw himself whole-
heartedly into his new task.

When Manstein, beset with grave anxieties about the Kiev region and
Crimea, discussed the subject on 7 November, Hitler, who was not open
to reason regarding the Crimea or Nikopol—on account of its

manganese ore mines—released three divisions involved in the shipments with instructions that they were to be used on the Crimean front and not in the fighting for Kiev. Thus he was accepting a high risk on the Eastern Front.

Air raid defence remained in the foreground. 'Aviation' was the decisive keyword for 1944, and Hitler considered the fast bomber to be the most important factor entering the equation. Repeatedly he asked how the Me 262 was coming along: he was impatient on account of the long delivery date for the aircraft.

On 8 November Hitler addressed Party veterans in Munich. As usual he spoke very frankly to this circle, mentioning the extraordinary severity of the fighting in Russia and the impressive achievements of our soldiers there. But he also referred to 'the bestial bombing raids' on German cities and the sufferings of German women and children and added: 'This war may last as long as it will but Germany will never capitulate.' The help of Providence was certain and would send us victory.

Despite the continuing adverse reports from the Eastern Front and about the air raids, a restful week was spent at the Berghof afterwards. The horizons were different, and one noticed of Hitler how relaxed he was in the old familiar private atmosphere.

When we returned to Wolfschanze on 16 November, Ambassador von Papen was waiting for Hitler. Papen knew that a few days previously the enemy Foreign Ministers had met in Moscow; Roosevelt, Churchill and Stalin would meet again shortly. Papen had long been carrying on a successful struggle to prevent the Allies drawing Turkey into their camp. Now he had a highly secret report to communicate: in Ankara the manservant of the British ambassador was supplying him with secret documents for cash. Papen had with him the first information about Operation 'Overlord' but few details at present. He saw the diplomatic situation as poised on a knife edge and said that the Crimea must absolutely remain in German hands if Turkish neutrality were to be maintained. Every fresh Russian victory endangered stability. Hitler concurred.

Firmness in Defence
The ability of our front to withstand really massive attacks never ceased to amaze me in the late autumn of 1943, but eventually the Soviets succeeded in driving a corridor 150 kilometres deep through the lines of the Second Army and Fourth Panzer Army between Kiev and Gomel. Places

such as Shitomir were recaptured, but generally the Russians did not capitalise on it. Their attacks against Army Groups North and Centre also faltered. In the south, against Army Group A, they crossed the Dnieper and pushed forward their front along a line Cherson–Nikopol–Krivoi Rog–Kirovograd. The penetration from Melitopol to the Dnieper was especially damaging. The Russians were very adept at identifying and attacking at the join between Army Groups.

On 20 November Hitler flew to Breslau to address senior cadets of all Wehrmacht branches in the Jahrhunderthalle—since the destruction of the Sportpalast this annual speech could not be held in Berlin—and the current officer intake took to heart his grave admonition that 'the *Volk*, if we lose, ends its existence'. Therefore every German soldier must be aware that 'this gruelling war, which our enemies accuse us of starting, but which they wanted, and have forced us into, can have no other ending than a German victory. In order to achieve this victory, everyone must be filled with a single unshakeable belief in our eternal Germany.' Keitel concluded the address with a recognition of Hitler, who left the hall to a storming ovation and shouts of *Sieg Heil!* from the cadets. He was not unimpressed by this echo.

The Me 262 Displayed

Air raids on 22 and 23 November caused substantial devastation to the heart of Berlin. The Gauleiter of Berlin, Dr Groeb, reported personally to Hitler and made particular mention of the outstanding morale shown by the people of the city over the two nights. Hitler was again filled with rage and anger against the Luftwaffe, which was never able to stop a raid taking place. He repeated these criticisms in bitter terms on 26 November at the impatiently awaited aircraft exhibition at Insterburg airfield. All those in some way responsible for aircraft production were present—Göring, Milch, Speer, Saur, Messerschmitt, Galland, Vorwald and others. In my opinion the Luftwaffe had repeated the error here of setting out mostly those models which were not yet ready for service. Hitler passed very calmly before the long line of aircraft, which included the newest version of the Me 109, the Me 410, Ar 234, Do 335 and Me 262. Milch accompanied him with full specifications to hand. Hitler was seeing the Me 262 for the first time and was very impressed by the look of it. He called Messerschmitt over and asked him pointedly if the aircraft could be built as a bomber. The designer agreed, and said that it would be capable of carrying two 250kg bombs. Hitler said, 'That is the fast bomber' and gave orders that the Me 262 should be built exclusively as such. Milch intervened at once to explain that only a number of the aircraft coming off the production line could be released to the bomber role, but Hitler insisted. Even Göring, when attempting to have Hitler's decision reversed a few days later, was rebuffed sharply. As it turned out, however, the Luftwaffe could only offer the type as a fighter-bomber because a true fast bomber would need extensive redesign for bomb carriage, release gear and sights. Hitler was forced to accept this. On our return to Wolfschanze I tackled him on the subject in the hope of saving the Me 262 for its fighter role. He replied that in principle I was right and he wanted as many fighters as possible for the Reich, bearing in mind the existing problems—the worst of which would be the Allied landings in France. We had to do everything to prevent this.

Teheran
The Teheran Conference took place on 28 November. Roosevelt, Church-ill and Stalin spent a week there with a large staff of officers and politi-cians. The results of this conference seeped through gradually, mainly through Papen's source in the British Embassy at Ankara. There had obviously been serious difficulties at Teheran, particularly on the subject of where the landings would take place. Roosevelt had got his way over Churchill for northern France; Churchill wanted to go for northern Greece. Hitler decided from this that Churchill wanted to drive a wedge between the Germans and Russians. The Russians would not agree to this as it would tend to rob them of the influence they wanted in the Balkans. Hitler assumed from Papen's reports that the invasion was still some way off and ordered a build-up of defence units on the Channel coast.

December on the Russian Front was less active than feared. The bomb-ing of the Reich had also slackened while the British concentrated on picking off the 96 V-1 launch ramps. They knocked out a quarter but these could be replaced. Apparently they worried the British and this gave Hitler a reason to step up production of these flying bombs. He regretted only that they were not immediately available for use.

In December Hitler ordered the setting up of a National Socialist Command Staff at OKW. General Reinecke was appointed Chief of Staff. The intention had been in the wind for some time and had been much discussed in Army circles. Hitler had been convinced of the need by Himmler, Bormann and many SS officers that his internal opponents were spreading anti-National Socialist propaganda through the fighting fronts. Most dangerous were the 'Seydlitz officers', who disseminated propaganda urging officers and men to give up fighting. Reinecke was instructed to form and train a National Socialist Command Officer Corps for the front. This went ahead in 1944. The organisation found some recognition since these NSFOs were active in the welfare field, but many commanders would not have them around. The way in which the war developed prevented the institution from realising its full potential.

Situation at the End of 1943

In 1943, for the first time in the war, I spent Christmas at home with my family. I was confronted by the realities upon my return to Wolfschanze. On 26 December Dönitz reported the sinking of *Scharnhorst*. The battleship had sailed out alone to attack an eastbound convoy in the Arctic and had been intercepted by a superior enemy naval force. Hitler was blameless here: for some time he had condemned the use of heavy units against enemy convoys as senseless.

The Russians had resumed their offensive on the Eastern Front; the first impressions suggested that a major offensive was brewing. Hitler spent New Year's Eve alone in his private rooms with Bormann. What was discussed between them is not recorded.

In 1943 the Russians had driven us back from the Don to the Dnieper and an Army Group Centre section from the gates of Moscow to the other side of Smolensk. It was difficult to divine Hitler's real beliefs about the situation. I attemped to form a picture composed of all the pros and cons. I had a number of conversations with him and noticed how often he contradicted himself. The Russian victories of 1943 had not worried him too much. The German front lines stood well in advance of our borders. There was still plenty of space in which to operate. The great danger, besides the increasing Russian pressure, seemed to be our failing strength. I was not sure if he was seeing things correctly. In my opinion we stood in a very much worse position altogether that at the end of 1942.

The Army Group commanders consulted him much more frequently, usually seeking leave to bring the front back to spare their forces and build up urgently needed reserves. But Hitler would rarely agree. The result was a severe blood-letting. The senior commanders had come to the stage where they despaired of ever understanding his leadership. For his part Hitler could not understand why the senior commanders had lost confidence in him. Yet he would fight on, for there was really no other way. Defensive successes of very short-term value reinforced his confidence, yet he hardly noticed the catastrophic casualty lists. The prospect of rest and replacement was so remote that most had given up hope of it. Despite all this, if the mass of fighting men looked with confidence to the New Year, this was due entirely to their belief in Hitler. To the extent that the commanding generals had lost their unconditional belief in Hitler, to that same extent the simple German soldier trusted in his unerring leadership. I had no doubt that this fact alone was responsible for the fronts holding together.

During 1943 the importance of the Waffen-SS had increased. At the beginning of the war, and more so since the beginning of the Russian campaign, Hitler had built up these divisions systematically. They embodied all his ideas for a fighting force. Division after division was formed, privileged as to its personnel and *matériel*. Thus there had slowly emerged a fourth arm of the Wehrmacht which by 1943, and more so in 1944, was put to especially endangered sectors of the front. Hitler was extraordinarily proud of these SS divisions and trusted in them and their commanders utterly.

At the year's end I reflected most frequently on how the bomber war would progress. It was quite obvious that we could never make up the leeway between the Luftwaffe and the Allied air forces. Hitler believed that the fighter groups would have new aircraft during the coming spring or summer. I told him that I considered this unlikely. I hoped only that the efforts of Milch to increase the production figures for the old well-known types such as Me 109 and FW 190 would be successful so that our squadrons would have at least have material replacements to be going on with. Nothing more could be expected for 1944. For some time I had not believed in victory, but neither did I foresee defeat. At the end of 1943 I was convinced that Hitler could still find a political and military solution. In this paradoxical belief I was not alone.

CHAPTER SIX

1944

The problems in the armaments field had been heightened by the enemy bombing of recent weeks, which had disrupted production severely. Repairs and rebuilding took time, and this time factor was critical. Speer had a knee injury and a pulmonary disorder, for which he was admitted to Hohenlychen military hospital. His representative for Army armaments was Saur, an unusually active rival of Speer with an unacceptably ruthless disposition. Milch was the minister with full authority for Luftwaffe armament; he was subordinate only to Göring. Saur was not in the least interested in what the Luftwaffe wanted and rubber-stamped the armaments decisions which suited Hitler.

Armaments Conference
On 4 January, before Speer's illness, Hitler had held an armaments conference at Wolfschanze attended by Milch, Keitel, Speer, Backe, Himmler and Sauckel, the main theme being the labour programme. Sauckel had pledged to procure four million workers, for which Hitler promised his full support. He was demanding increased output of the new U-boats and jet aircraft. He had gained a false impression at the Insterburg exhibition of the date of readiness and thought that the first machines with bomb-carrying and release gear would be available at the front in February. This was not possible because the bomb mechanism and sights had to be manufactured and would not be ready until May. He had not been advised of this.

With great satisfaction he learned that a special court sitting at Verona on 10 January had condemned to death all members of the Grand Fascist Council which had deposed Mussolini on 24 July 1943. Five of them were arrested and shot the next morning. Mussolini's son-in-law Ciano was amongst them. His wife Edda fled to Switzerland.

On 27 January Hitler delivered a long address to the Wehrmacht field marshals and generals. Two days beforehand they had received in Posen various instructions and had had to listen to a speech by Himmler. Hitler's speech at Wolfschanze completed the course. He spoke about the development of the National Socialist idea in the people as we had experienced it. There was a moment of drama about three-quarters of the way through it. Hitler had said, 'In the last contingency, if I as Supreme Leader should be deserted at any time, I must ultimately expect to be surrounded by the entire officer corps with swords drawn for my protection just as every field marshal, every commanding general, every divisional leader and every regimental commander expects that his subordinates will stand by him likewise in the critical hour.' At this Manstein made a loud interruption 'So will it be, *mein Führer*!' Hitler went on: 'That is fine. If that will be so, then it will never be possible to lose this war . . . I am glad to know that, Feldmarschall von Manstein.' But Hitler had interpreted this interruption in another sense. He saw in the remark a criticism of himself that he, Hitler, distrusted the officer corps. I have no idea if that was what Manstein was saying in a veiled manner. I did not have that impression at the time, for I was convinced of Manstein's honesty. Hitler continued to speak for another half an hour and then concluded with the words: 'I have no other wish than to comply with the natural law that says only he earns life who fights for it and is ready, if necessary, to sacrifice his life for it.'

The Crimea Lost

The war in Russia dragged on with undiminished bitterness. Hitler continued to demand that Nikopol and the Crimea be held, but both were lost in the course of the next few weeks, Nikopol on 8 February and the Crimea in the first half of May. Following the fall of the Crimea, Turkey blocked its supplies of chrome ore as Hitler feared she would. At other sectors of the front the Russians were being held, but these successes were only temporary. It was almost unbelievable how many new units the Russians were able to keep throwing into the fray whilst the same old German troops were gradually being worn down. There were no replacements in Germany; fresh divisions had to be brought up from the south and France. Hitler had to accept that the German perimeter was shrinking. On 10 April Odessa fell. At the end of the month the Russians were along the Tarnopol–Kovel line. Here they stopped when the muddy season arrived. Army Group North was being driven back more slowly, and after heavy fighting and casualties was at the Peipus Sea in March.

Manstein and Kleist Relieved

At the end of January Hitler had replaced von Küchler by Model. On 30 March he summoned Manstein and Kleist to the Berghof and relieved them of command. Manstein received the Swords to his Oak Leaves, but his dismissal left an unpleasant aftertaste. In both cases Hitler proceeded in such a tactful manner that Manstein thought Göring and Himmler had forced him out. That Hitler had decided to part with Manstein and Kleist was due to their disagreement with his current military thinking. It was also at this time that Zeitzler requested to be replaced. Hitler declined emphatically. Model was appointed to succeed Manstein while Schörner took over from Kleist. Hitler expected from them greater determination and ruthlessness in leadership. He said repeatedly that 1943 had cost the Russians many casualties and Stalin's might was beginning to disintegrate. Whether that was his true opinion I had no way of knowing. He fluctuated between sober observations and unfounded confidence. Whatever the source of the latter, it was not Zeitzler's grim situation reports. Hitler also spoke repeatedly of a possible breach between East and West in the Allied ranks. Here he was overvaluing certain Russian chess moves, behind which I saw Stalin's ice-cold calculations to render his allies pliant.

War in Italy

On the Italian Front, fighting resumed on 4 January. The British and American forces operated jointly and apparently not with particular harmony; moreover, their operations needed long periods of preparation. South of the Cassino Massif they made a slow advance. Even the successful American landings at Nettuno brought no immediate pressure on us. They needed eight full days before launching their first attack northwards. Kesselring used the time to erect a successful defensive line. Hitler had pulled troops out of France and the Balkans and demanded that an ignominoious defeat be inflicted on the Americans. On 14 February, the day before their next attack, the Americans bombed the monastery of Monte Cassino to rubble. The irreplaceable art treasures of the abbey had previously been brought to safety. There were no German troops in the monastery precincts but the Americans decided to destroy it all the same. It was an act of pure vandalism. The monks and other residents took refuge in the extensive subterranean vaults and suffered no casualties.

Air Attacks on Armaments Plants

The terror bombing of the Reich increased after New Year. On 11 January USAAF bombers made daylight raids on the Luftwaffe factories at Halberstadt, Oschersleben, Brunswick and Magdeburg. They lost 59 aircraft shot down for 40 German fighters. The Luftwaffe decided that this should go down as a victory. It had a certain deterrent effect because it put the Americans off daylight raids for a month, although on 20 January the British made a heavy night raid on Berlin which caused many civilian casualties. The armaments factories escaped significant damage. Goebbels telephoned his report to Hitler and next morning there followed another outpouring against the Luftwaffe.

On 20 February the USAAF resumed daylight raids accompanied by British and American long-range fighters. Their targets were the fighter factories around Leipzig and the ball-bearing works at Schweinfurt, Stuttgart and Augsburg. Some of these installations were up to 75 per cent destroyed, and fighter production declined by up to 800 machines per month. These recurrent attacks reduced the Luftwaffe armaments programme to such a sorry state that Milch visited Speer in hospital to see whether he would take over fighter production. Speer saw the necessity, and after five more days' continual bombing of fighter factories by the Americans the decision was taken to transfer Fighter Staff to Saur.

Rumours of Assassination

Some time in February Hitler's Press officer drew his attention to an article in a Stockholm newspaper which stated that a German Army General Staff officer had been found to assassinate Hitler with a pistol shot. Hitler sent for me, showed me the cutting and told me to do everything I could to prevent such an attempt being made. I discussed possible measures with the FHQ Kommandant, SS-Standartenführer Rattenhuber, who was responsible for Hitler's personal protection. We agreed that with immediate effect we ought at least to introduce a control of briefcases, if not also to search visitors thoroughly for concealed weapons. I asked Hitler how far the controls should go. He replied that all visitors should be under constant observation and heavy file cases for example should be watched. He declined to have the strict system of control which Rattenhuber and I had suggested. The new measures did not come into effect in East Prussia for a few days after this conversation. Meanwhile we travelled by his train to Berchtesgaden while the walls and ceiling of his bunker were fortified with more concrete. Upon our arrival I enquired as to what system of security for the control of visitors he proposed to introduce at the Berghof. He was averse even to discussing it and said he would speak with Rattenhuber. I do not know if her ever did; in any case, I never saw any visible change to the previous security measures.

Hanna Reitsch

On 28 February Flugkapitän Hanna Reitsch was invited to the Berghof to receive from Hitler the award of the Iron Cross First Class and a certificate designed especially by Frau Troost in Munich. The three of us took tea in the large hall. Hanna Reitsch quickly seized the opportunity to speak on her favourite theme of the day and suggested that a kamikaze squad be formed in Germany and if necessary deployed. She informed Hitler of the early preparations which were already in hand and asked for his blessing. Hitler was completely opposed to the idea of self-sacrifice. He spoke out against the idea at length, referring to the new military weapons under development by the Kriegsmarine and Luftwaffe and the imminent introduction of the new jet aircraft. Hanna Reitsch knew all about the problems of Luftwaffe production, including the long delivery date for the Me 262, and told Hitler so. He was taken aback by her frankness and retorted that she was not informed as to the present stage of progress and could therefore not judge the situation correctly. I was pleased that Hitler had heard of the production fiasco from another source. Yet he appeared unimpressed and preferred to rely on the false understanding he had and of which Luftwaffe Staff had not so far disabused him.

Hanna Reitsch did obtain Hitler's grudging consent to preparations for a kamikaze commando, although Hitler stressed that he did not wish to be kept informed of its progress in the preliminary stages. When Hanna Reitsch departed she left behind a long shadow. Hitler's doubts about the completion dates of the jet aircraft had been awakened. That evening I had a long conversation with him about her visit. He set very great store by her personal devotion to duty but remarked that suicide operations could not help the situation. I reminded him of her reservations about the series production and operational readiness of the Me 262. He replied that the Luftwaffe had informed him otherwise, and they must stick to the set dates without question. It was clear to me that evening that he was basing his expectations on a false premise. The Luftwaffe production estimates could only be realised if the centres of production remained undamaged. This could not be guaranteed because the British and American air raids were being aimed with great success at precision targets and the constant relocation of production areas was costing precious time.

Führerbefehl 11

At the beginning of March Hitler authorised the Army General Staff to issue Führerbefehl 11 for 'Strongpoint Commandants and Battle Commandants'. This directive explained that 'strongpoints fulfilled the same function as the earlier fortifications'. Their commandants were to be 'specially selected hardened soldiers'. There followed very detailed supplementary guidelines and orders respecting strongpoints—orders which made very high demands quite impossible of achievement in view of the situation. Hitler persevered with the idea of strongpoints, but in the event the various Russian and American offensives would simply roll over them.

On 2 April Hitler had the Army General Staff issue an order for further Army Group operations in the East. It stated that the Russian offensive to the south of the front had passed its climax: 'The Russian has worn down and divided his units. The time is now ripe finally to bring the Russian advance to a halt.' In the subsequent text, Hitler mentioned the break-out of Hube's Panzer Army from encirclement at Kamenets-Podolsk, which had succeeded despite heavy losses in men and *matériel*. There could be no talk of bringing the Russian advance 'finally' to a halt, however, and this order showed how Hitler was beginning to drift away from the true state of affairs.

My Uncle's Funeral

On 16 March—a few days before Göring's adjutant Bernd Brauchitsch and I had been promoted to Oberst ahead of seniority—Hitler granted me leave to attend the funeral of my uncle, who had died at the age of 87. The Göttingen Military Cemetery was a worthy resting place. I had a chance to speak to his son-in-law, Major von Borries. He was quartermaster of an Army Group North army corps and complained bitterly about the miserable supply situation. He had lodged repeated complaints with the appropriate OKH bureaux without success. This seemed inexplicable to me, and on my return to the Berghof I initiated enquiries into the foul-up. Borries told me later that at the end of July supply had been mysteriously restored.

Hungary Occupied

We remained at the Berghof—Hitler had invited my wife to join me there—until 16 July. On our return to Wolfschanze that day I saw a meeting scheduled with Admiral Horthy. Hitler was very put out by the latest Hungarian moves, which suggested to him a *volte-face* after the Italian example. Horthy arrived at Schloss Klesheim on the morning of 18 March. Hitler told him at once that German troops would occupy Hungary the next morning. Horthy replied that if that were the case he might as well go straight home. His departure was delayed by a fictitious air raid alarm and eventually he composed himself sufficiently to converse with Hitler that afternoon before boarding his train for Budapest. During the night German troops occupied Hungary. When Horthy arrived in Budapest next morning he found a German sentry at either portal of his front door. Thus was the Hungarian problem successfully resolved for the time being.

New Moves in Armaments Production

At the Berghof during the period March to May, Hitler's main interest had been armaments. The fronts in Russia and Italy had fallen eerily quiet. Hitler expected the invasion in France at any moment but the enemy seemed content to just continue the bombing. Rommel worked intensely at fortifying the Atlantic Wall. Hitler spoke very often about the new, secret U-boat types and jet aircraft, and told visiting armaments experts that if he had them he could prevent the invasion.

At the beginning of April Hitler pursued very thoroughgoing talks with Xavier Dorsch, leader of the Todt Organisation, about bomb-proof factories for fighters. What he had in mind here was the subterranean type of factory as at Nordhausen in the Harz mountains, where several thousand concentration camp inmates were working on the V-2. Dorsch received orders to look for other possible sites for underground factories.

In a conversation with Milch and Saur, Hitler agreed that, from March, the production of fighters had priority, and he ordered an increase in the monthly output of fighters for April. This order was a tacit admission that he now accepted the delay in delivering the Me 262.

Very heavy air raids on Berlin on 6 and 8 March, and on Nuremberg on the 30th, gave Hitler fresh ammunition to launch a blistering tirade at the Air Raid Defence organisation and the Luftwaffe. Here he overlooked completely the courageous engagements by our numerically inferior fighter force. Over Berlin the enemy had lost 79, and over Nuremberg 95 aircraft shot down. The Luftwaffe expressed satisfaction with the outcome, but Hitler demanded that higher numbers of aircraft be destroyed. This was not really possible because we lacked night fighters in numbers. Nevertheless the massacre of enemy bombers over Nuremberg brought about a reduction in British night raids.

A New FHQ?

A scheme which came in for much private criticism was the construction of a large new FHQ in Silesia near Waldenburg. The plan also meant that Prince Pless would have to vacate Schloss Fürstenstein. Hitler defended his instructions and ordered that the construction go ahead. Concentration camp inmates were set to work under Speer's direction. I visited this project twice in the course of the year and had the impression from the size of the undertaking that it would never be completed. I asked Speer if it would not be possible to influence Hitler to have it stopped, but Speer said that would be impossible. The work stretched far into the future and required huge quantities of cement and steel which were urgently required elsewhere.

Hitler celebrated his 55th birthday at the Berghof but was not in the mood for festivities. Before the midday conference he accepted the congratulations of his house staff and in the dining room settled down in a quiet corner to open a pile of presents from close friends. When Zeitzler arrived, however, he went at once to the hall for military discussions. Göring and Dönitz also put in an appearance to present the birthday greetings of their respective arms of service.

The Death of Hube

Another visitor was Hube, fresh from his dramatic success of extricating the First Panzer Army from the Kamenets-Podolsk pocket and breaking through to the German lines north of Czernowitz. It was a brilliant achievement, and Hitler expressed his special recognition by awarding Hube the Diamonds to his Oak Leaves and promotion to Generaloberst. Hube delivered a very detailed report about the state of the front, after which a long conversation ensued. Hitler was thinking of making Hube Army C-in-C. Schmundt had advised this but Hitler had not made the appointment at the time when the tragedy happened.

As Hube left the Führer's presence later that evening, I mentioned to Hitler that Hube was proposing to fly to Berlin in darkness and in an aircraft of the OKH courier staff. This needed Hitler's consent, which he gave, instructing me to select a good crew from the courier staff and to make a thorough preparation for the flight. I did so and had the impression that everything possible had been done to ensure a safe take-off. I was awoken in the early hours and learned to my horror that Hube's aircraft had crashed. Hube was dead, his companion Hewel injured. When I informed Hitler of the accident he received the news quietly as he had done two years before when Todt was killed. A few days later a memorial service was held at Schloss Klesheim at which Hitler was present. I flew to Berlin to attend the burial at the Invaliden Cemetery next day. I had known Hube since 1930 and had kept in touch with him ever since. I felt the loss of this outstanding man keenly.

Speer's Return

At about this time Speer came to Obersalzberg to inform Hitler that he had recovered sufficiently to resume work. As Hitler was currently more preoccupied by armaments than operations at the front, the best place to be was close to Hitler. During his absence he had been aware of the continuing intrigues to railroad parts of the programme and in some fields there was complete confusion. Certain personalities needed to be replaced. Firm, clear leadership was essential. He did not return to Berlin until mid-May, but he had all the strings in his hands again and attended the daily conferences to keep Hitler informed. These were the last few quiet weeks of the war. Speer considered that he had to maintain Hitler's confidence even if he had distanced himself inwardly from Hitler and ignored many of his instructions. Hitler was not deceived. He knew that Speer was no longer convinced of victory.

In these three months, March to May 1944, I had many conversations with Hitler, who began to confide in me thoughts which until then he had kept private. Once he said that despite his lack of confidence in victory, Speer was the only man who understood the infrastructure of the armaments empire. The industry recognised him unreservedly and I once heard it said, 'When we need especially important war materials,

Speer is the only person who can get them rushed through.' After Speer had resumed his grip on affairs the trust between Hitler and Speer was quickly restored.

Hitler and Göring

I often received Hitler's views about Göring. He knew the Reichsmarschall of old and and described him as 'brutal and ice cold' in a crisis: 'He is an iron-hard and ruthless man. In the most difficult of crises Göring is the right man to have on the spot.' His vanities and love of luxury were superficialities which fell away when the hour came. I was surprised that Hitler still held him in such high regard. I had often been present recently when Hitler had sent for Göring to receive a sharp rebuke. When I told Hitler that I could not reconcile this sort of thing with his positive judgement of Göring, he replied that he had to be sharp with him occasionally because the Reichsmarschall was inclined to issue orders without bothering to ensure that they were carried out. Göring was often wounded deeply by these criticisms. Once he confessed to me, 'Hitler treats me like a stupid boy'—and that was just how it looked when Hitler gave him a telling off. Over the last two years I had had cause to mention certain matters to Hitler which amounted to a criticism of Göring. I was always nonplussed at how Hitler accepted these reports in silence. I never knew if he ever spoke to Göring about any of them, but if he did I am sure that he never let on that I was the source, for Göring retained the same friendliness towards me to the end.

How Hitler's respect for Göring was reciprocated I observed during a journey to Berlin in Göring's private train in the autumn of 1943. At the evening buffet, in a very relaxed atmosphere, Göring told me of Hitler's positive attitude towards me personally. He also spoke of the high regard in which Hitler was still held by the German people. This confidence was based on the belief that in Adolf Hitler Providence had sent them the man who would rectify all the injustices inflicted on Germany since November 1918. This idea went so deep that a German defeat was unimaginable to them. I saw from this remark that Göring was still firm in his belief in Hitler, for he was the type of man who called a spade a spade.

Peaceful Days at the Berghof

In these many weeks at the Berghof—except for the regular situation conferences—Hitler returned to the old routine that had prevailed pre-war. He enjoyed very much the table conversations he had with my wife. Usually they spoke about our children or the farming on the family estate. It was embarrassing for me when he told her occasionally how happy he was to have me on his staff. He thanked her frequently for having forged such a good friendship with Eva Braun. From many evening fireside chats I realised that Hitler was really a man without contradictions. Despite many assertions to the contrary subsequently, I could not say that he was always changing his opinions about things. His judgements of people, historical personalites and history remained the same. He spoke a great deal about his ideal of the European State in which it would be his objective to fight Jews and Communists and to destroy their influence in the world in every respect. He believed firmly that Providence had given him this task. He had an astonishing 'sixth sense' for events, and it was disturbing now to observe how his contact with reality was tending to slip away.

Anger Over the Me 262

At the daily situation conferences the enemy build-up for the Channel invasion, and the resumption of operations in Russia and Italy, could be discerned as imminent. At the centrepoint of Hitler's considerations was the Me 262. In the end his desire to have it as a fighter-bomber failed owing to unsurmountable technical difficulties, principally the alteration to the centre of gravity in the fuselage: a bomb-carrying capacity practically deprived it of airworthiness. It was definitely completely unsuitable as a bomber. In a long talk at Obersalzberg on 23 May Göring explained all this to Hitler, who refused to accept the report. As far as possible he wanted 'all superfluous equipment' to be removed from the aircraft to make weight for at least one 250kg bomb. Milch, Galland, Petersen—the commanders of the Luftwaffe test centres—and others were unable to convince him that it would not work. Thus we simply had to wait until Hitler found out the hard way.

I set everything down in a memorandum and took up the subject with him again one evening. I succeeded in convincing him of the special technical difficulties of the jet in comparison to propeller aircraft. Hitler conceded that altering the purpose of the Me 262 from fighter to bomber would create technical problems, but these had to be taken into account. I explained that my reservations were valid only for the change in purpose; as a fighter the type was first class. It was a very long conversation.

Hitler regretted only that the jet bomber design had not been contracted for earlier. I answered him by pointing to the postponement of the Luftwaffe production programme in favour of the Army since 1940.

These conversations about the Luftwaffe led to a decision at the end of May that the entire responsibility for Luftwaffe production should come under the umbrella of Speer's ministry. The transfer was made in early June, after which Milch was relieved of his duties and retired to his hunting lodge north of Berlin. He was in the picture as no other about Luftwaffe production problems and knew that the air force was not adequate for the demands to be made on it in the near future. During the spring, when I visited him with my wife, we had a long talk and therefore I knew his honest opinion as to how the war was likely to proceed. He had never been shy of stating his views to Hitler and Göring, but the problem with Hitler was that he was always looking for a new solution and would not meet a problem head on.

Attacks on Our Hydrogen Works

In May the USAAF began daylight raids on our hydrogen works. The Leuna Werke at Merseburg, and at Plönitz north of Stettin, were the first to be attacked. The damage was substantial and reports stated that production would be suspended long term. Hitler insisted on an immediate resumption of production. A vast force of Todt Organisation workers was set to the task of rebuilding, and after a few weeks the factories were almost as good as new until fresh bombing put them out of action again. In subsequent months we always managed to repair bomb damage at hydrogen works in a relatively short space of time to enable the fuel requirements of the Wehrmacht to be met, even if they had to accept severe rationing.

A New Job

On 22 May Speer invited me to be his liaison officer to Hitler at FHQ, Hitler having previously given his assent. Speer was now so engrossed in his task that he found it advisable to keep Hitler informed with running reports. Almost every week he sent me a memorandum to pass on. This would be as likely to contain information about damaged factories as statistics about panzers, aircraft and munitions. Hitler usually read these reports upon receipt and would have me note down his reply to phone through to Speer at once. Co-operation like this between the two of them was very effective. Speer expected the Americans and Russians to launch their major offensives in 1944 and believed that we would not be able to withstand the pressure.

On 11 May an artillery hurricane of forty minutes' duration heralded the resumption of fighting on the Italian Front. Kesselring's units acquitted themselves well, and it was not until 3 June that the Americans were at Rome. Kesselring ordered that there should be no fighting in the city itself and placed his divisions around Rome in such a manner that there would be no street fighting. Even the bridges over the Tiber he had left intact. During June and July German forces withdrew into the Appenines. In August the Americans assembled their first small bridge-head across the Arno.

At the beginning of June Hitler devolved all responsibility for the Italian theatre to Kesselring. It was extraordinary how it became an independent minor threatre with no especial problems except enemy air superiority. Their aircraft flew constant raids against roads and railways during daylight hours, so that German forces moved only by night. Despite this, Kesselring succeeded in holding the front together.

Invasion

The invasion began in the early hours of 6 June. Hitler had been expecting the landings from the beginning of April, whereas OKW considered that no invasion need be reckoned with in 1944 at all on the grounds of the prevailing unfavourable weather conditions. On 4 June Rommel had gone to Ulm for a few days' leave while other army commanders and many General Staff officers were not at their respective HQs. One had the impression that there was a low state of alert in force. On 5 June wireless monitoring had reported indications that the Allies were planning something extraordinary, but neither General Dollman's Seventh Army, which stood directly on the invasion front, nor the OKW at Berchtesgaden, was advised. The general reaction in Normandy seemed to be one of awaiting developments.

In the darkness on 6 June an enormous armada headed for the French coast between the Orne estuary and the eastern side of the Cotentin peninsula near Ste Mère-Église, the sector where Hitler had always anticipated the invasion.

The most punishing blow that morning was the parachute drop by three divisions into the Seventh Army's sector. Enemy air superiority was clear-cut: their aircraft patrolled the skies almost unmolested and our troops were unable to move by day. Hitler was informed of the invasion that same morning. During the midday conference Jodl reported the early details, which left no room for doubt as to the massive scale of the troop landings. Our coastal defences were outnumbered and reinforcements were having to be brought up during the short June night. Hitler expressed relief and said that it would be possible to defeat the invasion. This was expecting a great deal of our troops. Using his air superiority, the enemy had gained a foothold and had succeeded in establishing landing heads on the coastal stretches which could not be removed. By that same evening it was already clear that the invasion was a success.

I was unable to understand Hitler's attitude. He still seemed convinced that the invasion force could be thrown back into the sea despite the enemy's air superiority and the huge amounts of material coming ashore unchecked. The situation was that the Army stood alone, and Hitler was forced to recognise for the first time what enemy air supremacy really meant. His many conversations with Speer on the subject of finding something to oppose it on equal terms were completely unrealistic. I took the opportunity to speak to Hitler about these ideas for the Luftwaffe. I said it was out of the question to think that an upsurge in aircraft production could be brought about in a few weeks. We had to do what we could with the existing fleet, but we were hopelessly inferior to the enemy. He listened quietly. I think he probably accepted what I said, but he still continued to ply Speer and Göring with great demands for aircraft construction.

The V-1

The first batch of V-1 flying bombs was ready for despatch in the second week of June, but the initial launch was a flop. At the last moment OKW brought forward the operation by two days and this interfered with the timetable for completing the heavy prefabricated launching ramps. Two nights later 244 V-1s started off. Recconnaissance aircraft reported numerous fires in and around London. The deployment of the V-1, and from September the V-2 rocket, caused heavy damage in the British capital. The campaign was a triumph for Milch, who had been forcing the project through under great difficulties since mid-1942. Hitler expressed his satisfaction to Milch. The programme lasted only until US and British forces overran the territory in which the launch ramps were sited.

On 16 June I flew with Hitler to Metz, where we joined a road convoy to FHQ Margival near Soissons. Here Hitler had arranged to talk to the Western Front field marshals. This was a thoroughly unpleasant reunion. That morning Rundstedt reported on events over the preceding ten days and implied that he could not eject the Allies from France with the forces at his disposal. Hitler was enraged and pointed with his usual flourish to the V-1 and the Me 262 jet which would soon be making its appearance. The field marshals demanded that the V-1 be used against the build-up of military forces in southern England and the landing places in France. This was not possible because the flying bomb dropped when its revolution counter reached a fixed point and could not be aimed at a target. In the afternoon Hitler had a private conversation with Rommel. I did not find out what was said until a few weeks later. Rommel attempted to convince Hitler that the war was lost and that no effort should be spared to bring about a negotiated peace. This was the last thing that Hitler needed to hear from a field marshal. Voices were raised as Hitler endeavoured to bring Rommel round to his own point of view, but eventually he saw that it would not work. We returned to Metz in the afternoon of 17 June and flew from there to Salzburg. The visit to Margival had been singularly unfruitful, but at least we knew how things stood with the Allied landings.

Allied Advances in the West
When the Americans took the Cotentin peninsula and Cherbourg Hitler flew into a rage and demanded the fullest possible report. This did not affect the catastrophic development. By 20 July the Allies had gone on to erect a front which stretched from the Dives estuary on the west to the west coast of Cotentin at Lessey through St Lô. Hitler viewed this with unease but at least accepted, if with the greatest difficulty, that the enemy had seized the initiative. His prospects were now reduced to hopes of a breach in the Anglo-American alliance. He was firmly convinced that this breach would be decisive for the outcome of the war in Germany's favour and he said as much to all of the many callers at the Berghof from Wehrmacht, state and industry. There were many who left his presence confident and optimistic after this dialogue with him. In his speech to senior officers in the Platterhof at Obersalzberg on 22 June he did not deny the gravity of the situation but expressed to this discriminating circle the hope and belief that the breach would leave the German Reich

free to carry on the struggle. The German officer must be an example and possess the strength to lead his men, come what may. His listeners departed confident, their belief in Hitler reinforced.

The Death of Dietl

That evening General Dietl arrived. There was a danger that the Finns were thinking of a peace treaty with the Soviets. Hitler wanted to concentrate on this theme, but Dietl was concerned with other problems too. He considered that Hitler was badly informed about northern Finland and Norway and had a false picture of the situation. We were surprised at Dietl's clarity of purpose and his sharp tone. He would not let himself be deflected from his agenda. Hitler said little and conceded Dietl's demands for more men and materials. When Dietl left, Hitler complained that only very seldom did he get to hear reports presented in such a manner since most generals, through either temperament, tact or awe, did not feel at liberty to be so candid. Hitler wished only that all his generals were like Dietl.

The subject of his admiration left the Berghof late that evening on a schedule which would return him by air to Norway next day. It came as a terrible shock to learn that his aircraft had crashed on the Semmering, killing all aboard. This loss hit Hitler as hard as the death of Hube three months previously. He confessed this in the obituary which he delivered during the state memorial ceremony at Schloss Klesheim a few days later. He had known Dietl since the early 1920s and referred to him as that officer 'who on the one hand made the hardest demands of his men but on the other was caring as to the fate of his subordinates, to whom he was a true father and friend—a National Socialist therefore not in name only but by his will, by conviction and from the heart'. And this was a good description.

A Second Landing?

The heavy fighting on the invasion front resulted in the submission of confusing and often contradictory reports from the various battle HQs and command posts. The SS units involved in the hardest fighting were still confident. The sober reports of Rundstedt and General Geyr von Schweppenburg, C-in-C Panzer Group West, struck a different chord. To clarify matters from the end of June, Hitler had invited Kluge to attend all military conferences at the Berghof, unsuspecting of Kluge's close connections to resistance circles (although he had not joined them unconditionally). The atmosphere at the Berghof was friendly, and Hitler had such confidence in Kluge that on 1 July he made him Rundstedt's successor, Geyr von Schweppenburg also being relieved of his post.

The 'Foreign Armies West' bureau at OKW was of the opinion that there were about sixty Anglo-American divisions in England. This estimate led Hitler to assume that a second landing would occur in the Pas de Calais, and he reinforced the divisions of General von Salmuth there. The estimate was false since the Allies had no more than fifteen divisions in England, and these were also intended for the Normandy beaches. Hitler was convinced that his new C-in-C West would succeed in erecting a strong defensive front.

Army Group Centre Shattered

On 22 June in the East—the third anniversary of the German invasion of Russia—the Red Army began its offensive against Army Group Centre, their largest and most successful operation of the war. At first it appeared that the Russians' attack was composed of several minor operations, but once they had battered the first gaps in the German lines a major tank attack developed on the Vitebsk front and was quickly succeeded by further attacks. The Russians paved the way for every advance by air attacks and a heavy artillery barrage before sending in their massed tank groups. Busch, C-in-C Army Group Centre, asked Hitler for permission to abandon the strongpoints, but Hitler declined and demanded that every centre should be held.

The Reich was now under threat from the direction of France, Italy and Russia. Hitler reiterated his strict order that every square metre of territory was to be defended to the last. It was everywhere obvious that the enemy strength was either superior to our own or far superior. Hitler could not see this and considered the Army reports exaggerated. Busch, C-in-C Army Group Centre, was replaced by Model, and Lindemann, C-in-C Army Group North, by Friessner. But these changes of command altered nothing.

Army Group Centre had lost 25 divisions—about 350,000 men. A 300-kilometre long gap had been torn open along the front and the Russians were pouring through it towards the German frontier. On 9 July Hitler flew to his East Prussian FHQ. In his entourage were Keitel, Dönitz, Himmler, Jodl and Korten. From the Eastern Front came Model,

Friessner and Generaloberst Ritter von Greim, the Luftwaffe C-in-C Centre. The Chief of the Army General Staff, Zeitzler, did not come. Since the beginning of the Russian offensive Hitler had had a number of shouting matches with him. Zeitzler did not share Hitler's military policy ideas and was at the end of his tether. Hitler never saw him again.

The conference was aimed primarily at pushing up new units to the front. Model and Friessner both had a somewhat optimistic outlook. Requirements indented for would be met within the next few weeks, provided that the Russians did not undertake any surprise thrusts in the interim. Dönitz stressed the need to hold the Baltic ports, which were important for working up the new U-boat types. That afternoon Hitler flew back to Salzburg. I had the impression that he still had a positive view of events on the Eastern Front.

Final Days at Obersalzberg

At Obersalzberg, during one of the daily conferences, I had occasion to leave the room and before returning sat in the annexe which was screened from the room by a curtain. I overheard Hitler praising me for being the only officer who always expressed his opinion openly and without timidity. This observation gave me the determination, at this critical hour for the Reich, to remain bold. I did not re-join the conference since I would not have been able to look any of them in the eye.

The final days ever spent at Obersalzberg were calm and serious. Hitler wanted to return to Wolfschanze but had postponed his departure because the conversion work on his accommodation bunker was still incomplete. At this time I gained the impression that he saw defeat ahead. I inferred this from comments he made when speaking of the new weapons and their effect. These would bring us success, he said. He would never give in. Everything strengthened his conviction: 'I will never capitulate.'

Hitler often discussed Luftwaffe reconstruction with me. Now he had decided to concentrate entirely on the production of fighters. These would have the highest priority. Everything else would be stopped. He expressed the hope daily that the first jets would soon be arriving in front-line squadrons. I could not support this hope: the Me 262 could not be expected for at least another six months. My great fear, which I did not conceal, was lack of fuel; some Army Group Centre units had reported severe shortages. Hitler said that what it amounted to was a struggle to

protect the most important production centres and maintain the airworthiness of fighters. He acknowledged the fuel problem but said we must
never give up the chance to obtain the upper hand. How we were supposed to do that without any fuel seemed to escape him.

On 15 July he decided to return to East Prussia next morning. The
Berghof circle was much reduced and there were few guests around. He
had become much calmer in himself. On that last evening before retiring
he went into the large hall, moved once more down the long line of
portraits, looked at each—and took his leave of them. Then he bade Frau
Wolf and my wife good night, kissed the hand of both, went up the steps
to the bedrooms, turned, made a warm gesture of farewell and left the
hall. It was the last goodbye.

Next morning we flew to Wolfschanze. The situation conference began at 1300 in the barracks annexe. It seemed as though we had never
been away. Hitler was given quarters in the finished 'Guests' Bunker'. I
admired his resolve. The strength of his will and nerves impressed me.
He was a little more round-shouldered than before and he carried himself less well, but his mind was clear. For him this was a new beginning at
FHQ. In these military surroundings he was in his element. Bad reports
flowed in from all points of the compass. I had the impression that the
Army was near exhaustion. There could no longer be any doubt about
the enemy's superiority.

On 17 July, in the West, Rommel received head wounds when the
open car in which he was travelling to the front was strafed by fighter-
bombers. His driver was killed. When Rommel had recovered sufficiently
he was returned to Germany, and he never went back to the front.

Two days later Kesselring arrived at FHQ. On 20 July he celebrated
forty years of military service and in recognition he was due to receive
the highest decoration, the Diamonds to the Oak Leaves and Swords of
the Knight's Cross. It was an enjoyable visit. Despite heavy attacks by
American, British, Polish and French forces, none had succeeded in col-
lapsing his Italian front. Hitler spoke to him in a very appreciative manner about his cleverly calculated defensive battle and praised the fight he
was putting up against the stiffest odds.

The 20 July Bomb Plot

The next day was 20 July. Hitler was expecting Mussolini in the early
afternoon and the situation conference had been brought forward half

an hour to 12.30. It was a warm summer's day and those of us attending the conference assembled before the barracks hut. This circle included Puttkamer, Bodenschatz and Graf von Stauffenberg, who since 1 July had been Chief of Staff to Generaloberst Fromm, C-in-C Reserve Army, and had attended at the Berghof a few days previously to present a report. Hitler wanted to explore the idea of new panzer and infantry formations, and today's conference was to receive information on the possibilities. Hitler welcomed with a handshake each officer standing before the barracks before leading the way at once into the situation room, where other senior officers were assembled. Amongst these were Keitel with his ADC John von Freyend; Jodl together with Major Büchs his Luftwaffe General Staff officer, and Oberstleutnant Waizenegger, 1st General Staff officer; Korten; Buhle, Chief of the OKW Army Staff; Schmundt; Heusinger; Warlimont; Fegelein; Voss; Oberst Brandt, 1st General Staff officer; Kapitän zur See Assmann, 1st Admiral Staff officer; Scherff; envoy Sandleithner; Borgmann; Günsche; and two male stenographers, Berger and Buchholz.

The conference opened as usual with Heusinger's report on the Eastern Front. I was standing a little to the side discussing the agenda for Mussolini's visit with the three other adjutants. Heusinger made a point which interested me, and I moved to the opposite side of the table to obtain a better view of the map. I had been there for a few minutes when the bomb exploded. The clock said 12.40. I lost consciousness for a few seconds. When I came to I saw around me a ruin of wood and glass. I staggered to my feet, got out through one of the window frames, then sprinted around the hut to the main door. My head was buzzing, I had been deafened and I was bleeding from the head and neck. At the door a terrible scene greeted me. Severely injured officers lay around on the floor, others were reeling around and falling over. Hitler, sure-footed and erect, was led out by Keitel. His uniform jacket and trousers were torn but otherwise he seemed none the worse. He retired at once to his bunker for medical attention. Eleven persons were found to have serious injuries and were taken to the military hospital four kilometres distant.[18] Everybody else had injuries in some degree, the majority with perforated eardrums.

I ran to the neighbouring signals barracks and passed orders to the duty officer, Oberstleutnant Sander, to block all outgoing signals except those from Hitler, Keitel and Jodl. Next I went to the Führerbunker, where I found Hitler sitting in his study. As I entered I saw that he had the facial expression of a person who has faced death and come through it almost unscathed. He asked after my injuries and said that we had all had enormous luck. The conversation turned to the incident. Hitler dismissed any idea that Todt Organisation workers, who had been refurbishing the barracks a few days previously, might have been responsible.

By now Graf Stauffenberg had been missed and a search was made. It emerged that shortly after the beginning of the situation conference he had slipped out to the annexe on the pretence of having to make a telephone call. Without waiting for the connection to be set up, he said he had forgotten his map case and returned to a car in which Oberleutnant von Haeften his orderly officer was waiting. The SS FHQ-Kommandant had meanwhile raised the alarm and sentries had instructions to allow nobody to pass. Stauffenberg's car had arrived at the outer barrier but could not go through until permission had been obtained by telephone from the Kommandant's adjutant. This officer knew Stauffenberg, had taken breakfast with him that morning and assumed that Stauffenberg had to return to Berlin for service reasons. He saw no connection between Stauffenberg's hasty departure and the explosion. Thus Stauffenberg had an open road to the airfield, from where he took off for Berlin aboard an He 111 of the Army Quartermaster General.

As these details gradually became known, Stauffenberg's guilt was obvious. Himmler, now nominated C-in-C of the Reserve Army, received full powers for the criminal investigation and after a short stop at Wolfschanze flew to Berlin to be closer to events.

It was not possible to form a clear picture by phone. The flight from Rastenburg to Rangsdorf took two hours, the drive to the Reich War Ministry about another hour. Thus neither Himmler nor Stauffenberg could reach Bendlerstrasse until after 1600. This allowed us a few hours to get patched up, and I sought treatment from an Army medical officer. Göring's personal physician also took an interest in me on my return, confirmed my concussion and ordered me to bed. Göring even had an SS guard posted at my door to ensure that I did not attempt to get up. This was ridiculous, for I was the least badly hurt of the adjutants, being able to walk and fit for limited duties, for which Professor Brandt gave me permission during the course of the evening. This was necessary, for Hitler was very busy. After dinner and the evening conference we talked. He told me that Schmundt and Borgmann were very seriously hurt while

Puttkamer was confined to bed with a knee injury. This meant that I needed another aide, and I asked him if I could have Oberstleutnant von Amsberg to assist me. He had been Keitel's ADC and knew the ropes at FHQ. Hitler agreed at once. What most concerned him now was who should be Chief of the Army General Staff. Zeitzler was on the sick list and Hitler did not want to see him again. He was thinking of Guderian as his successor. I advised him against this apointment and suggested other candidates. I had in mind Buhle and Krebs. But Hitler settled for Guderian.

Many more details came in that evening from Berlin. Goebbels had summoned Major Remer, commander of the Berlin Wachtbatallion, and set up a telephone conversation with Hitler in Remer's presence. Hitler told Remer to restore order by force of arms. Generaloberst Fromm, who had been replaced by Himmler as C-in-C Reserve Army and whose stance was not unequivocal, had, after some vacillation, taken the initiative in the Bendlerstrasse. He had had the ringleaders arrested and shot. These were Stauffenberg and von Haeften, General Olbricht and his Chief of Staff Ritter Mertz von Quirnheim. Generaloberst Beck was given the opportunity to take his own life. Hitler was extremely annoyed at these measures and ordered immediately that those arrested were to be brought before the People's Court.

That evening, after Mussolini's departure, Goebbels pressured Hitler into making a brief radio announcement. Goebbels said that there was great uncertainty amongst the people, which only a direct speech by Hitler could assuage. Hitler allowed himself to be persuaded and spoke that evening. He named the would-be assassins and said that 'a quite small clique of stupid officers, ambitious, unprincipled and criminal' had wanted to remove him. 'I interpret it as a confirmation of the intention of Providence,' he said, 'that I shall continue to my goal as I have done previously.'

Late on 20 July Hitler was obviously saddened to receive news of the death from his injuries of stenographer Berger. On the 22nd General Korten, Chief of the Luftwaffe General Staff, and Oberst Brandt of the General Staff also died. It was discovered that the latter had belonged to the resistance. A strange role was played by the head of Wehrmacht Army Signals Liaison Organisation, General Fellgiebel. He remained at FHQ after the explosion, congratulated Hitler on his survival and was arrested on 21 July as a member of the resistance. He was later executed.

According to the medical staff, Schmundt was so seriously injured that even on the most favourable prognosis he would not be able to resume duty for several months. Hitler missed him sorely. General Burgdorf took charge of the Army Personnel Bureau and in October, after Schmundt's death, became Wehrmacht adjutant.

Hitler's condition was worse than at first thought. His hearing was damaged and he had recurrent pain in the arms and legs. The nerves of his left arm were damaged. Only his strong will and the heightened sense of mission kept him upright. Repeatedly at situation conferences he would speak in a sharp and coarse manner and make demands of the Army and Luftwaffe which were simply not possible.

Hitler spent more time with me than usual discussing the rebuilding of the Luftwaffe. I was surprised that these conversations were quite normal and no criticisms were levelled at absentees. I told him that only in the East did we have continuing prospects for success: in the West, in view of the enemy air superiority, we had few opportunities. He admitted that I was right but insisted that he would never capitulate. Henceforth events would determine that our opponents in the East, increasing in strength and fighting power, would soon be capable of making the strategic breakthrough there. Hitler responded by saying that the Soviets held us in such awe and respect that they would never dare to attempt it. This was true initially.

A few days after the Bomb Plot, Goebbels came to FHQ for talks. It was his heartfelt desire that Hitler should order 'total war'. Hitler agreed and nominated Goebbels 'Reichs Plenipotentiary for Total War', to which effect he signed an edict on 25 July listing the Plenipotentiary's most important duties. This edict did not really change anything, for we had already been engaged in 'total war' for some time. All it did was weaken Speer's authority.

At about this time Richthofen came to FHQ to report himself fit for duty after a head operation. Hitler received him after the evening situation conference. Richthofen requested him to end the war. I gasped in horror: Hitler was not in the mood for talk of this nature. Yet in this small circle—just the three of us—he was open and relaxed, and said he saw no prospect of obtaining an acceptable peace for Germany. The discussion rambled on about this and that for ages. Hitler respected Richthofen, who always knew the right way to put his ideas across without being presumptuous or subservient.

Retribution

Daily reports were received from Himmler's staff in Berlin about the progress of the investigation. Each contained fresh names of resistance conspirators. The list showed clearly that the resistance had its foundations in conservative circles. In fact the nobility was so strongly represented that voices began to bay for action. Noisiest was Party organisational leader Dr Ley. After Hitler forbade him to speak publicly things began to quieten down.

The stream of reports which Fegelein laid before Hitler was unceasing. After a few weeks, when the investigation had more or less ground to a halt, the leading figures of the resistance were in custody and the trials had begun before the People's Court, Hitler ordered an end to the flow of paper. The military situation compelled him to direct his attentions elsewhere.

Fegelein's subsequent behaviour was repugnant. He was not merely content to present reports about the results of the trials but took pleasure in passing round photographs of the executions. I refused to look at them. Hitler merely glanced at the prints reluctantly in the same way that he would look at photos of bombed German cities. With him it was simply a case that he shut his eyes to the consequences of his orders. I cannot recall a single visit to a burning city or a residential block reduced to rubble after an air raid. In exceptional cases he would make a hospital visit.

His main concern remained the bombing. He always came round to this even in conversations with visitors. He still believed firmly in the completion of the jet aircraft and in using them operationally in northern France. He knew my opinion on this but refused to admit it. He saw the Me 262 as the last great chance to bring about the change in Germany's fortunes.

The Russians had pushed on and by the beginning of August they had taken Brest-Litovsk and Kovno. In the fighting of the next few weeks, Army Group North would be cut off. Shortly before the Russians reached Warsaw there was an armed uprising by the Polish resistance. Himmler ordered it to be put down ruthlessly and the SS did so, inflicting heavy casualties on the Poles. Farther south the front had been forced back almost as far as the Hungarian frontier.

In northern France August brought fresh successes for the enemy. The American breakthrough at Avranches opened up all Brittany. Hitler ordered a counter-attack from east to west across the base of the Cotentin peninsula. This made no tactical sense and in any case never got off the ground because of unopposed enemy air superiority.

My Health Deteriorates

During these crises in early August my headaches increased in severity and I collapsed. Bed rest was ordered. I managed to get Keitel to lend me his Luftwaffe adjutant Major von Szymonski. This he did very grudgingly. Hitler agreed to this solution and let me rest. I kept to my bed at FHQ. I needed peace and quiet to allow the consequences of my concussion to heal. My recovery dragged on for almost a month. At the end of August I was granted leave of convalescence.

I have no clear recall of those three weeks in bed. Hitler himself remained upright only with effort, and what I learned from Szymonski and von Amsberg did little to help my recovery. On the occasions when I visited Hitler I found him engrossed in planning a huge new offensive on the Western Front with freshly formed panzer and fighter units. I asked him why he did not concentrate all his forces against the Russians and received the answer that he could attack them later provided that the Americans were not in Berlin. First of all he must have space on his western border. I did not understand his thinking and I doubt whether anybody else in Germany could have either. Everybody thought it was preferable to allow the Americans to take the Reich so that the Russians could be held off as far as possible from the eastern frontier. Hitler did not share this view because he feared the power of the American Jews more than the Bolshevists.

On a visit to my bedside Hitler spoke to me about Göring's faults. He would not let Göring fall, however: his achievements were unique and it might be that he would need him again one day. It was clear to him that Göring had failed with the Luftwaffe, not least because of his idleness and partiality towards old cronies. But when it really mattered, Hitler said, he would want Göring at his side. He still had confidence in him. I replied that I was of a different opinion, but Hitler shook his head. The Luftwaffe had been given a new Chief of General Staff who would soon set himself zealously to his task. There was much to do. I remained silent, for it was obviously impossible to convince Hitler to the contrary. The situation in the Luftwaffe was muddled for there were actually two Chiefs of the General Staff—Kreipe, a crony of Göring, and Koller, who was standing in for Korten. Amsberg and Szymonski came almost daily with tales of Hitler's gripes against the Luftwaffe. Meanwhile the enemy was advancing calmly on the main fronts.

Convalescence and Recovery

I reported to Hitler on my departure at the end of August. He was in the rebuilt conference room in which the bomb had exploded five weeks previously. He stooped a little more than before the Bomb Plot. I had the impression that he was not yet fully recovered. He greeted me warmly and extended his wishes for a speedy recovery. Of military matters he did not speak, except to hand me the special wound badge he had instituted for survivors of the Bomb Plot. It varied from the usual issue in that the steel helmet and swords were positioned higher to make space for the inscription '20th July 1944' and his autograph.

I took the night train to Berlin and went from there to my in-laws' estate at Halberstadt. Here I felt very low. A year previously my wife had taken the children and some of the furniture and moved in with her parents at Nienhagen to await the war's end. The attacks on Berlin were becoming worse. Our house had been the only one left standing in the street: the rest had either been reduced to rubble or burnt out. At Nienhagen the war seemed far away but an incident I remember well was of a heavy bomber formation crossing a marvellous blue autumn sky. Our fighters got in amongst them and scored heavily in the fine weather. A burning four-engined bomber spinning in flames from a heavenly blue sky made an eerie picture because the distance robbed it of sound.

Hitler sent a handwritten note to my wife conveying his best wishes for my recovery. I was surprised that he could find the time to write. My wife replied with a letter of thanks. I interpreted the letter as a hint to resume duty as soon as I could. In mid-September she drove me to the health spa at Salzbrunn in Silesia. Within four weeks I had made a relatively rapid recovery. I had to take the cure and spent hours walking in the countryside..

In Salzbrunn it seemed like peacetime. Our hotel was reserved mainly for wounded soldiers. Not least on account of our friendship with Karl Hanke, Gauleiter of Silesia in Breslau, whom we had befriended pre-war, we were well accommodated and cared for. He visited us several times at Salzbrunn and showed us round the district. This was of

215

especial interest for me because of the construction of the FHQ near Waldenburg in Silesia. So far, other than the foundations, there was nothing to see. Little progress had been made at Schloss Fürstenstein either. I considered the work at this FHQ completely superfluous and my first view of it told me I was correct. Later I was given to understand that the work had been abandoned.[19]

Szymonski's Visits

Szymonski visited me twice at Salzbrunn. Both times he arrived weighed down with dreadful tidings, but he had a sense of humour and always managed to depart in high spirits. The Russians were at Goldap and closing in on East Prussia. FHQ would soon have to be evacuated. I told Szymonski that he should arrange to transfer to Zossen near Berlin all less important parts of FHQ. As for the air situation, there was hardly a battle-ready unit. The Luftwaffe was out of it. The hydrogen, rubber and ball-bearing centres had all been severely hit again. The USAAF was concentrating on destroying key industries. It was everywhere a picture of catastrophe.

Szymonski told me about Hitler's psychological condition. On 26 September Himmler informed him about resistance activities in 1938 and 1939 by Canaris, Goerdeler, Oster, Dohnanyi and Beck. From this it was clear that the attack dates for the Western campaign had been continually fed to the enemy. Other documents provided a history of the failed attempts to depose or assassinate Hitler. Hitler reacted to these reports with a breakdown in health. At the end of September he complained of severe stomach and intestinal colic. Dr Morell diagnosed a psychologically induced gall bladder condition. Hitler languished in bed for several days until resuming work, very slowly, at the beginning of October. Schmundt's death on the first of the month would have added to the shock. I knew that in recent months his most confidential conversations had been with Schmundt.

Szymonski told me that at the end of September Ritter von Greim had come to FHQ. Hitler wanted to make him C-in-C of the Luftwaffe whilst allowing Göring to remain in the post nominally. In view of the hopeless military situation I assumed that Greim had declined to work anywhere near Göring. As for Kreipe, who had recently been deposed, we assumed that Party people had done the dirty work. Since the Bomb Plot, Fegelein had had Kreipe watched.

Szymonski was visibly embittered when he brought me the news of Rommel's death, which was undoubtedly on Hitler's order. Rommel had been given the opportunity to commit suicide so that his family should not suffer. His membership of the resistance had been discovered. We thought it unlikely that he would have been a driving force—he had probably been lured in by his Chief of General Staff, Speidel.

The only reasonably positive report was news of the first V-2s on London at the beginning of September. A large number had gone astray but many had caused serious damage. The British took a dim view of rocket attacks and Hitler expected much from this weapon. Szymonski also reported on the abortive British parachute drop at Arnhem; on the fighting for Aachen; on the defection of Hungary; on the British landings in Greece and the capture of Athens; on the loss of Antwerp; and finally on the Polish uprising in Warsaw, which had been put down on 2 October. Next he mentioned Hitler's plans for the Ardennes offensive with the objective of re-taking Antwerp. I asked Szymonski why Hitler wanted to do that: even if he succeeded, Antwerp was not the place from where to make a decisive stab anywhere. Szymonski replied that Hitler wanted to gain time for the completion of new weapons. I said 'Which?', but Szymonski did not know.

In mid-October I drove to Nienhagen to resume convalescence. On the 22nd Puttkamer rang and asked me if I could possibly return. The Luftwaffe was 'Subject Number One', and permanent discord had developed between Hitler and Göring. I told him I would set out next day. I did not really feel up to it, but it was obvious I had to help Hitler. Thus my convalescence came to an abrupt end.

Return to Wolfschanze

I arrived back to a transformed Wolfschanze in the morning of 24 October. The Führerbunker had become a colossus of concrete with walls seven metres thick. Three other bunkers had been similarly clad. The former wooden structures had 60cm concrete splinter protection. After being brought up to date generally, Puttkamer explained the worries being voiced by Hitler about the Luftwaffe. The negotiations with Greim about becoming Luftwaffe C-in-C were dragging on and Puttkamer pressed me to obtain some kind of solution.

In the Adjutantur General Burgdorf had taken over the Army Personnel Bureau and become Chief Adjutant following Schmundt's demise.

He had brought in a young front officer with the Knight's Cross, Major Johannmeyer, to assist. Amsberg and Szymonski had returned to normal duties, and after Christmas Borgmann would step down as Army adjutant.

From the front there was only unfavourable news. In East Prussia the Russians were at Goldap. We had just won back Gumbinnen, where the Soviets had been raping and murdering the female population, and ransacking and then torching the houses. Chaos reigned in the streets. The OKH expected a Russian offensive in the southern sector of the front daily. Some German divisions had been partially rested, but the substantial losses of panzers could not be made good.

The Balkan peninsula had been abandoned. German units were making an orderly retreat from Greece by way of Bulgaria and Romania and then through Yugoslavia. The Western Allies were advancing towards the whole western frontier. Hitler was preparing the Ardennes offensive for about 1 December provided there was no Allied offensive beforehand.

The air situation was causing major concern. The USAAF and RAF were treating Reich airspace as their own. Our air defence was insignificant. The Allied bombers were going for pinpoint targets such as oil refineries, aircraft works, rubber factories and supply organisations. Hitler's rage at the Luftwaffe was understandable, but the guilt lay not with the Luftwaffe itself—there was a whole string of causes, which began with the neglected armaments programme of 1940.

Puttkamer mentioned that at the end of September, Hitler had agreed to Goebbel's demands for a Volkssturm. All Germans aged between 16 and 60 were eligible for call-up. The Party centres were given responsibility for the force but it lacked weapons and equipment.

Intentions, Reflections, Illusions

When I reported to Hitler at midday he gave me a hearty welcome. He wanted to talk during the course of the evening. The working day began as usual with the situation conference, at which Guderian and Wenck were also present. Jodl made a statement about the preparations for the Ardennes offensive. As Hitler had ordered Kreipe not to appear again, the Chief of the Luftwaffe General Staff, Christian, delivered the Luftwaffe report. Admiral Voss represented the Kriegsmarine. It was relatively quiet on both major fronts and Hitler had had time to scheme the Ardennes offensive. Everything seemed to revolve around this operation.

That evening I had the first of numerous conversations with Hitler which began mostly in the hour before midnight and lasted up to ninety minutes. Hitler was calm and businesslike. He had had a number of talks with Greim. Actually he wanted to make him Luftwaffe C-in-C without relieving Göring of his post. Greim had made a suggestion for a command structure which did not quite match his own ideas. Greim had maintained the dialogue and both wanted to find a satisfactory solution. I asked Hitler if Göring knew anything about these discussions and he said he supposed so. I told him I could not imagine that Göring would voluntarily resign his position and added that I no longer believed a fundamental change in the Luftwaffe were possible—it was more or less wrecked. Factory airfields were coming under repeated air attack. The British seemed to know precisely when a batch of aircraft was due off the line. Then they would attack. It was my opinion that this could only be stopped if an RAF force were massacred on one of these pinpoint raids. At the moment that was simply not possible; if one day we had the Me 262 as a fighter, then we might. Hitler got very annoyed at this and held forth about the skill of the jet-fighter pilots. I told him we had to think in realities.

Another evening Hitler spoke about the Bomb Plot and the subsequent trials. He said that Himmler's reports had caused his breakdown. No person could imagine what pain he had had to bear. Everything had been betrayed—the preparations for the French campaign, the dates of the attack and the objectives of the first operations. Even the beginning of the Russian campaign had been betrayed. There was probably nothing more that remained a secret in Germany. Most sinister had been the work of Admiral Canaris. Goerdeler had been very much involved: he was the one who had confessed. He was talking his head off while Canaris was still denying everything. The mass of the arrested conspirators had become involved more or less incidentally, Hitler said. The number who were fully in the picture was quite small. General von Tresckow, for example, had had a hand in everything and had committed suicide once he recognised soberly that the Bomb Plot had failed.

I mentioned to Hitler the case of my cousin Borries and the supply problems of his corps in Kurland. He had just informed me that supply had been mysteriously restored following the failed Bomb Plot. Hitler admitted in a disheartened manner that so many conspirators came from the 'educated circles' in which he had always more or less had blind faith. What pained and disgusted him was not that they had betrayed 'him', but Germany. 'I had known for some time,' he said, 'that the "better circles" of our people were against me. But the trick in times of crisis is not to become fickle, and if that is achieved you have a source of strength which can never dry up.'

Hitler mentioned the fighting on the fronts. The quiet situation on all fronts now showed that the enemy needed a breather. He was himself waiting for the moment when the Anglo-American coalition broke up. He could not imagine that the British would accept a permament American presence in Europe. I replied that I differed. Churchill's politics proved that he stood shoulder to shoulder with the Americans. Anyway, the Americans were so strong in Europe now that they would suit themselves as to how things were done. Hitler did not respond to this.

In the afternoon of 1 November Hitler had a long private talk with Greim. When I asked Greim afterwards about the outcome, he said that for the time being nothing had changed. I was glad that this had been the decision. Although I could find much fault with Göring, a change of C-in-C at this time served little purpose. Hitler admitted that I was right, but said that a new Chief of the Luftwaffe General Staff had to be appointed. I suggested General Koller, who as Chief of the Luftwaffe Command Staff seemed to understand the problems; he had calm and poise too. This coincided with Göring's ideas, and so Koller became the last Chief of the Luftwaffe General Staff.

The 'Areopag'

On 11 November Göring convened an 'Areopag' tribunal in the Luftkriegsakademie at Berlin-Gatow.[20] General Peltz, a bomber man, had been selected to chair the meeting. Amongst those present were all the big fighter-bomber names—Galland, Maltzahn, Gollob, Trautloft, Lützow, Steinhoff, Nordmann and Streib—and the bomber men Harlinghausen, Baumbach, Knemeyer, Storp, Diesing and others—an illustrious assembly. Göring opened the convention, saying that the Luftwaffe had failed and we had to look at ourselves critically in order to turn the page. The rules of the tribunal were that he, Göring, must not be criticised and the Me 262 had to be left out of the discussion. With these limitations the 'Areopag' was so much hot air, for these were two fundamental causes of all our misfortunes. Göring called upon those present to help him resurrect the Luftwaffe, then left. Peltz took over. I could not help thinking that Peltz had an unenviable task. He knew that an 'Areopag' was a tribunal with unlimited powers, but Göring had set restrictions. In attempting to avoid that which could not be discussed, the discussion meandered down many blind alleys. The whole thing was a dreary forum which harped on about the National Socialist influences within the Luftwaffe, especially amongst the pilots, and led to a conclusion which said nothing. The final protocol discussed between Hitler and Göring was no more inspired. The meeting broke up in dissatisfaction. It was stigmatic of a Luftwaffe in dissolution: 'too little too late', the fighter pilots probably thought as they climbed up into their cockpits.

A Hopeless Situation

I returned to Wolfschanze in a state of depression. As so often in recent months, I wondered about Hitler and his purposes. How could we win the war with the forces we had distributed around Europe? Our hope was now a split in the enemy alliance or, put simply, a miracle. The fighting strength of the Waffen-SS was substantially better than that of the Army, but even they could not carry on without weapons and ammunition. I did not know whether Hitler understood the catastrophic situation in the Army and Luftwaffe or if he preferred to deceive himself. The planned Ardennes offensive seemed to me to be a sideshow that would succeed for as long as the winter conditions kept the enemy's aircraft on the ground.

Hitler repeatedly emphasised the National Socialist spirit which 'welded together the fighting forces', but in 1939 he had begun the war without speaking in that vein. Now he said that the British had to recognise the importance of his war against the Soviet Union. Yet from the beginning Britian had stood shoulder to shoulder with the Russians against us. The Americans knew only one enemy in this war—Germany. We were at the end of this great struggle and there remained for Hitler only the question of his personal destiny. He mentioned the problem on numerous occasions. In the last days at Wolfschanze, between 16 and 20 November, I heard him speak about it. When Jodl suggested that FHQ be transferred to Berlin so as to be nearer the Ardennes, Hitler said that he would never leave East Prussia. The war was lost. He said this several times. But Bormann succeeded in convincing him. In the afternoon of 20 November Hitler boarded his special train and left Wolfschanze for ever.

On 14 November the British had attacked on the Meuse towards Roermond and Venlo in Holland but without achieving a significant success. At the same time the Americans had had little success in an attempted penetration deeper into the Reich further south. They had carried out air raids on towns in their intended field of advance and Düren near Aachen, Jülich and Heinsberg were completely destroyed. However, they made poor progress forward, being forced back between Düren and Jülich, and at Metz they encountered heavy resistance. Hitler looked on with a baleful eye. He was fearing for his Ardennes surprise. He had invested great hopes in this offensive and was already seeing in his mind's eye the German spearhead rolling into Antwerp.

In East Prussia German troops had had to cede more territory and had either withdrawn into the fortified area at Königsberg or been forced back to the Vistula. One of these armies was commanded by General Hossbach, who celebrated his 50th birthday on 21 November. Hitler sent him a cheque for 50,000 Reichsmarks as a gesture of confidence in his former adjutant.

We arrived in Berlin on the 21st. Next day Hitler had a small polyp on his vocal chords removed at the Charité hospital by Professor von Eicken and was ordered not to speak for seven days. On 28 November the first US naval convoy docked at Antwerp and from now on the Americans had no problems of supply.

On 10 December we left Berlin, arriving early the next day at Ziegenberg near Bad Nauheim, where there was a fine old castle which Speer had had rebuilt and refurbished at the beginning of the war. Hitler had assured him then that he would never set foot in it and instructed Speer to build barracks and bunkers in the nearby woods. We lodged in the latter while C-in-C West and his Staff were quartered in the Schloss.

The Ardennes Offensive

In the last two days of our stay Hitler assembled the commanding generals and divisional commanders for the Ardennes campaign into two groups of about twenty persons each and attempted to persuade them that the enemy coalition would soon break apart. He set all his hopes on it. He reminded them of how Frederick the Great, in the darkest hours of his war, had stood alone and triumphed: then, as now, the enemy alliance would founder as a result of this imminent offensive. He demanded that the enemy be engaged to the end. If every man would only think of success, of victory, then we would not fail. With such words as these Hitler attempted to unite the senior commanders. With an attack in a small area, using the last battleworthy units still at his disposal, he seriously believed he could bring about the disintegration of the enemy alliance. I was appalled that this should be served up to the generals as a reasonable argument, for the enemy superiority was such that no enduring success was possible.

The offensive began on 16 December. The weather was overcast and no enemy aircraft appeared until Christmas Eve. Dietrich's Sixth SS-Panzer Army and Manteuffel's Fifth Panzer Army were the mainstay of the attack, which was under the command of Model.[21] Manteuffel made good progress and only Bastogne held out. Dietrich, battling further north, had to batter down more resistance and remained further back. On 24 December the weather cleared and enemy aircraft appeared. This ruled out any further movements by day. Some units were short of fuel. Shortly after Christmas it became obvious that the adventure was fruitless. My fears were fully confirmed. Our offensive, with between 28 and 30 divisions—among them twelve panzer divisions—ground to a halt at Monschau-Echternach at the year's end. Our units had taken heavy punishment and were in no state for fresh operations.

No Way Out

Even Hitler could not close his mind to this. One late evening I was with him in the air raid bunker. He appeared to me to be in despair. Never before or subsequently did I see him in such a state. He spoke of taking his life, for the last hope of achieving victory had gone. He reproached the Luftwaffe and the 'traitors' in the Army. He said something like, 'I know the war is lost. The enemy superiority is too great. I have been betrayed. After 20 July everything came out, things I had considered impossible. It was precisely those circles against me who had profited most from National Socialism. I pampered and decorated them. And that was all the thanks I got. I ought to put a bullet in my head. I lacked hard fighters. Model and Dietrich are such. And Rudel. Now there's a successor for me. Intelligent. What are his views on art and culture? He should come.' He continued: 'We will not capitulate, ever. We may go down. But we will take the world down with us.' I have never forgotten his words. I have never spoken to anybody about this conversation until now. It made it finally clear to me that Hitler would never seek to negotiate peace and would rather drag everyone down in his defeat. The path had been laid: it led to that very unconditional surrender upon which the victors were insisting.

On 29 December Hitler instituted the Knight's Cross with Gold Oak Leaves, Swords and Diamonds. He stipulated in the deed that the decoration could only be awarded on twelve ocasions. That day and the next he spent time with General Thomale discussing political problems, the completion of the new panzers and when the latter could be got to the front. Guderian followed next. He expected a new Russian offensive in the first days of January and wanted divisions withdrawn from the Ardennes to the Eastern Front. Yet Hitler vacillated. He approved the transfer of four divisions in Hungary to defend the Romanian oilfields, but that was all.

Thus ended 1944, in a mood of hopelessness. The last prospects of a success of the Western Front had disappeared; new, difficult operations lay ahead in the East. Apart from the occasional local success, the Luftwaffe war effort was almost invisible. The Allies had almost total air supremacy. What Hitler really thought about the situation nobody quite knew. Officially he spoke only of continuing the battle in the hope that the enemy alliance would fall apart. What we were supposed to make of that nobody knew. What we did know at FHQ was that of himself Hitler neither could nor would take a step towards a solution. The year 1945 would bring an end to the war, but it was doubtful if we would be alive to see it.

CHAPTER SEVEN

1945

In his New Year speech to Wehrmacht and Volk, Hitler spoke openly about the war situation. He referred to the international plans to dismantle the German Reich. It remained only for the German people to put up a successful resistance to 'the attempts of our enemies to strangle us'. He spoke of the attempt on his life, which was a turning point in German history. I was convinced that even in this quite hopeless situation Hitler still had the confidence of a broad cross-section of the people, who simply would not believe that the Reich could be defeated under his leadership. Personally, after the autumn of 1944 I saw his death as the only way out. That he shared my opinion might be inferred from the suicidal thoughts he sometimes expressed.

On the morning of 1 January the Wehrmacht C-in-Cs and the Chiefs of the General Staff assembled at Führer Headquarters to offer their best wishes for a successful New Year—a sentiment which I am sure they all expressed with their tongues in their cheeks. After the situation conference Hitler invited Oberst Rudel into the circle of generals. He spoke a few words of recognition and praise for Rudel's selfless devotion to duty, presented him with the recently instituted highest award for bravery and mentioned his 'unremitting and provenly highest heroism . . . his unique fighting success as aviator and warrior'. What Hitler and Rudel discussed behind closed doors after the midday meal I was never able to discover.

A catastrophe befell the Luftwaffe the same day. Göring had planned a strike by almost a thousand aircraft on the Western frontier against various ground targets. Preparations for Operation 'Bodenplatte' were kept strictly secret; nevertheless, the attack was greeted with heavy enemy anti-aircraft fire. On the way back our aircraft flew over accurate German flak, the batteries not having been informed of the operation on the grounds of secrecy. We suffered heavy losses which could not be made good. 'Bodenplatte' was the last major operation undertaken by the Luftwaffe.

On the occasion of his 52nd birthday, Göring called at FHQ on 12 January to receive Hitler's warmest congratulations. That day a massive Russian offensive began in the central sector of the Eastern Front. Behind heavy artillery fire a large mass of tanks smashed through the German front line and headed for Upper Silesia and the Oder. The Red Army took Baranov on the first day and Kielce on the third. Hitler attempted vainly to close the breach by bringing up a corps from East Prussia. He realised that this was the beginning of the end: in the evening of 15 January he travelled to Berlin and, apart from one visit to the front, never left the German capital again.

The great Russian offensive stretched from Baranov to the north of Warsaw and was opposed by exhausted, groggy German units. The Army Group commanders and Chiefs of the General Staff advised Hitler to have his forces fall back to allow a versatile response, but Hitler would not hear of this. He insisted vociferously that the front hold firm and, as so often before, that no ground be yielded. This left our divisions in a desperate situation and frustrated any hopes of an organised defence. Some commanders took it upon themselves to arrange their men as the situation demanded, but Hitler soon detected this sort of independent spirit and removed the offenders. On 15 January Harpe, C-in-C Army Group Centre, gave way to Schörner, on the 26th Rendulic replaced Reinhardt and on the 30th Hossbach stood aside in favour of Müller. Hossbach was a victim of the Party demagogues: the Gauleiter of East Prussia, Koch, sent to Berlin such scornful reports about Hossbach's leadership that Hitler felt obliged to sacrifice him.

Military Command in Crisis

In these first weeks of 1945 the military command was in crisis. Hitler stuck to his old principle—which may have been justified in the winter of 1941 but not now—not to surrender a single square metre. The superiority of the Russians along the entire front was so great, however, that no general could stand up to the steamroller and survive. The entire population of East Prussia had taken flight. The highways were blocked with refugees who obstructed the passage of Army vehicles. It was almost impossible to cross the Vistula into the Reich proper and the Russians forced the civilians to the Baltic coast, where their only hope was evacuation by the Kriegsmarine. The Soviets crushed many such treks. Civilian sufferings were unimaginable and the casualty figure enormous.

At the end of January the Russian southern front forged onwards from south-west of Breslau to the Oder. The consequence of this advance was the loss of the Silesian industrial area. The city of Breslau was encircled but held out with heavy losses until the general capitulation on 6 May.

To halt the Russian advance in the centre, Hitler formed a new Army Group, 'Weichsel', commanded by Himmler. It was a ragbag of stragglers and retreating units used as a stopgap to gain time and, needless to say, was viewed with scepticism by military experts. When the Russians reached the Oder they halted along a line south of Küstrin–Frankfurt an der Oder and along the Neisse to near Görlitz while Zhukov attempted to shorten his lines of supply to the rear.

In the West at New Year Anglo-American forces were hoping to beat the Russians to Berlin, and that they failed was due to the strong discipline of the German divisions. Their fate was inevitable and bitter resistance replaced hopelessness.

In January I travelled again to the Harz, to Ohrdruf in Thuringia. This was a military exercise area where a new FHQ was under construction. The works were proceeding only slowly. I could not see any point in having them speeded up.[22] The great subterranean factory not far from Nordhausen, in which concentration camp inmates helped manufacture large numbers of V-2 rockets, interested me more. The prisoners seemed well treated and were in good physical condition so far as I could determine, but it was nevertheless a depressing sight to watch this forced-labour workforce, who hoped to purchase their lives by their industry, at work in the extensive underground galleries. In the final analysis it all seemed rather pointless by this stage.

On 30 January Hitler broadcast to the German people for the last time. What else could he ask for than a fight to the last? 'We will survive even this crisis,' he said. 'In this battle, it is not inner Asia that will triumph, but Europe.' Many of his listeners still clutched at the straw of the 'miracle weapons' which would turn the tide at the last minute.

A few days later we received the first reports of the meeting on 4 February of Roosevelt, Churchill and Stalin at Yalta which discussed the carving up of the Reich. Hitler was informed about this conference but was still curiously disinterested, rather as if it had nothing to do with him any more.

Dresden

On 13 and 14 February the United States Army Air Forces and Royal Air Force made two appalling air raids on Dresden. It was not thought at the time that undefended cities overflowing with refugees would be a target for a mass raid of this kind. This was sheer terrorism devoid of any military sense against a defenceless civilian population. The devastation exceeded anything that a German city had suffered previously. More than 12,000 buildings and 80,000 homes were destroyed. The beautiful old city was lost for ever. The death toll was put at between 135,000 and 300,000; the exact number was unknown because of the huge number of refugees.[23] It was astonishing how the rescue services managed to continue functioning. With these final heavy air raids on Dresden the German people understood at last the mentality of the Western Allies. After Dresden Hitler said frequently that he was going to renounce the Geneva Conventions, but Jodl always managed to dissuade him from this step.[24]

Last Speech to the Gauleiters

Hitler summoned the Gau- and Reichsleiters to the Chancellery on 24 February. Mutschmann, Gauleiter of Dresden, was bombarded with questions about the fate of the city. The Gauleiter for the Rhineland was also at the centre of attention and and spoke of the fighting in the West. Gauleiter Koch of East Prussia did not appear; his Gau was almost completely encircled by the Russians. Hanke was holed up in beleaguered Breslau. Hitler came in for criticism, but when he entered the room, stooped and older-looking than his visitors had seen him previously, he received a sympathetic reception. His speech began with reflections on the Weimar period and the first years after the seizure of power. Finally he came to what his audience was waiting for—the present. He spoke of the decisive hours of this war. The year 1945 would decide the next hundred years. His references to new naval and Luftwaffe weapons made no impression. During lunch Hitler—forced into the Chancellery and death's hands—attempted to convince his listeners that he alone could correctly judge the situation. But the powers of suggestion he had employed in the past to mesmerise this circle were gone. It was at this meeting that he said, 'We have liquidated the class warriors of the Left, but unfortunately we forgot to strike out against those of the Right. That was our great sin of omission.'

Hopes for the Me 262

During February Hitler entertained the fighter pilot Hajo Hermann, who was of the opinion that the time had come for ramming, and suggested to Hitler how this should be done. Yet Hitler still showed no interest in this suicidal method and spoke of the new fighters which would shortly bring in new fighter tactics. He also mentioned Göring's plan to form the first jet fighter squadron in southern Germany. He expected great things of these pilots. The formation of this squadron, achieved despite severe difficulties, was the result of the long internal squabbling which had culminated in the abysmal Areopag. Under the command of Generalleutnant Galland, the squadron had the best-known and highly decorated fighter pilots of the Luftwaffe—Lützow, Steinhoff, Hohagen, Krupinski, Barkhorn, Bär, Herget, Bob and Eichel-Streiber. Operations were limited to a sphere centred on Riem near Munich, and the great successes expected by Hitler failed to materialise. Lützow did not return from one of its missions and Steinhoff was badly wounded.

The Noose Tightens

Since 16 January the daily situation conferences in the New Reich Chancellery—when opened in 1939 a superlative edifice of mosaic and marble—now began at three in Hitler's large study there, the large room in the old Chancellery which had been the the venue since the beginning of the war having serious bomb damage. The Army General Staff was at Zossen, south of Berlin, from where Guderian regularly made the journey to report on the rapidly approaching Eastern Front. The circle attending these conferences had grown larger. Bormann and Himmler were always present, and Ribbentrop and the Chief of Police, Kaltenbrunner, frequently. The conferences lasted for two to three hours and gave Hitler the opportunity to ruminate at length on the precarious situation. The result would be a shuffle of forces which might be scarcely battleworthy, if not imaginary, and his ideas did not often reflect the true situation.

The most painful reports were those concerning the enemy air raids. The British and Americans flew over the western Reich more or less as they pleased, bombing residential areas and attacking the supply organisation, the armaments industry or hydrogen works. They were apparently in possession of the most accurate information about factories. These attacks crippled the production of all kinds of war materials.

During March, Würzburg and Nordhausen were reduced to rubble, and Halberstadt on 8 April.

After the daily situation conference Hitler often took tea with his secretaries in a small office of the old Chancellery. I was occasionally drawn into this circle. Hitler would discuss subjects unconnected with the war as a diversion. On one of these breaks he suddenly decided to dictate my wife a letter, which she has kept, recalling our frequent meetings.

At about this time Speer went his own way. He knew that defeat was only a few weeks off. He was on the friendliest terms with Guderian and, escorted by his Army liaison officer, Oberstleutnant von Poser, travelled far and wide throughout the Reich consulting Gauleiters and military commanders on ways to mitigate the order to destroy essential installations. In this way, and at no small personal risk to himself, Speer was able to save many important facilities from destruction. After 15 March he presented to Hitler his final report, 'The Industrial Situation March–April 1945 and Its Consequences', which consisted of ten typewritten pages without appendices setting out the situation clearly and frankly and the implications he drew from it. Although Speer's reports contained only bad news, Hitler would always take them to his bunker to read when alone. Speer stated in this report that we should do everything 'to enable the people, if only in the most primitive way, to maintain a basic standard of life', and he continued: 'We have no right at this stage of the war to ourselves inflict destruction to the detriment of the German people. We have the duty to leave behind us the possibility to start a reconstruction in the more distant future.' Hitler allowed Speer more rope than anybody else to say such things. In better times they had worked so closely together that Speer was probably the only person who could go so far with Hitler without being in fear of his life.

On 15 February Hitler went to the front for the last time. Near Frankfurt-an-der-Oder he visited Army units and General Busse's Ninth Army Staff. He had collected himself, disguised his injured arm and made a good impression. But the more discerning amongst his listeners no longer believed what he had to say. It was patently obvious that they had to hold the Oder, and just as certainly they knew that because of the enemy's clear-cut superiority it was going to be almost impossible to stop the Russian juggernaut once it really got under way. Hitler considered this visit to the front especially important and believed he had bolstered the troops' confidence.

On 19 March he issued an order to all military commanders—his official 'answer' to Speer's last memorandum. In this so-called 'Nero Order' Hitler ordered that all military communications, signals, industrial and supply installations as well as ancillary works within the Reich which might be of use in any way to the enemy immediately or in the forseeable future were to be destroyed. It was not really possible to put this order into effect since the scale of destruction was already enormous enough without having to introduce a 'scorched earth' policy.

Events picked up at the end of March. The Americans had evidently decided to steal a march on the Russians. On 22 March they crossed the Rhine at Oppenheim and on the 24th at Wesel. The Ruhr was taken within the next few days. Model's Army Group became encircled and after its determined resistance ceased on 17 April Model took his own life. The Americans advanced eastwards in numbers, finding only patchy resistance, and on 11–12 April they reached the Elbe at Magdeburg. British forces north of the Americans found only weak resistance on their way through Westphalia and had little difficulty in getting to Bremen and Hamburg. We gained an impression from the reports that the population in the Reich, especially in north-west Germany, accepted the Allies with relief. They had simply had enough. We understood this but Hitler could not. He sharply criticised their attitude but could no longer influence events in western Germany.

Hitler's last goal was to hold off the Russians' onslaught and prevent their crossing the Oder. Himmler was replaced as C-in-C Army Group 'Weichsel' on 20 March by Generaloberst Heinrici. Himmler had come in for severe criticism from Hitler. Where he had needed to find fault with him—and there was little of a positive nature to say—Hitler had not spared Himmler's blushes. Finally he had decided to shed the military amateurs. Whether he knew anything at this time of Himmler's feelers to Sweden about an armistice or peace treaty—an act completely contrary to the SS motto *'Meine Ehre heisst Treue'*—I cannot say, but I do not discount it. In any case, the relationship worsened appreciably from the end of March.

On 29 March Hitler got rid of Guderian after several violent confrontations. Outwardly the dismissal was couched in terms of 'obligatory leave', initially for six weeks, but the break was final. In past weeks numerous arguments had arisen as a result of the very reasonable proposals Guderian had made and to which Hitler preferred to close his mind. The fact that Guderian remained on good terms with Hitler may have been due in part to a misunderstanding as to how his dismissal had come about: he thought he had been forced out by other interests. His successor was Krebs, in whom Hitler had great confidence and whom he had long esteemed both for his personality and as a qualified General Staff officer. He had first come to Hitler's notice in the spring of 1941 in the odd scene enacted at the Moscow railway terminus on the occasion of the departure of the Japanese foreign minister, when Stalin had engaged Krebs in a demonstrative conversation. As the last Chief of the Army General Staff, Krebs had less work to do than the commander of Berlin Wehrkreis III. He committed suicide in despair after his first meetings postwar with the Red Army when he saw the type of people they were. That same day Hitler also parted company with his long-serving Press Chief Dietrich. The relationship between them had recently deteriorated. Goebbels had never trusted his subordinate and he merely put up with Dietrich because Hitler wanted to keep him. At last, probably with Bormann's support—Bormann and Dietrich rarely spoke—Goebbels got his way and Dietrich had to go.

Farewell to My Wife

On 5 April I travelled to Nienhagen for the last time to bid farewell for ever to my wife and three children. I knew that Hitler wanted to remain in Berlin, that the war would soon end and that it was unlikely that I could escape from Berlin with my life. There were certainly worried faces in Nienhagen, but the people were well-groomed and composed and lived together harmoniously. Spring had arrived. My wife was expecting our fourth child but let none of her anxieties show. It was a comfort to know that she was well cared for. Next day I made the difficult return journey to Berlin. The sun shone, the countryside slumbered peacefully but I was heading back to hell. Perhaps it was a good thing that we were so stressed in Berlin and had little time for morbid reflection. I was able to phone my wife for a few weeks more until the Americans cut the lines.

At the end of March Hitler was surprised by the arrival of Eva Braun at the Reich Chancellery. She had come of her own free will. Hitler wanted to send her straight back to Munich and gave Hoffmann the job of persuading her. Despite his efforts, she was quite determined that she wanted to be at Hitler's side and from then on she lived in the bunker in a room adjacent to Hitler's private quarters and accustomed herself completely to the atmosphere of bunker life. She always dressed carefully and taste-fully, was an example to all in her conduct and showed no sign of weak-ness to the very last. At the time I was lodging in a basement room in the housekeeper's wing. Towards the end I moved into a bunker room stuffed full of housekeeper Kannenberg's clothing and requisites.

Last Days in the Bunker

At the beginning of April Hitler promoted Schörner to field marshal. The Press statement announced that Schörner 'as scarcely any other German general, is a symbol of the unshakeable steadfastness of Germa-ny's defences in the East'. In this Hitler was referring to Schörner's ef-fectiveness as C-in-C of Army Groups in Kurland, Silesia and the Pro-tectorate.

On 13 April Vienna fell. A few days earlier, on 8 and 9 April, the executions of Admiral Canaris and General Oster had been announced. A rumour spread that the Admiral's diaries had been found, which of themselves gave ammunition enough to condemn him. If this were true, it surprised me that such a careful man as Canaris, an opponent of Hit-ler from the beginning, should have kept a diary.

It became the custom after the situation conference that Johanna Wolff—Hitler's private secretary—and Admiral von Puttkamer would come to my room for coffee. We kept up this informal arrangement as a diversion from the hopelessness of our plight. We talked mainly of the past. In the last week of April, during a conversation, Hitler asked me quite suddenly about my future plans and intentions. I replied that as his adjutant I had no choice—I would remain with him in the bunker. He greeted this with the brief observation that in view of the uncertainties he needed to have around him people in whom he could trust.

On 12 April Kesselring visited Hitler for the last time, probably to receive instructions first-hand. Hitler left no doubt that he had not yet given up. Kesselring was obviously not deceived and probably decided that henceforth he would follow his own inclinations. Outwardly he was still the optimist: this was the ingrained way he had to encourage his men, to get them to put their shoulders to the wheel when matters seemed at their worst. He had been to my in-laws' estate a few days previously and brought news of my wife.

In the evening of 12 April Goebbels arrived with news of Roosevelt's death. He informed the bunker inhabitants that the event signified the turn in Germany's fortunes. He saw a working of the 'historical Almighty' and said that 'Justice' was becoming visible once more. Hitler took a more sober view devoid of optimism, although he did not rule out the possibility that the death could have political consequences for us. He reminded everybody that Roosevelt had had a ruthless attitude towards Britain and it had always been his objective to destroy that very colonialism by which Britain had achieved her greatness. Goebbels insisted on clutching at the straw, however, and even influenced the Press to cast Roosevelt's death in a positive light. He was hoping thereby to highlight the contrasts between the West and the Soviet Union and foment discord. Earlier that day Speer had arranged the final concert of the Berlin Philharmonic. Their hall was still partially intact. Together with Speer and Dönitz I listened to the finale of *Götterdämmerung*, Beethoven's Violin Concerto and Bruckner's 8th Symphony. Afterwards we returned to the Chancellery across the ruins of the Potsdamer Platz.

In order to provide a leader for Germany should the Reich be divided into two halves, north and south, on 15 April Hitler issued a decree vesting leadership in Dönitz and Kesselring respectively. Hitler appealed next to the soldiers of the Eastern Front. He was expecting hourly the Russian attack across the Oder. Recently he had held frequent telephone conversations with General Busse, C-in-C Ninth Army, and made available to him all the weapons he could muster. His last hope was to repulse this Russian attack. He declared: 'Berlin remains German. Vienna will be German again. Europe will never become Russian.' Referring to Roosevelt's death, he concluded: 'Now that Fate has taken from us the greatest war criminal in history, there will be a decisive change in this war.' I have no explanation today what this optimistic statement was supposed to achieve, nor what Hitler himself believed, so intermingled were his ideas of fantasy and reality. For myself, I was quite sure. The Russians and the Americans would occupy the German Reich. There was nothing to suggest that they would stop at some point short of taking every single square metre. I never shared Hitler's belief in a breach of the East–West alliance. His political thinking anticipated events, but I thought that the ideological differences would not take effect until after the war had ended. Any hope of peace on this basis was therefore illusory and an unconditional surrender was inevitable.

The Russian offensive across the Oder began on 16 April with a ninety-minute artillery barrage—one of the biggest in military history. When the Russians attacked, they were held off. Another ninety-minute barrage followed that afternoon, after which the Russians broke through the German lines north of Küstrin on the west bank of the Oder. On the 17th and 18th they crossed south of Frankfurt and began to amass. Shortly after this our whole Oder front collapsed, offering the Red Army the opportunity to reinforce their penetration with armour. During the next few days they combed forward in a line stretching from north of Berlin near Oranienburg to the south of Berlin near Zossen. No military acumen was needed to see that the intention was to encircle the Reich capital. Opposition was patchy. In the south the armies of Busse and later Wenck were forced ever further westwards across the Elbe. To the north of Berlin stood the last German groups under Generalleutnant Heinrici and SS-Obergruppenführer Steiner. But these, outnumbered and exhausted, were soon forced back too. In the days up to 23 April Hitler interfered repeatedly in the conduct of the German defence but saw ultimately that it was futile.

The best situation reports were being delivered by Oberstleutnant de Maizière. As a rule he stayed up at night to draft the day's events. His style was terse, clear, devoid of pathos and without refinement. Most listeners were very impressed, and even Hitler, who could no longer expect to hear anything agreeable from the Eastern Front, took pleasure in the precise manner of presentation and valued Maizière's reports, black though they might be.

For the situation conference of 20 April, Hitler's 56th birthday, Göring, Dönitz, Keitel, Ribbentrop, Speer, Jodl, Himmler, Kaltenbrunner, Krebs, Burgdorf and many others were present: Hitler accepted their birthday wishes and then went immediately to the business of the day. Afterwards Hitler had several private conversations. Göring asked Hitler to be excused since there was something urgent he had to attend to in southern Germany: probably he would only be able to get there by road. With that he took his leave. I had the impression that inwardly Hitler had rejected him. It was an unpleasant moment. Dönitz also took his final leave of Hitler, receiving the brief instruction to take over the government in north Germany and prepare himself for an honourable fight to the finish. Hitler's words implied great trust in Dönitz. Of others present, such as Himmler, Kaltenbrunner and Ribbentrop, he parted without much ceremony.

That day it seemed to me that Hitler was wavering about remaining in Berlin. A general spirit of unrest pervaded the bunkers; a portent of upheaval was in the air. Puttkamer was sent with two NCOs to destroy all papers at Obersalzberg. I asked him to burn my diaries which I kept there. He promised to do this and confirmed on his return that they had been burnt, together with Schmundt's notes. Fräulein Wolf and other members of the personal Adjutantur now prepared to leave the bunker. In the late evening we gathered in Hitler's small living room for drinks— Eva Braun, Hitler's secretaries Gerda Christian and Trautl Junge and his vegetarian cook Constanze Marzialy, plus Schaub, Lorenz and myself. The war was not mentioned: Gerda Christian was good at getting Hitler to talk on other subjects.

On 22 April Keitel and Jodl urged Hitler to leave Berlin. He was still undecided when a furore occurred during the situation conference. The reports submitted by the various commanders of the armies fighting for Berlin were contradictory. It seemed that each was putting up his own private fight but that an organised resistance was not possible. Krebs could not resolve the difficulty. It was not clear whether it was a consequence of the Russian superiority or the collapse of our own command structure (if this was still possible). Hitler became very irate. He ordered everybody from the room with the exception of Keitel, Jodl, Krebs and Burgdorf and then unleashed a furious tirade against the Army commanders and their 'long-term treachery'. I was sitting near the door in the annexe and heard almost every word. It was a terrible half-hour. After this outburst, however, he had at least made up his mind about his destiny. He ordered Keitel and Jodl to report to Dönitz in northern Germany and continue the war from there. He, Hitler, would remain in Berlin and take his own life.

After Keitel and Jodl had departed, Schaub was given the task of destroying the contents of Hitler's personal safe in the bunker and then make his way to Berchtesgaden to burn any remaining private papers he found there.

Hitler's close circle was being reduced almost hourly. One noticed how each was preoccupied by private thoughts. There was a peculiar atmosphere abroad that day. Only Goebbels' State Secretary, Dr Naumann, who had arrived in the bunker a short while previously from the Propaganda Ministry, seemed phlegmatic.

On 23 April Dr Goebbels issued a Press and radio statement that Hitler would remain in Berlin and command 'all forces assembled for the defence of Berlin'. On this day Hitler transferred all other responsibilities to Dönitz and Kesselring. He kept with him as his only military advisers Krebs, the latter's General Staff officer Major von Freytag-Loringhausen and the young cavalry captain Boldt, who was in charge of telephone communications whilst these remained possible. Besides these were present Bormann, Goebbels, Hewel, Voss, Hitler's pilot Baur, Burgdorf with his adjutant Oberstleutnant Weiss, Heinz Lorenz as Press Officer, Johannmeyer and myself from the military Adjutantur, plus Günsche of the personal Adjutantur in the Chancellery bunkers.

Göring Dismissed; Greim Appointed

That afternoon Göring's telex arrived, the first copy for Hitler, the second addressed personally to me. I read the text at once: '*Mein Führer!* In accordance with your decision to remain at your battle HQ in the fortress of Berlin, are you agreed that I take overall command of the Reich at once with full freedom of manoeuvre at home and abroad in pursuance of your edict of 29.6.1941 as your representative? If I do not receive your answer by 2200 hours, I shall assume that you have been deprived of your freedom of action, in which case I accept that you award me the provisions of your edict to act for the welfare of Volk and Fatherland. You know what I feel for you but cannot find the words to express in these worst hours of my life. God protect you and despite everything allow you to come here as soon as possible. Your loyal, Hermann Göring.'

I was horrified and feared the worst, since there could no longer be any doubt about Hitler's uncompromising attitude and his complete break with his former entourage. I went to the Führerbunker at once, telex in hand, and found Hitler sitting with Bormann discussing it in the common sitting room. Hitler saw at once that I was in the picture and said merely, 'What do you think about it? I have relieved Göring of his post. Are you satisfied now?' I replied, '*Mein Führer*, too late.' A long conversation ensued in which Hitler attempted to understand Göring's intentions. I took the text literally and gave my opinion that Göring actually believed that he could still negotiate with the Western leaders. Hitler condemned this as utopic.

In the afternoon Speer came to the Führerbunker to take his leave of Hitler. They discussed Göring's behaviour, but Hitler stood firm by his decision to relieve Göring of all his posts and to have him held in 'honourable house arrest' at the Obersalzberg. This was an extremely unpleasant and completely unnecessary reaction. Hitler was undoubtedly influenced by Bormann, who sent the enabling telex to Obersalzberg. While speaking privately that evening with Hitler about Göring, I saw that he had some sympathy for his behaviour but was of the opinion that, as his Deputy, Göring had to act under Hitler's own instructions. There was no possibility of negotiating with the enemy. Hitler ordered me to have General Ritter von Greim summoned to Berlin so that he could appoint him as Göring's successor as Luftwaffe C-in-C.

On 24 April the enemy ring around the Chancellery was drawn a little tighter. Russian units between the Anhalter and Potsdam railway termini were advancing very slowly and cautiously, taking no risks. This enabled contact to be maintained with the new military commander of Berlin, General Weidling, whose battle HQ was to the west of the city. He commanded LVI Panzer Korps, which had fought a rearguard action to Berlin all the way from the Oder. Weidling attended the situation conference in the bunker every day.

On 25 April Soviet and American troops met up at Torgau on the Elbe. The relief attack of Army Wenck, Hitler's last hope, had failed near Potsdam. Next day Wenck began disengaging from heavily superior Russian forces to withdraw westwards across the Elbe. The centre of Berlin lay under increasing Russian artillery fire and soon the first shells hit the Chancellery ruins. Also on the 25th the USAAF made a theatrical, meaningless raid on Obersalzberg. Hitler had long expected it, but now, in the last days of the war, thought it unlikely. He knew that there were good air raid shelters for the residents and therefore did not concern himself unduly.

Late in the afternoon of 26 April Ritter von Greim arrived, accompanied by Hanna Reitsch. Greim had been wounded during the flight and had to be treated at once by Dr Stumpfegger. Hitler visited Greim in the first-aid room and had a very frank conversation with him, mostly about Göring. Then he spoke about what lay before the Luftwaffe in the next few days. Hitler expected the Luftwaffe to take part in the final battle for Berlin, even though he knew that there were no battleworthy units left. With this order he reached the high point of his self-deception. He promoted Greim to field marshal and appointed him C-in-C of the Luftwaffe.

Greim, practising forbearance throughout, told me that he would stay here in the bunker to the last; Hanna Reitsch made a similar request to me. On 27 Hitler decided that Greim should leave the city as soon as possible. On the 28th I succeeded, with the greatest difficulty, in getting his Fieseler Storch clear to start, after which Greim and his companion got out of the shambles and reached Rechlin—a very meritable achievement.

The Last Days

During 27 April Hitler spoke to me of my future plans. I told him I had none but would wait and see how things developed before deciding. I knew that my wife and children were safe. Hitler gave me a cyanide capsule in case I encountered a difficult situation with no way out. I put the poison away safely. Hitler then surprised me by saying, 'I have decided to order the commander of Berlin to break out. For myself I will remain here and die in the place where I worked so many years of my life. But my staff must also attempt to go. Most of all, it is important to me that Goebbels and Bormann should get out safely.' Thus, after originally insisting on being surrounded by people he could trust to the last, he had now reversed his intention. I asked Hitler whether, in view of the circumstances in Berlin, he believed that this break-out stood any chance of success. He replied, 'I believe that the situation has now changed. The Western Allies will no longer insist on the unconditional surrender demanded at Casablanca. It appears quite clear from the foreign Press reports of recent weeks that the Yalta Conference was a disappointment for the United States and Britain. Stalin must have made demands which the Western Powers conceded only reluctantly for fear that Stalin would otherwise go his own way. I have the impression that the three big men at Yalta did not leave as friends. Now Roosevelt is dead, and Churchill has never loved the Russians. He will be interested in not allowing the Russians to advance too far through Germany.' Hitler decided that I should go too, and attempt to fight my way through to Dönitz and Keitel.

I reported this conversation with Hitler to Krebs and Burgdorf at once. Krebs told Weidling of Hitler's change of view and ordered him to prepare an outline plan for the orderly break-out. We attended this conference on tenterhooks. Reports were all bad. After initial successes, Army Wenck had been driven back by the Russians. Hitler relapsed into apathy as he often did in these final days. Weidling's plan for a break-out depended on Wenck's thrust succeeding. As this now seemed unlikely, Hitler said that the idea of a break-out was hopeless.

The same evening Hitler spoke at length with Goebbels, who for some time had been planning to die in Berlin with his wife and five children.

Hitler attempted in vain to dissuade him but eventually agreed that the family could move into the bunker.

That same day, 28 April, the BBC announced that Himmler had offered capitulation to the Allies. According to this report, he had met the Swedish Count Bernadotte in Lübeck on the 24th and set out his ideas. At about this time Fegelein rang me. He told me of the goings-on and in response to my enquiry as to his own whereabouts he said that he was 'in the city'. I did not take this amiss at the time and only thought it strange after hearing the BBC bulletin about Himmler's dealings. The latter Hitler dismissed with contempt and it had obviously annoyed him. Probably he had expected it of Himmler, and during the day his bitterness at Himmler's activities increased. He ordered Fegelein to report to him, but he could not be found: an SS squad discovered him at a flat on the Kurfürstendamm dressed in civilian clothes. He was brought to the Reich Chancellery, where a drumhead court-martial was held. After a short hearing Fegelein was found guilty of desertion and sentenced to death. The sentence was carried out immediately.

During the day numerous reports made clear that the remaining German forces had been forced out of Berlin, were dispersing or had been thrown back across the Elbe into the Western sector. Berlin could no longer be relieved, and Hitler accepted this fact.

After the evening meal Hitler sent for a registrar to marry him to Eva Braun. We congratulated the couple and Eva Hitler accepted our best wishes in full knowledge of her role and imminent death. We filed into his living room for a short celebratory drink. All residents of the bunker participated and we made the effort to think of old times. It was a rather eerie situation. Hitler's marriage at this hour, at the end of his life, was to thank Eva Braun for coming of her own accord to be with him during the last hours of the Third Reich and to share his fate.

Hitler now dictated two testaments, one political and the other private, and signed them at 0400 on 29 April. I was very surprised to be invited to witness the private testament with Bormann and Goebbels. Considering his approaching demise, the political testament was a depressing certificate of self-deception. The various anti-Jewish sentiments expressed were an embarrassment. I also found odd and completely meaningless the testamentary settlement of succession and the installation of a new Reich Government. The unlucky incumbent would have had little freedom of action. The private testament began with an emotional offer of gratitude to his wife, who was determined to die with him. There followed a disposition about his art collection intended for Linz and general bequests for family members and collaborators. Bormann was nominated as trustee.

Hitler had virtually entered seclusion, although he kept himself informed during the day of the fighting. He no longer interfered in the proceedings. The hitherto normal mood of hopelessness in the bunker sank to a new low. Sorrow, depression and despair spread and the masks dropped. Each asked what he could do after Hitler's death. Hitler's mood was unstable and one could not easily follow his thinking. The time was long gone when we maintained an 'official' attitude of respect in speaking of him. All expressed their opinions frankly. We recognised Hitler in all honesty as a great man—not in the moral sense, of course, but as a political revolutionary, for whose achievements we would always have respect and from whom we still maintained a correct distance. Spiritually the flame in him still burned brightly.

Flight from Berlin

At midday on 29 April I asked Hitler if he would allow me to attempt a break-out to the West. He considered this straightaway and said only that it would probably be impossible. I replied that I thought the way to the West would still be free. As to the danger of my intention, I had no illusions. Hitler gave me written authority to go and said I should report to Dönitz. That afternoon I made my preparations and decided to take 'light gear'—haversack and machine pistol. I took part in the evening situation conference and reported to Hitler afterwards. He gave me his hand and said only *'Alles gute'*—best of luck. What happened in the bunker subsequently I know only by hearsay.

Together with the old man of the Adjutantur, Mathiesing, I went through the subterranean corridors of the Chancellery to the eastern exit near the garages and left at midnight on 29 April, the last of the military adjutants and Hitler's close military entourage to emerge alive.

As I stepped out of the Chancellery I saw before me an absolute inferno. A confusion of cables, rubble and tram wires lay around—ruins, bomb craters and artillery craters. There was a serious fire in the Potsdamer Platz area. The whole city was enveloped as far as one could see in a mixture of smoke and fog from the many fires crackling on all sides. I wondered what was worse—to be here under Russian bombardment or awaiting death in the bunker. We headed north along the Hermann Göring Strasse to the Brandenburg Gate, bore left towards the zoo, along the East–West axis, past the Victory Column to the railway embankment, made another left turn and after a few steps reached the large municipal air raid shelter.

On this walk through the burning and mostly destroyed city I felt an enormous relief. With every step it became clearer to me that I had nothing left to do. It was all the same to me whatever happened now. I was free at last of all the responsibility and depressing burden of the Hitler years.[25]

Notes

Notes supplied by the Publisher, except where specified otherwise

1. It is inexplicable why the British historian David Irving should assert in the Foreword to his book *Hitler and his Generals* (1975) that my diaries are 'probably in Moscow'. Another statement by Irving astonishes me: I am supposed to have put at his disposal 'unpublished contemporaneous manuscripts and letters' and 'subsequently took the trouble—together with others—to read through many pages of the text based upon them'. I do remember several visits by Irving, when I answered some questions; but the rest is untrue.—Author

2. Published as *Inside the Third Reich: Memoirs*, 1970.

3. *Restpolen* was the remainder of Poland. The purpose of Germany's war with Poland was to resolve the questions of Danzig and the Polish Corridor. The Polish surrender would be negotiated on the basis of how the remainder of Poland would be treated.—Translator

4. Churchill, who was still First Lord of the Admiralty at this time, had long been 'seen in Berlin as the leading western warmonger' (Ian Kershaw, *Hitler, 1936–1945: Nemesis*, 2000, p. 230).

5. At the time, the Soviets were developing a brand of pan-Slavism aimed at Bulgaria and Yugoslavia in particular.—Translator

6. Presumably the figure of two million includes prisoners-of-war from Belgium, the Netherlands and France, since the whole Belgian Army in 1940 was only 600,000 strong.

7. Gürtner (1881–1941) was the high official in the Bavarian Justice Ministry appointed to solve the political murders in revolutionary

Munich in 1919. In February 1924, as Minister of Justice, he worked behind the scenes to influence the judges in favour of Hitler at his trial and put through his release from prison contrary to law. As Minister of Justice in the National Socialist Government he introduced the law proclaiming the Röhm *putsch* of 30 June 1934 to be justified as 'the means of State defence'.—Translator

8. Rommel only had the 5th Light (later 21st Panzer) Division in Libya at the time (late March) and would not receive the 15th Panzer Division until May. He had, however, been ordered not to make any aggressive moves until the latter had arrived.

9. The problem with the Ju 88 A-4 series was the delivery of the more powerful Jumo 211 engines, which were intended for the summer of 1940 but were not available until early 1941.—Translator

10. Nevertheless the heavy cruiser *Lützow* sailed with orders to break out into the Atlantic in June 1941 and in December 1942. On the first occasion she was torpedoed off Egersund by aircraft and on the second returned to her Norwegian anchorage after the 'Regenbogen' fiasco.—Translator

11. Kesselring was not just C-in-C Luftwaffe but also, as C-in-C South, the overall German theatre commander in the Mediterranean.

12. The Royal Air Force had been bombing Germany from the summer of 1940, but the raids had not constituted a serious threat to the German war effort. What began in March 1942 was something different—a true second front. The French factory bombed on 3 March was the Billancourt Renault factory and the actual deaths numbered 367.

13. The Heinkel He 177 was one of the most trouble-plagued and accident-prone aircraft ever built.

14. There were also American landings at Casablanca. Oran is further away from Sicily than Algiers, and it is not clear how the Allied landings at Algiers could have been repelled with no Axis forces present

at the time in French North-West Africa—and the fact that Hitler ordered something did not mean that the Wehrmacht had the where-withal to comply.

15. In fact it was Manstein rather than Hitler who oversaw the operation.

16. The Germans capitulated at Stalingrad on 1 February 1943.

17. In fact it was the PzKpfw V (Panther) and PkKpfw VI (Tiger) that interested Hitler for 'Zitadelle'.

18. In fact only four were seriously wounded. See Gitta Sereny, *Albert Speer: His Battle with Truth*, 1995, p. 441.

19. According to Igor Witkowski in his book *Supertanje Bronie Hitlera* describing his excavations into the remains of this FHQ, the development was a series of very long, vast galleries burrowed into a mountainside. Work was said to have been done here on six or seven projects, including the V-2 and A9/10 rockets, the Ursel anti-ship rocket for Type XXI U-boats and the Rheinbote.—Translator

20. The 'Areopag' was a tribunal with unlimited powers to inquire into the subject matter of its reference.

21. Dietrich's Army was just the Sixth Panzer for the Ardennes offensive; it was retitled Sixth SS when it moved to Hungary for the Lake Balaton offensive, to distinguish it from the Sixth Army, with which it would be operating.—Translator

22. According to the German authors Harald Fäth and Dieter Meinig, the FHQ at Ohrdruf, commenced in 1938, was a deep, vast underground facility descending through at least five levels.—Translator

23. For a detailed review of the figures for the death toll at Dresden see *The Irving Judgment: David Irving v. Penguin Books and Professor Deborah Lipstadt* (Penguin, London, 2000). Mr Justice Gray (at p. 334) concludes: 'The true death toll was within the bracket of 25–30,000.'

24. According to the noted German historian Günther Gellermann in his book *Der Krieg der nicht stattfand*, 1986, Hitler ordered an attack against New York in which six U-boats would fire off rockets and shells filled with sarin nerve gas in reprisal for Dresden, but Jodl talked him out of this plan.—Translator

25. With the help of a Hitlerjugend battalion, von Below and Mathiesing crossed the Havel river to Havelberg where, after obtaining civilian clothes from a farmer, they registered with the civilian authorities under false names on 4 May, and each obtained an identity pass and ration book. They lived by odd jobs for a month until parting at the beginning of June. Von Below now worked his way towards his in-laws' property at Wanzleben near Magdeburg. He arrived there on 20 June and was reunited at Nienhagen with his pregnant wife and three children. At the Wernigerode clinic—where his fourth child Christa was born on 28 July—von Below was recognised from his photograph in the 3 September 1939 issue of the *Völkischer Beobachter* and forced to flee. He found shelter with friends in Bonn and decided to use the time studying economics at the University. He was betrayed to the British authorities on 7 January 1946 and arrested. He took exception to the treatment meted out in the British interrogation centres where he was lodged and took his revenge by inventing a nonsensical tale about 'the special mission I was given by Hitler to bring secret orders to Keitel', which appeared subsequently, to his great satisfaction, in Hugh Trevor-Roper's book *The Last Days of Hitler* (1947). Von Below was given the highest security classification and was transferred to Nuremberg prison on the basis of being a material witness in the spring of 1947. He volunteered for catering duties to pass the time and spoke with many accused or convicted members of the former SS and Wehrmacht. Von Below was granted his final discharge on 14 May 1948.

Index